D0557791

HUMAN ON THE INSIDE

HUMAN ON THE INSIDE
UNLOCKING THE TRUTH
ABOUT CANADA'S PRISONS

GARY GARRISON

University of Regina Press

© 2014 Gary Garrison

All rights reserved. No part of this work covered by the copyrights hereon may be reproduced or used in any form or by any means—graphic, electronic, or mechanical—without the prior written permission of the publisher. Any request for photocopying, recording, taping or placement in information storage and retrieval systems of any sort shall be directed in writing to Access Copyright.

Printed and bound in Canada at Marquis.

Cover design: Duncan Campbell, University of Regina Press.
Copy editor: Anne James.
Text design: John van der Woude Designs.
Cover photo: "Prisoner in old jail" by Lou Oates / iStockphoto

Library and Archives Canada Cataloguing in Publication
Cataloguing in Publication (CIP) data available at the Library and Archives Canada web site: www.collectionscanada.gc.ca and at www.uofrpress.ca/publications/Human-on-the-Inside

10   9   8   7   6   5   4   3   2   1

University of Regina Press, University of Regina
Regina, Saskatchewan, Canada, S4S 0A2
tel: (306) 585-4758 fax: (306) 585-4699
U OF R PRESS   web: www.uofrpress.ca

The University of Regina Press acknowledges the support of the Creative Industry Growth and Sustainability program, made possible through funding provided to the Saskatchewan Arts Board by the Government of Saskatchewan through the Ministry of Parks, Culture, and Sport. We also acknowledge the financial support of the Government of Canada through the Canada Book Fund and the support of the Canada Council for the Arts for our publishing program. This publication was made possible through Culture on the Go funding provided to Creative Saskatchewan by the Ministry of Parks, Culture and Sport.

This book is dedicated to the staff and volunteers of Mennonite Central Committee Alberta and its affiliates, MCC Canada and MCC USA.

If only there were evil people somewhere insidiously committing evil deeds and it were necessary only to separate them from the rest of us and destroy them. But the line dividing good and evil cuts through the heart of every human being. And who is willing to destroy a piece of his own heart?

— Aleksandr Solzhenitsyn, *The Gulag Archipelago*

CONTENTS

ACKNOLWEDGEMENTS

To staff of Mennonite Central Committee Alberta: Gord Hutchinson, Tom Brownlee, Moira Brownlee, Elly Klumpenhouwer, Janet Anderson, Kae Neufeld, Don Stoesz, Ken From, Abe Janzen, Suzanne Gross, Melanie Weaver, and Peter Worsley. I am grateful to all of you for your friendship, camaraderie, collegiality, and support. I am grateful as well to all other MCC Alberta staff, volunteers, and donors and to the Mennonite community that nurtures and lives the Mennonite culture of social justice and peacemaking.

Chaplain Sr. Elizabeth Coulombe and I started this book during a conversation over lunch at Edmonton Institution, the Max. I am grateful to her and to other chaplains at the Max and at Bowden Institution who supported me at various stages of my prison work, even if their help wasn't directly related to this book: Oliver Johnson, Paul Vanderham, Don Stoesz, Hardy Engler, Thelma Pelletier, and Teresa Kellendonk.

Three people I interviewed and can thank by name are Roy Chudek, Sarah Salter-Kelly, and Moira Brownlee. I am also deeply grateful to everyone else I interviewed and cannot name, and to all prisoners, staff, victims, and their families, and to everyone involved in the criminal justice system who does his or her best to make our communities safer.

The volunteers I met and worked with could have easily chosen to spend their time at home with their families, taking in sports or cultural events, dancing, or walking in the park instead of going into prisons. I honour you for your choice to befriend prisoners you had never met, even though you might never know what impact your visits had on the prisoners.

To Linda Goyette, Jocelyn Brown, Margaret Macpherson, and Jason Lee Norman, writers-in-residence who helped me at various stages of the project, from the book's early stages to finding a publisher. To Alice Major, the Living Room Poetry Collective, the Edmonton Stroll of Poets Society, and all my other friends who helped me become a better writer.

To David McLennan and everyone at the University of Regina Press who read the manuscript, decided to publish it, and worked with me to get it into its final form.

To my mother and all the other members of my family, especially Sara, who encourage me to keep moving forward.

ABBREVIATIONS

AVP   Alternatives to Violence Project

COSA   Circles of Support and Accountability

CSC   Correctional Service of Canada (also referred to as Corrections Canada)

D&S   Detention and Segregation, the part of a prison where prisoners are kept in isolation from others, either for punishment or for their own protection; sometimes referred to by people outside the system as solitary confinement

FASD   Fetal Alcohol Spectrum Disorder

M2W2   Man-to-Man, Woman-to-Woman; a prison visitation program, operated in Alberta by the Mennonite Central Committee

MCC   Mennonite Central Committee

P2P   Person-to-Person, a prison visitation program in Saskatchewan, operated by MCC Saskatchewan

Pop   General population, all of the prisoners in a prison except for those in Detention and Segregation, or Protective Custody

SHU   Special Handling Unit or super max unit, one security level higher than a max

TRU   Transfer and Release Unit (at the Max, this refers to Protective Custody units, since the Max has had no bona fide Transfer and Release Unit for many years)

INTRODUCTION

Nothing in life is to be feared, it is only to be understood.
Now is the time to understand more, so that we may fear less.
—Marie Curie

C stumbles across the scene of an accident: a crumpled van, blood, and bodies strewn across the highway. C has basic first aid, but he's frozen and helpless in the middle of all the twisted metal, gore, screams, and agony. His best friend dies in his arms. Two other friends are dead too. Five others he knows lie there with broken necks, arms, and legs. For a week C drinks to blot out the memory. He doesn't even know he's killed somebody until the police come to arrest him.

K's parents are always drunk. K sees them throw chairs, tables, bottles, and each other through the windows of their house so often he thinks that's how relationships work. When he's eight, he sees his aunt back a car over his mother in the driveway. He remembers watching her shift into drive and run over his mother again to make sure she's dead.

S's mother is a drug addict. He's beaten and sexually assaulted by his mother's boyfriends. Starting at age seven, he frequently runs away from home, lives on the street, and parties with older friends. He's in and out of the young offenders' centre and group homes. Once he's out of elementary school, he does break and enters and steals cars to support himself and to buy drugs and booze. After he gets his first federal sentence, he slashes his arms, not to kill himself but for the high the pain gives him.

H holds off taking drugs until grade nine, despite pressure from friends. Once he's into the drug scene, he experiments with LSD when his depression becomes extreme. He kills his sister instead of himself simply because she happens to be there.

P's father teaches him how to mainline heroin at age six. He assaults another boy at school with a stick, and his mother turns him over to a group home. He holds the group home staff hostage at knifepoint for three hours. His principal demand is for a gun so he can shoot himself. P is in and out of prisons, group homes, and psychiatric hospitals for sixteen years, from the age of ten.

Prisoners' stories like these are not usually part of the public debate about crime, punishment, justice, and public safety. They rarely get told in newspapers or on television. Politicians who hear stories like these are careful about what they say because their opponents will twist their words to make it look like they're on the side of murderers and pedophiles. Nothing, it seems, is a more effective vote-getter these days than fear: of terrorism, public debt, taxes, poverty, cancer, death, crime, criminals, and a host of other things.

When I visited prisoners in Edmonton Institution (the Max) and Bowden Institution, I met many people who wondered why people like me were taking the prisoners' side—so they claimed—instead of the victims' side. Sometimes prison staff obstructed prison visitors like me for supporting murderers, rapists, pedophiles, and drug dealers. They saw the brutality of the crimes and put roadblocks between us and the prisoners. They would decline to circulate official memos that authorized our visits. They'd violate the system's rules about testing us for traces of drugs on our clothing and delay us at the front gate or even turn us away. They'd give prisoners too little time to gather for their walk to the visiting room and not let them come when they weren't fast enough. Sometimes they'd simply decline to notify the prisoners we were on site waiting for them.

The fact is, though, that it's not a simple either/or choice to support criminals or victims. It's not always even a clear judgment that the worst offenders are only offenders and not victims themselves. In the abbreviated stories of prisoners C, K, S, H, and P, the offenders were abused as children or suffered from a mental illness or post-traumatic stress. I say this not to excuse their crimes but to recognize that these men are human beings who had to deal with circumstances far more difficult than most of us have known. In fact, the prisoners I worked with—with few exceptions—have accepted personal responsibility for their crimes and for the irreparable damage they caused. They have deliberately chosen not to blame somebody else for what they did.

The first priority of the Correctional Service of Canada (CSC, and also referred to throughout this book as Corrections Canada) is the "Safe transition to and management of eligible offenders in the community."[1] The agency officially recognizes that prisoners can only be safely reintegrated into the community if individuals and groups from the community are involved in the process. The main purpose of this book is to show the larger community how that looks to the people who get involved, why they do it, and how we all benefit by having less fear and more understanding and, consequently, greater safety and security.

A key part of the con code in prison is that the guards and the staff are the enemy. The guards have a similar, unwritten code of conduct. Both groups protect their own even in extreme cases, even if it means letting someone get away with murder. Nevertheless, every prisoner and every guard is a human being, and that fact sometimes supersedes both these codes. I've even seen people on both sides of the divide shed tears for people on the other side. As a person with a community agency, I support both groups. I'm also on the side of the police, the chaplains, the native Elders, the victims, and all the potential future victims in the community. A longtime staff person I worked with at the Max told me it was wrong

---

1 www.csc-scc.gc.ca/about-us/006-0002-eng.shtml

to have the prison eleven kilometres away from where city people lived. He said the prison belongs downtown where everybody can see it and learn that the guards, staff, management, and even the prisoners are still part of the community, that they belong to us and we to them.

This is not an academic criminology textbook. It does not attempt to be comprehensive; for example, the work of chaplains, Elders, psychologists, judges, lawyers, and journalists is only mentioned in passing. It presents stories of prisoners' lives and circumstances in order to un-demonize them so readers can understand how much people outside prison have in common with people inside. It offers readers the opportunity to visit a prison vicariously and to participate in an Alternatives to Violence workshop. It includes personal stories of victims, staff, volunteers, and community agencies. These stories show that we are all human persons with a role in supporting each other and making our communities stronger and our streets and homes safer. The first step is to engage with others' stories "to understand more, so that we may fear less."

Fear has built walls, iron gates, barbed-wire fences, and armies of guards, police, and prosecutors to protect us. We agree as a society that these things are necessary, but do the walls have to be so high that they cut us off completely from prisoners who need contact with us if we are to be safe when they get out? Do the walls have to be so thick we cannot learn from other people some vital truths about ourselves? From a security perspective, the best way to make a building safe is to lock it down completely and let nobody in or out. It's also safer to stay at home than to go out. Safest of all is to stay in bed all day. But is that the kind of safety we want for ourselves and our communities?

CHAPTER 1

THE PRISON BREAK-IN

In every cry of every Man,
In every Infants cry of fear,
In every voice: in every ban,
The mind-forg'd manacles I hear
— William Blake, "London"

I lived with my family in a silo in Edmonton's Mill Woods sub-division from 1978 to 2002. Our home was a chocolate-brown, aluminum-sided, suburban bi-level, but it was still a silo. We attended St. Theresa's Roman Catholic Church, our kids attended Catholic schools, and we rarely crossed paths with non-Catholics whose kids attended public schools. We were separated from the rest of Edmonton by industrial and commercial districts and a freeway. Mill Woods was all middle class and working class people, very much like us. A silo within a silo within a silo.

I worked at the Alberta Legislature as editor of *Hansard*, the official report of the Assembly's debates. That was another silo. I worked under the Speaker, whose department was part of the public service but not part of "the government," which was run by the majority party in the House. Our department—the Legislative Assembly Office—served all the parties and had rules unique to us, like exclusion from the public service union, even though we were clearly public servants. The public service is a silo too. Public servants get benefits, pension plans, and job security unheard of in the private sector; they also work in a tightly controlled, hierarchical, political environment.

I call these things silos, but they were and are a lot like prisons. Even some of the language we used during my time in the public service was like prison lingo. People approaching retirement—even if it was ten years away—would talk about how many years, months, and days they had left to serve before they were free. When positions were cut and people were laid off, they usually got a generous payout, which was called "the golden handshake." People like me had well-paying jobs we'd been in a long time, but if we got tired of them or wanted to change careers, we had little hope of moving to another job with similar pay somewhere else. We called our situation "the golden handcuffs."

In June 2000, I burned out. For a while I couldn't even read a book or stand up for more than fifteen minutes at a stretch, and I napped all the time. When I regained some of my strength, I felt empty and didn't know what to do with my life. A counsellor suggested I try to meet people who were unlike me. He said that would open my eyes to a different world and help me see myself in a different light. So, in September 2001, I made my first trip to Edmonton Institution (the Max) and visited a man serving a life sentence for murder. I broke into the Max to get out of my own prisons.

In July 2002, I became the coordinator of the M2W2[2] prison visitation program I'd been volunteering for. My job was to pair prisoners with volunteers who came in to visit once a month. I talked to prisoners on their units and in the metalworking shop at the Max, where they could learn useful skills like powder coating and

---

2   M2W2 sounds like R2D2, George Lucas's cute little robot from Star Wars, but it's an abbreviation for "man to man, woman to woman." The name states the essential principle that this prison visitation program is simply—and profoundly—a matter of one person reaching out to meet another person. The comparable program in Saskatchewan is called Person to Person and is commonly abbreviated as P2P.

welding. I met them in the prison school, the Aboriginal cultural centre, the chapel, the gym, and even in the sweat lodge, where we all wore only gym shorts and towels. My job was to find prisoners who would volunteer to come on our visiting night and meet with a person from the outside.

M2W2 is a program of the Mennonite Central Committee that began in Alberta over twenty-five years ago. Its main purpose is to provide personal contact for prisoners with somebody who's part of the larger community. The volunteers come into the prison on the second Friday of every month, listen to prisoners, and informally mentor them, one-on-one. Visitors model for them how to live a normal life, something many of them have never seen.

To recruit prisoners and maintain the program's visibility at the Max, I went there every Tuesday. I nearly always started my day off in the chapel by having lunch with one or both chaplains. One of those Tuesdays about two years into my doing this work is particularly memorable.

///////////

The Roman Catholic chaplain, Sr. Elizabeth Coulombe, invites me to share my life story with a group of prisoners at an evening chapel service. I agree to come, hoping I'll find more prisoners to join the program.

"Some of you know me," I tell the ten men sitting in a circle of orange, hard plastic chairs. "I coordinate the M2W2 prison visitation program. What you may not know about me is how I ended up here. By 'here' I don't only mean 'in this prison.' I mean in Canada, in Edmonton at the Max, as coordinator of M2W2."

"I just realized a funny thing about my being in here," I continue. My heart starts pounding so loudly I can hear it. Suddenly, I'm afraid that if I tell them about me, they'll think I'm a wimp. Once word gets around, I could lose the trust I've built with prisoners throughout the Max these last two years. If a new prisoner—a "fish" in prison lingo—came in with a history like mine, he'd be a target for fists, kicks, and even knives ("shivs"). In the sixties and seventies men like me were savaged in the U.S. media and shunned by the community. My own father said he was ashamed of me for leaving the United States and coming to Canada. I'd worked at a newspaper in Toronto where a pressman could scarcely contain his rage at my "cowardice." His face turned fire-engine red whenever we crossed paths. I marvel now that he didn't wind up and punch me in the nose.

But it's too late to back out now. I take a deep breath and forge ahead. "If I hadn't come to Canada in 1970," I say, "I would've gone to prison for dodging the draft. That was the height of the Vietnam War. I had just graduated from Saint Louis University. I grew up in Kansas City and Pueblo, Colorado, but I was born in Muskogee, Oklahoma."

"So you're an Okie from Muskogee, like in the song?" Somebody laughs.

"Yeah. That's me," I smile. "Unlike the Okie in the song, I did grow my hair long. I had a lot more then, and it was curly. People told me I had a pretty fair Afro for a white guy." More chuckles.

"The point I want to make is that I came to Canada because my own country threatened me with prison if I didn't join the army and kill people. And here I am at the Max visiting you guys." I look around at their faces. I know that a few of them are in on life sentences because they took another person's life. I see a few headshakes and grimaces, but most of them are as still as bronze statues. I ask them, "What would you think about being put in prison for *not* killing somebody?"

"Far out!" somebody says.

"I woulda gone," says another.

"Yeah, man. It woulda been fun. And the travel!"

"I didn't come here to talk politics," I say. "But politics are part of life wherever you go. Some of you probably think you're in here for political reasons, that you didn't get justice because you couldn't afford a good lawyer, because you're part of a racial minority, or you aren't as educated as the police, the lawyers, the judges, and the prison guards you have to deal with. There's a lot of truth in that."

"I came to talk about where I came from. I left behind all my friends and relatives in 1970 to protest the Vietnam War. I was alone except for the woman I married. We stood together against the killing. After we raised three children to adulthood, in 2002 we broke up. I realized she wasn't the person I thought I married. Maybe she had similar thoughts about me. By that time we couldn't even talk to each other. Now all three of my adult children are gone, and I'm the only one of the family left in Edmonton." Then I tell them how I found the strength to move forward and develop a new life for myself. After I've said my piece, we have an informal discussion over coffee and cookies, and then the guards come to escort the prisoners back to their units.

When I return to the Max the next Tuesday, Sister Elizabeth and I talk about the chapel service. She tells me that a day or two afterwards, many of the same men came back to the chapel. One of them opened up about his life. She says that telling his story helped him understand himself better, gave him hope for the future, and convinced him he has the power to determine his own destiny. Sister Elizabeth thanks me for leading the way. She plans to encourage more prisoners to tell their life stories too.

That gets me thinking. I've just read Studs Terkel's *The Good War* and *Working*, landmark oral histories about World War II and life in various workplaces, and I see in my twenty-two years' experience of editing *Hansard* at the Alberta Legislature a talent for translating oral speech into written text. "Maybe I could interview some prisoners," I say, "and we could make a book out of it."

When Sister Elizabeth and I first draft plans for the book, we decide on a simple, three-part formula for prisoner interviews: (1) Where do you come from? (family background, life before prison); (2) What is prison life like for you?; and (3) What are your hopes for the future, and what will you do to keep out of trouble when you get out? We agree that anonymity is essential, that I will include no prisoner's name in the book, that I'll edit out all place references. We want these to be real stories, and we want the prisoners to feel free to talk without fear of retribution or ridicule.

The prisoners' life stories would be just the start. The book would give prisoners a chance to tell their stories and to be heard; it also would shine a light inside the prison and let readers face their fears of crime, of prisoners, and of parts of themselves they don't want to acknowledge. Our proposal appeals to the higher-ups in the prison because they want to do what they can to help prisoners improve themselves and because they know that, ultimately, the community is safer when people on the outside have a better understanding of people on the inside. Our proposal fits into the system's interest in the restorative justice model, which refocuses the traditional emphasis on punishment and security as part of the effort to heal the damage crime does to individuals and the community.

So I get permission to come in with a tape recorder. I spend between sixty and ninety minutes with each prisoner who agrees to an interview. I invite thirty prisoners to participate, I get twelve prisoners' oral histories, and I transcribe and edit them all. I preserve each prisoner's speaking style, as I had so many MLAS' speeches in *Hansard*. I share the transcripts with my supervisor, with coworkers, with the prisoners involved. As editor of *Hansard*, I published about sixty large volumes comprised of many thousands of pages of MLAS' speeches; what I've got now is a text that's as full of repetition and posturing and as unengaging as *Hansard* ever was. Why would anybody publish it? Why would anybody read it? The journey from editor to author looks like a mile-high Grand Canyon wall in front of me. I'm afraid I'll never make it to the top. I'm low on energy, still recovering from my family breakup and from my burnout at the Legislature two years before that. So I set the project aside.

That was ten years ago. The book Sister Elizabeth and I had in mind is very different from the book you have in your hand now. I started this project thinking I would simply be the facilitator in a process of prisoners opening up about themselves, and then other prisoners who read those first stories would open up too. It was going to be a story avalanche, and the sound of my voice would trigger it. All I had to do was invite prisoners to speak and then get out of the way. I would be the catalyst. During the years the project was on hold, I learned how much the rules of my *Hansard* life were still part of me and how far I still had to go to break away from them.

In 2003, I'd already taken the first step, even though I didn't realize it. I'd started writing poetry. The next step involved music. I remember a conversation with Paul Vanderham, who was an M2W2 volunteer. He asks if there'd be interest in starting a music program for the prisoners. His guitar helped him survive his marriage breakdown, he says, and he's convinced music will help prisoners heal too. So Paul and I begin a monthly music jam session, singing and playing music with prisoners. After about a year, Ken From, the provincial manager of M2W2, asks us to provide music for an evening on restorative justice at the Inglewood Christian Reformed Church. We agree.

When we get together to pick songs, we start with "Folsom Prison Blues," "Cold, Cold Heart," "Knockin' on Heaven's Door," "Bad Moon Rising," and "The Weight." The prisoners at the jam sessions love those songs. But we wonder: Isn't this event as much about the community as it is about the prisoners? Shouldn't we sing about the work we do, something educational or inspiring? Tom Brownlee, the coordinator of M2W2 at Bowden at the time, plans to sing Mary Gauthier's "Karla Faye" for a similar event in Calgary. It's about the life and execution of Karla Faye Tucker, a convicted double murderer in Texas. We practice it a few times, but neither of us feels right about it. Even reports from Calgary that the audience loved Tom's performance of "Karla Faye" don't change that.

At one of our practices I say to Paul, "'Karla Faye' would work if this was the United States, but we haven't had capital punishment in Canada for 40 years. Wouldn't it be way better if we sang a song about prison visitation?"

"Yeah," he says. "But there isn't one."

Two weeks before the event, we have another practice. We try "Karla Faye" again, but it doesn't go well. I tell Paul I've written a chorus for a song about prison visitation. He reads it and says, "You may have something here, but it's only a chorus. And there's no music. We have to go with what we've got."

Paul leaves and I go to sleep. I'm back in the visiting room at the Max. A visitor and a prisoner chat one-on-one at each table as they sip coffee and share jelly donuts. Then I'm lying on a lumpy mattress in a cell. My brain clenches. My gut knots. I breathe in quick, short pants. Then I'm inside a coffin buried under six feet of dirt. I claw at the wooden lid until my fingers bleed in a desperate attempt to get out into the open air. Then I'm back in Mount Pleasant, Iowa, in 1989. It's the middle of the night. I gasp, wheeze, choke. It's a major asthma attack. I'm gonna die. My breaths get shorter and shorter. I wake up. I bolt up out of bed at 3 a.m. My pajamas are drenched in sweat. My heart is racing.

Later that morning, I sit down and rough out three verses. I fine-tune it over the next few days, but I still have no music and no title. I show it to Suzanne Gross. She's a visitor at the women's prison at the time and a personal friend. She has a PhD in music, teaches piano, and writes musical arrangements for her choir at the First Mennonite Church. She sets it to music in a week. Two days before the Inglewood event, we sing it for Ken From and two other prison visit coordinators: Elly Klumpenhouwer, who has been involved for nearly twenty years and runs the visiting program at the women's prison, and Gord Hutchinson, who runs M2W2 at the Drumheller prison. Everybody loves it. When we go to the event, I sing the verses solo, and Elly, Paul, and Suzanne join in the chorus. The audience gives us a long round of applause.

The song is called "Human Too," the last words of the last verse. It's the essence of the twelve prisoner interviews I did: seventy thousand words of transcribed text and twenty hours of interviewing condensed to 258 words, all performed in under four minutes. It's about what happens for prisoners when an ordinary person comes into prison and brings in the fresh air and sunlight, the freedom and empathy the prisoners crave. It reflects how prisoners tell me they feel when somebody they don't know comes out of nowhere and takes an interest in them before they even meet. Takes enough interest to drive for an hour or more through fog, snow, ice, darkness, and minus forty degree temperatures to talk about weather, sports, politics, a walk in a park.

The song is about being locked in an eight-by-twelve-foot cage for twenty-two or twenty-three hours a day and suddenly getting into open air. It's about the odour of stale gravy and french fries and vomit and sweat and urine and the bleach residue on the floors and walls from their daily cleaning. It's about the gray cinder blocks, the tiny barred windows, the 24-7 surveillance cameras. It's about the grind and clank of iron barriers between prisoners and the outside world. The constant orange halo of mercury vapour lamps encircling the compound all night, swallowing up the darkness, blurring the boundary between dream and reality. The constant, visceral fear of the guards, of the other prisoners, and having nobody to trust. The movie replaying over and over in each prisoner's head: the blood and gore of the crime scene, the victim screaming, the prisoner's wife and kids weeping as he's led away in handcuffs after the trial, the victim's family torn apart by the prisoner's fit of rage. It's about the same day again and again with every head count, every pat-down, every tasteless meal. It's about the rifle shots from the guards' firing range pop-pop-popping in the background.

The song was a good step forward, but it didn't go far enough. I still had a way to go to finally get this book. I realized that because of the way privacy laws were evolving, the book could use only one of the twelve interviews I'd done. I tried to interview more prisoners, but by that time the political culture had changed, and I couldn't get the official permission I needed. So I looked for a few ex-prisoners and interviewed them. I also realized that the prison and the prisoners were central but still only part of the picture. I discovered Sarah Salter-Kelly, whose mother was murdered in 1995, and she was willing to talk about her healing journey. I found a former prison guard who told me about her life inside. I got to know some sex offenders and people who worked with them. I met David Milgaard and learned about wrongful convictions.

The next critical step was when I decided in the summer of 2010 that I couldn't do M2W2 anymore and still write the book. Sister Elizabeth and I initiated the project as a way to free prisoners to speak. I had to free myself from the routine of going to the Max every Tuesday and Bowden every Wednesday. I needed to stop subjecting myself to the prison routines and the drug scanning machine at the front gate and the constant fear of being turned away. I was institutionalized myself and had to get out. I also knew that even though my intent always was to be mostly positive about Corrections Canada, I could well be banned from federal prisons when the book came out. The new political culture had reasons for not allowing me to interview more prisoners.

I got a warm send-off from my colleagues at Mennonite Central Committee Alberta when I quit. Many of them wished me well with the book and said they were eager to see it in print. One thing I didn't anticipate was how hard it was to work on the book without the routine imposed by regular employment. I couldn't work with the job, and I couldn't work without it either. I feared the freedom even though I had chosen it myself. Many days I felt isolated and alone. I feared I would fail, that the project would never get finished, the book would never be published, my words and the words of others who spoke to me would never be heard.

I often remind myself that my loneliness and isolation are nothing compared to a man who is locked up, to a sex offender afraid of his addiction and unable to be open about his past, or to someone whose mother or father or spouse or child was murdered or to a person who was raped. All I have to do to break free any day is get on the Internet, send some emails, pick up the phone, or walk out my front door.

Contemporary brain research has concluded that eighty percent of the human brain is designed primarily to handle externalities, to relate to our environment and to other people. The brain is primarily a social organ. The company I keep affects me to the core. My brain develops neural pathways for self-expression, self-defence, and other social activities. Another fact about the human brain is that some pathways get overused and some shrivel up from neglect. Like a prisoner stuck in a way of life or a drug habit, I get stuck in unhealthy thinking and behaviour patterns — a middle-class, suburban silo, for example — unless I do something to break out. As William Blake suggested in his poem "London," "mind forg'd manacles" are as real as iron ones.

CHAPTER 2

A VISIT TO THE MAX

*When you guys come here to visit and I go to the visiting room,
it's like I've been released. I'm free, even though it only lasts an
hour and a half.*
— A lifer at the Edmonton Institution, the Max.

'm in a car with three other men. We're driving northeast from
Edmonton on Highway 15, the Manning Freeway. It's Friday
night, the second week of April, and five months of winter are
mostly melted off the brown suburban lawns that flank the right-of-
way on both sides. We're going to the prison for our monthly visit.
Halfway between northeast Edmonton's farmland-swallowing
suburbs and Fort Saskatchewan, we pass Henwood, the Alberta
Alcohol and Drug Abuse Commission centre for addictions treatment. We pass the turnoff to Alberta Hospital, the region's inten-
sive treatment mental hospital. We pass the onion-topped tower of
a Sikh temple just off the highway, its curves and corners and walls
intricately decorated with gleaming blue-white-green-red mosaic
tiles. This small piece of India is in stark contrast to the mowed
brown stubble fields and the mostly treeless prairie fanning out in
every direction.

A little farther on, we see a stand of poplars and pines. Light
standards peek out above the trees. A small green sign beside

the highway says EDMONTON INSTITUTION in white letters. An arrow points left. We turn onto a chip-sealed road, like so many thousands of others that connect isolated prairie farmsteads to the rest of the world. Willow thickets on both sides of the road block wind and snow in winter. Now they preserve the last patches of snow, next to ditches where snowmelt collects, stands and, in July, breeds mosquitoes. Buds swell on the bushes. In the roadside swamp dried cattails bob in the westerly breeze.

Edmonton Institution. The Max. The Big House. The only maximum-security federal prison in Alberta. The place most high-profile, dangerous murderers, rapists, child molesters, bank robbers, and drug dealers on the prairies go immediately after their convictions make headlines and their mug shots appear on the evening news. In Canada, people sentenced to two years or more of prison time go to federal prisons; shorter sentences are served in provincial jails, like the one a little farther down Highway 15 in Fort Saskatchewan.

We turn right, past a large, concrete Edmonton Institution sign. We pass several black-and-white signs warning us this is the property of Corrections Canada, that it is under constant surveillance, that vehicles here are subject to search. We park in the visitor section of the lot and walk toward the main gate. Three volunteer visitors and I cross a hundred metres of pavement, cradling in our arms four boxes of Tim Hortons donuts, the gooiest and sweetest they had in the display case. As we approach, the evening sun glistens off graceful spirals of razor wire, a miles-long tinsel-like garland strung along the top of a twelve-foot-high chain-link fence. To the left, a glass-enclosed lookout perches on a concrete pillar. We cross the perimeter road ahead of a black Correctional Service of Canada pickup truck, one of two that circle the premises night and day.

One of us who has a free hand pulls open the outer door. Its glass and black metal is identical to the doors of office buildings, doctors' offices, and stores all over town. We step inside. A gray steel door separates us from the waiting room. To get past it, we have to get out our driver's licences and put them on a retractable metal tray. Once they're all on it, the tray slides back into a massive wall of bulletproof, reflecting glass. As I step closer to the glass, I see the shadow of a guard checking our names against a list on a clipboard. After about a minute, the tray slides out again. We each pick up our licences. The gray steel door hums. Its bolt retracts. I grasp the brass handle in my right hand and slowly pull the solid steel slab toward me. It must weigh 200 pounds. It feels like an airlock on a spaceship.

In the anteroom, between the first bolted steel door and a second one further on, we meet six other volunteers who arrived ahead of us. One of them has a three-inch-diameter white paper disc in his hand. He swipes it across his shirt and puts it in the guard's open, latex-glove-covered hand. As carefully as a surgeon handling a tissue sample, the guard takes the paper between the thumb and index finger of his right hand and places it in a slot on the Itemizer (sometimes called the ion scanner). After a few seconds, the guard peels off the gloves, throws them in the waste bin, records the results in a logbook, and moves on to the next volunteer.

The Itemizer is technology designed to detect minute traces of illicit drugs. Drugs are a big problem in all Canadian prisons, despite numerous attempts to eliminate them. Prisoners tell me drugs are easier to get in prison than on the street. There is a huge demand for drugs in the prison. Drugs are a way to escape. Many prisoners have been using drugs to escape from something most of their lives. Once, a prisoner's girlfriend got caught trying to smuggle in a small amount of LSD. An officer told me if she'd succeeded, the prisoner with the drug would have had more power in the prison than the warden, at least for a while.

All visitors are subject to Itemizer scans and may be denied entry to the prison if they test positive on it. Occasionally, a volunteer does test positive. In those cases, a supervisor normally comes out and asks the volunteer a few questions, like "How long have you been a volunteer at the Max? Are you bringing illicit drugs into the institution this evening?" and "Do you have any idea how a trace of heroin/cocaine/marijuana/LSD could have gotten onto your shirt?" In the years I've been going into the prison, I've hit positive on the machine many times, and so have other volunteers. A few have been turned away. We've been told by various people, including prison staff, that simply touching a twenty-dollar bill, sitting next to a drug user on a bus, handling student essays, or using certain types of cleaning fluids or hand lotions can result in positive hits. We've also been told that the Itemizer never makes a mistake.

Once we're all clear, we sign in, stash our wallets, keys, and coins in lockers. We walk through a metal detector, just like the ones at the airport. If it beeps for anyone, red lights flash, and the guard uses the hand-held detector on him. We don't have to take off our shoes, but sometimes we're asked to turn our pockets inside out, so the guard can make sure we're not smuggling in money or other contraband. Since tobacco was banned from federal prisons in May 2008, cigarettes are contraband. One cigarette, for prisoners desperate to smoke, can be worth ten dollars or more on the inside.

Our coats, the donuts, and the pop go on a conveyor belt and through an x-ray machine. I also put through a grocery bag containing six decks of cards, in case anyone would like to play. They have cards in the visiting room, but they're always dog-eared and sticky. Clean cards are a treat for the prisoners. Then we go through steel doors two and three, walk into the open air, inside the fence. We cross an open paved area between the fence and the main building. To our right are two house trailers with small grass yards front and back. Each contains a child-size swing set. The chain-link fencing around them is only four feet high, like in any urban neighbourhood. This is where inmates can book private family visits and spend private time with spouses, children, and other relatives. We enter the main building, hang up our coats outside the Visitation and Correspondence Office, and pass through steel door four into the visiting room.

As we enter, we open the donut boxes and place them on separate tables, with a small stack of paper napkins beside each one.

The tables are plate glass, over half an inch thick, each one on top of a steel pillar bolted to the concrete floor. Square steel tubing branches off each pillar to support four circular, steel seats. I put my bag of playing cards on one of the seats. A shiny steel cylinder six inches in diameter sticks up about an inch in the middle of each table. This cylinder contains a microphone so guards can monitor our conversations. The cylinder also makes card playing more difficult.

The room's entire west wall is a window, glass reinforced with steel bars. Through it we see the perimeter fence and the parking lot where we came from. In the east wall is the door where the prisoners come in. Next to it is another large window, of one-way reflective glass. From behind this window, visitation and correspondence staff control the doors, observe activities directly and on video monitors, and communicate to people in the room through loudspeakers.

On this night eight prisoners saunter into the room with us through steel doors five and six. Three days ago, on Tuesday, fifteen told me they were coming. They each committed two, three, or five dollars from their prison accounts to pay for the snacks, but the missing seven apparently have higher priorities than money, snacks, and visitors. A dropout rate of fifty percent or more is typical for programs at the Max.

M2W2 stands for "man to man, woman to woman." Its original purpose was to connect individual volunteers with individual prisoners so that, over time, they could develop a relationship. On this occasion, though, we have two prisoners talking to four volunteers. When I started going into the prison in September 2001, all the volunteers were matched up one-on-one with prisoners, as the program originators envisioned when they started the program twenty-five years ago. It operates in one form or other at four federal prisons in Alberta (Edmonton, Bowden, and Drumheller Institutions, as well as the Edmonton Institution for Women). Some prisoner/volunteer pairings have lasted decades and continue long after the prisoner is released.

The program's objective is dead simple: friendship. Prisoners do not open up to prison staff or to other prisoners because that would make them vulnerable to ridicule or physical attack, or they fear what they say could be used against them when they have parole hearings or need something from the system. But volunteers come from outside the system, from outside prison culture. Volunteer visitors have no power over the prisoners, do not file reports, and are, for the most part, unintimidating physically. None of these volunteers bulks up to fend off attacks from his neighbours, as prisoners do.

Trust is rare in prisons. When an M2W2 volunteer meets with a prisoner one-on-one month after month, the prisoner gradually ventures out of his prison comfort zone and engages in more personal conversations as his trust grows. In the latter years of my going to the Max, M2W2 saw fewer and fewer continuing visitor-prisoner relationships; nonetheless, prisoners still valued the possibility of trust and friendship.

The eight prisoners squint as they come through the door. Like coal miners rescued a week after a cave-in, they're unused to so much daylight. They wear prison-issue blue jeans and their best white T-shirts. A few have on unzipped prison-issue dark green cotton jackets. Some are clean-shaven, one has curly shoulder-length black hair, another a ponytail, one a sparse and scraggly black beard. Most of them have on their feet white or black running shoes in various stages of aging. One wears a pair of dazzling white Nike Air Jordans that just came out of the box. The prisoners smile and extend their hands to the volunteers. Many of them have never met before. Once the formalities are over, they each pick up a couple of napkins, grab two or three of the most heavily sugar-coated, goo-filled donuts, and sit down.

Gradually the hum of conversation fills the room. A few men play cards. "Tens" is a popular game for four players, and cribbage is good for two, three, or four. Except for the bars on the windows, this could be a church social or a drop-in centre. The man I sit with I've talked to a number of times before. I'll call him E. He's in his early twenties, but his skin and mannerisms make him look seventeen. He's a year and a half into a life sentence. He won't have his first parole hearing for another nine years. His hands are steady as he raises a half-eaten Boston cream to his lips, but his voice trembles even as he exudes bravado.

"I almost went to gym tonight instead, you know." He takes another bite and surveys the room. His lips are coated with icing sugar and vanilla cream. He lowers his voice and adds, "Too much drama. I'm really sick of this place." The conversation jumps from the Edmonton Oilers to a conflict with a guard to his tentative hope of a transfer to Grande Cache, a minimum-security prison in northwestern Alberta, on the edge of the Rocky Mountains.[3] When I ask him what kind of work he'll look for when he gets out, he says, "I'm sure something will turn up. I can do just about anything." He had been taking welder apprenticeship training in the prison but quit because he didn't like the pressure he got from other prisoners to smuggle pieces of metal out of the shop and back to the unit to make into weapons. I didn't ask him what kind of pressure, and he didn't tell me.

At 8:40 a guard behind the glass flashes the lights off and on, the signal that we have five minutes left. About thirty seconds later, the door opens and two guards in dark blue uniforms enter and motion the prisoners toward the exit. The prisoners and volunteers shake hands and say goodbye. One of the larger prisoners grabs a glazed chocolate donut, the last one in the box, and shoves it into his mouth whole as he heads out the door.

When they're all gone, we gather up the empty bottles, stuff the empty donut boxes and chip bags into the garbage can, and head back out through steel door four, across the open area, through three and two, collect our keys and wallets and IDs. All of us wish the guards good night and walk out the front door as steel door one clanks shut behind us. The power bolt buzzes, slides, and releases us back to the earth.

---

3   Grande Cache Institution recently became a medium-security prison.

As we cross the parking lot, I take an extra deep breath of damp April air. A thunderstorm blew through while we were inside. The lingering ozone tingles against my face and inside my lungs. "Did you have a good visit?" I ask Tom, a retired engineer who was paired up with a prisoner he'd never met before.

"Yeah," he nods, hopping over a puddle three feet across. "D and I mostly talked about the Oilers. He missed half the game tonight to come see me. Towards the end he got into his childhood. He used to play goalie in sneakers because his parents couldn't afford skates."

D is an Aboriginal man from northern Alberta. As with virtually all of the prisoners, I don't know what crime he was convicted of. I don't know how many victims he may have harmed, robbed of life savings, of a loved one, of life itself. I don't know how many women he may have raped, how many children he may have molested, how broad a trail of destruction his drug deals and addictions may have left behind: women driven to prostitution, men to robbery, assault, and murder, children beaten, abused, and abandoned, all because of one young man feeding their addiction to heroin, cocaine, or crystal meth.

I do know that during the four years he's been in prison, eighteen members of his extended family have died. He found out two weeks before our visit that his mother died of a drug overdose six weeks previously. Relatives withheld the news from him. They wanted to spare him the grief of requesting permission to attend a funeral and being denied again. Some maximum-security prisoners can go to family funerals in shackles. If they go, they bear the weight of their crimes and shame like the ghost of Jacob Marley dragging a long, heavy chain behind him. In those cases, four armed and uniformed prison staff stand guard, to ensure the safety of prisoner and society, their presence making a spectacle of the prisoner who has come to mourn.

Under those conditions, it's clear why many prisoners don't apply for passes to funerals. They prefer to spare themselves and their family the shame they personify. They choose instead to curl up on bunks in their eight-by-twelve-foot cells. They weep into their pillows. They stare at the glossy gray concrete walls around them. They crank up their stereos until nobody within fifty feet can hear himself think. They watch hockey reruns, infomercials, news, David Letterman, all-night cable TV movie marathons until they fall asleep. Then they do it over again the next day.

\\\\\\\\

As Tom and I talk, our shoes crunch against the limestone chips and sand left over from the long, snowy winter. With the others in our group, we enter the visitor section of the parking lot.

"Hey, you guys, look up there," Jim raises his arm forty-five degrees and points. "Sandhill cranes heading north. Must be two or three hundred of 'em."

They might have been a swarm of aphids but for the slow, graceful sweep of their tiny wings.

"They must be a couple thousand feet up, at least," he adds.

Black silhouettes against a twilit northwestern sky. The leading V forms and re-forms continuously as cranes switch places in the slipstream. The flock's outline curves and blurs toward the back. Cirrus veils streak north to south, pink, purple, gray on periwinkle blue that fades to black toward the eastern horizon. We stand and stare. "Bwonk! Bwonk! Bwonk! Bwonk!" drifts down to us like a bass drum rhythm line in a symphony.

As the leading birds move away, the stream behind stretches farther and farther south and east, where thousands more pepper the sky. They sketch a broad fan of Vs, a mighty river out of the dark flowing toward the fading rays of the sun.

For a moment, I am a crane at the head of a great flock, cutting into the wind, muscling forward, my eyes squinting against a steady rush of air. I flex and lift my wings until my chest aches, drop back into the crowd, float forward on the slipstream. When my lungs recover, I add my voice to the collective chant, celebrate our imminent homecoming, bless our nests and the chicks that will be born in them.

If the men locked up inside the prison could see and hear those cranes, what would they feel? They can't look up, though. They're confined to their cells and only have tiny, barred windows to look through, windows that let in very little air or sound from the outside world.

I get into the car, and the four of us ride back toward the city, where our families and friends, our jobs and leisure activities are waiting for us. I wonder what it would be like to be cut off from all of that for five, ten, twenty years, or even more. I'm glad I'm able to give my presence to prisoners for a few hours a month and then return to my own life. What would be left of me if I had none of that, if I had to live with only myself and a toilet, a sink, a bed, a television, and four gray walls every day of the week? What if I had nobody outside who wanted to visit me?

CHAPTER 3

EARLY INTIMATIONS OF HELL

Ever to be eaten with flames, gnawed by vermin, goaded with
burning spikes, never to be free from those pains.
—James Joyce, *A Portrait of the Artist as a Young Man*

If you want to distract people, give 'em a video screen. It could be a Play Station, a Nintendo DS, a smart phone, a desktop or laptop computer. It could be a retractable overhead monitor in an airplane. It could be a television. Federal prisons in Canada do their best to ensure that every prisoner has at least a basic television in his or her cell. They do this because every hour a prisoner spends watching sports, movies, or even the news is an hour the prisoner is not using to cause trouble or wallow in self-pity.

When my family got our first television in 1956, we lived in Overland Park, Kansas, a suburb of Kansas City. We had our choice of three channels, 4, 5, and 13. Broadcasts were from 6:00 to 9:00 p.m. Everything was in black and white. We soon developed a family tradition on Sunday nights. We watched *The Wonderful World of Disney* and *The Ed Sullivan Show*. Every day after work, Dad sat down in his easy chair, a glass of bourbon in hand, and invited Walter Cronkite into our living room to give us the CBS evening news. At the end of every newscast Uncle Walter looked us in the eye and declared, as if he were the burning bush on Mount Sinai, "That's the way it is, Monday, August 22, 1962" — whatever it was that day.

I had freedom. I could go outside and play with my brother, sisters, neighbours, and friends whenever I wanted. I felt the wind blow across my face, smelled the sweet forsythia blossoms that obliterated our backyard fence every spring, heard robins sing high up in the black-walnut tree in the vacant lot across the street. I laid on the grass and watched cumulus clouds parade across the endless blue sky, this one a horse's head, that one a fire-breathing dragon, the next a fluffy sheep with a long line of lambs trailing behind.

I had a dog, Pepper, a black mongrel with golden-brown eyebrows. Nearly every day I wrestled with him in the yard and took him for walks. I took him to the grass playground down the hill, let him off his leash, threw a stick as high and far as I could, and rewarded him with a hug when he brought it back to me. Sometimes Pepper got distracted. When another dog came to the playground, he barked, ran over to it, and started to play with it. I yelled at him, cajoled and coaxed him to come back. He didn't care. The only way to get him was to tackle him and clip the chain around his collar. Whenever I gave Pepper a beef bone to gnaw on, that would become his universe. He snarled and bit me once when I attempted to play with him in the middle of a chew. I had Pepper four or five years. As he aged, he got crankier and snarlier, more and more independent, more frustrated by the fence around the yard, the leash, the loneliness. One cool, bright March Sunday afternoon, my father drove us out to a farmer's field half an hour away and turned Pepper loose. Pepper ran away and never looked back.

I had freedom, but I had a schedule every weekday: up at 7:00, brush teeth, get dressed, eat breakfast, walk five blocks to Queen of the Holy Rosary School, start school at 8:00 with daily Mass, go out for recess 10:00 to 10:15, lunch 12:00 to 1:00, recess again 2:30 to 2:45, dismissal at 4:00, a five-block walk home. My lessons were by the clock, forty-five minutes each: Math, Reading, Religion, Geography, History, and sometimes Band. At home I had chores suited to how

old I was at the time. I had to set the table, wash dishes, peel potatoes, carry out the garbage, sweep the floors, scrub the toilets, cut
the grass, make salad, fold the laundry, et cetera, at one time or
another, sharing the jobs with my brother and two sisters. From
grade four onward, I always had homework to do, but I got to play
after supper until dark. I went to the Johnson County Library every
week and read all the baseball novels they had. I listened to Kansas
City Athletics games on KCMO radio every weekend. I rode my bike
around the neighbourhood, played kick the can with neighbourhood kids, played baseball, football, and basketball on driveways,
in backyards, and in the public school playground a block away.

Every Saturday night I had to take a bath to get ready for Sunday.
Every Sunday morning at 8:30 a.m. I dressed up, piled into the back
seat of our milk-green-and-white 1956 Oldsmobile Super 88 with
my brother and two sisters, and rode to Queen of the Holy Rosary
Church for 9:00 Mass. My mother was a lifelong church volunteer.
She was an organist in her parents' church from the time she was
nine. She has belonged to the Legion of Mary, the Altar and Rosary
Society, and the Nocturnal Adoration Society, and done whatever
the pastor or the parish needed. My dad was a tenor in the choir.

Every Mass began with the Confiteor, which is Latin for "I confess." The priest and altar boys kneel at the foot of the altar and
recite the prayer in Latin as everybody in the pews reads along in
their missals: "I confess to Almighty God, and to you, my brothers and sisters, that I have sinned." I was an altar boy from grade
three to grade eight myself. In the middle of the prayer everyone
at Mass clenches a fist and strikes his or her own chest right above
the heart, and says "through my fault, through my fault, through
my most grievous fault."

The Mass re-enacts the Last Supper, when Jesus used bread and
wine to establish a new covenant with his followers. The message
I got from the Jesus the priest conjured up was: "I gave up my life
to rescue you from your sinfulness. Now you owe me." Above the
altar hung a larger-than-life marble cross with a giant plaster Jesus
nailed to it.

In grade three I didn't understand any of this. I soon learned that every time I didn't do what my parents told me or I disobeyed a teacher or took one of my sister's toys without permission, I was committing a sin and driving a nail deeper into Jesus' hand, ripping open the flesh on his back with a barbed whip, and spitting in his bleeding face.

I heard over and over again that I was conceived in sin, even though I had no idea what sex was or what "conceived" meant. I heard that because of the sin of Adam and Eve, I and all of humanity were born into sin. I came to know in my bones that as a human being I am as addicted to sin as an alcoholic is to whiskey. Whenever I even indulged in thoughts against God's law, I committed yet another sin and deepened my shame. I carried God around inside my head like a surveillance camera that never shuts off, even when I'm asleep.

My only way out was to follow the teachings of the priests and the pope, confess my sins in a dark, curtained booth, and acknowledge my shame before God and the church at every opportunity. Otherwise, I'd be condemned to a prison of unending fire and lung-searing, skin-boiling stench. Next to hell, a life sentence without parole in the worst prison on earth would be a picnic. At least in a prison, death would release me; in hell, I'd already be dead. There'd be no passage of time, no release date, no chance of escape, and nobody could ever visit me.

Some people believe there is no life after death, that when a person dies, that's simply the end. When a person kills, that's another story. That's something the dead person's family and friends never forget, since their lives are changed profoundly and forever. The killer also has to live with the memory for the rest of his life. That memory alone can be a kind of prison, a television program that repeats itself over and over and over. A person can change the channel for a while, but the program seems always to come back and repeat.

CHAPTER 4

IN CANADA WE HAVE LIFE AFTER DEATH

A person is more than the worst thing he has ever done.
— Helen Prejean, *Dead Man Walking*

n 1965, Steve Jones, a spoiled eighteen-year-old from the Maritimes, moves into a Toronto apartment with a twenty-seven-year-old woman. In a fight over the woman with another man, Steve kills him with a knife. If he'd done it five years earlier, he could have been hanged.

In Canada, with varying degrees of success, we've tried both execution and life sentences to punish murderers and protect the community. Until 1961, a person convicted of murder was automatically sentenced to death. Judges had no discretion. That year a new law defined two types of murder, capital and non-capital. Capital murder was either premeditated, or committed during another violent crime like armed robbery, or took the life of a police officer or prison guard. The last time Canada executed someone was 1962. Canada abolished capital punishment in 1976.

Now a person convicted of first-degree, premeditated murder automatically receives a sentence of life-twenty-five.[4] That means

---

4   The Protecting Canadians by Ending Sentence Discounts for Multiple
    Murders Act came into effect in 2011. It provides that for multiple
    murders,...

he or she must spend twenty-five years in prison before parole is possible, and after that the prisoner is on parole for the rest of his or her life. In fact, everyone convicted of murder in Canada is called a lifer for two reasons: they've taken a life, and they remain in the custody of Corrections Canada for the rest of their lives, whether in prison or out on parole. A life for a life. People convicted of other degrees of murder have lower numbers than twenty-five attached to their life sentences, sometimes as low as five. A lifer, out of prison for ten years, joked to me that he'd be on parole until thirty days after he died. He said that's how long it takes for the death certificate to circulate through the bureaucracy and his file to be closed.

Being eligible for parole doesn't mean they'll get it. I've met prisoners who got life-ten and life-seven, who have already been in prison for eighteen and twenty years and don't know if they will ever get parole. Even if the lifer gets parole, he or she is always only a step away from the federal prison he or she was released from. Each one can be summarily imprisoned for actions many of us on the outside do without even thinking, like having a beer or missing an appointment.

In 1991 Corrections Canada began supporting a program called LifeLine. Its funding was terminated in 2012 because the minister responsible claimed it "wasn't producing any results that improved public safety."[5] At the time, LifeLine in-reach workers across the country were supporting 4,300 people serving life sentences. People involved in LifeLine disputed the minister's claim, but without success. An in-reach worker did three things: he was

---

...a person can be sentenced to serve up to three life-twenty-five sentences concurrently. That means someone who murders three or more people could get a life-seventy-five sentence. The first person convicted of multiple murders who is subject to this provision is Travis Baumgartner. The judge sentenced him to a life-forty sentence.

5   CBC News, April 18, 2012, www.cbc.ca. Despite the government's claim, the program was effective enough to persuade the state of Colorado to model a new program there based on Canada's LifeLine experience.

a sign of hope for lifers in prisons, supported lifers living in the community, and shared his own personal experiences with people in the community. Steve Jones (not his real name) was one such worker. I often crossed paths with him when I was involved in M2W2. He invited me to his home in 2009 to talk about his work and his life.

\\\\\\\\\\

July 28, 2009. It's a dry summer in Edmonton, throughout all of central Alberta in fact. Canola fields that should by late July be lush and full of waving golden blossoms are varying shades of pale green and pockmarked with large brown patches of dust. But on this Tuesday morning as I drive south of Edmonton on Highway 2, those patches are black with rain. Two continuous, thin puddles shimmer in the right lane's driving ruts, and off to the west the trailing edge of the storm is breaking up into powder blue. The sun is gradually getting brighter.

I turn right onto a secondary highway, head west for a few kilometres, and look for the small white numbers on the green rural street signs that identify the range roads and township roads branching off north and south. I quickly learn that at one hundred kilometres an hour, by the time I read the number I'm looking for, I'm already past the turn. The highway I'm on has no shoulder, and so I pull off and stop on a built-up, flat patch of grass beside the road, a parking spot for farm equipment. Staging points like this are common as mosquitoes on the prairie, places for trucks and tractors to get from pavement to field and back again. I turn around, and soon I'm on a narrow gravel road heading north.

A kilometre off the blacktop, the first house on the left is a tidy, compact two-story white building with green trim. I turn into the driveway. North of the driveway is a barn several times the size of the house. Its roofline sags like a sway-backed horse. Daylight shines through dozens of places in the roof where shingles have come loose and fallen away. Its once-red paint is dull as rust, brown-gray like dried blood. The lawn is lush, green, and well-manicured. Like many farmyards, it is full of vehicles. But this place looks more like a well-kept used car lot than a junkyard. More than a dozen cars and pickup trucks line up in neat rows. Thistles and quack grass have been trimmed around the running boards, tires, and shining bumpers. Despite their being driven here through dust or mud, they are clean and sparkle in the sun.

I park my car and approach the door. A small terrier tethered to a post in the yard yipyipyipyipyips and sprints back and forth at the end of his chain. A slightly lower-pitched bark from inside the door answers yip for yip. A man comes to the door and lets me in. He's about 5'6", medium build, with a head full of gray hair, a neatly trimmed gray mustache, and a beard stained nicotine-brown on the right side of his mouth. He offers me a seat and a coffee. I ask for a glass of water instead and sit down. He sits across the kitchen table from me once he refills his mug. It's 9:30 a.m. and still cool outside; inside it's humid and muggy and smells of damp dog and burnt-out cigarettes.

I turn on my tape recorder. "Steve, you've just passed your thirty-fifth anniversary of being out of prison. You started your job as a LifeLine in-reach worker the day before your thirtieth anniversary. What was it that appealed to you about LifeLine?"

He sucks on his cigarette and clouds the air between us with smoke. He waves his right hand above the kitchen table, as if painting a pink sunrise in broad, sweeping stokes. "The concept appealed to me. I could see that my family was thrilled with the idea because I wouldn't any longer be crawling over roofs and walls and so on in the construction business. They felt I was getting too old. I was fifty-seven or fifty-eight then.

"My predecessor was hired back in '97. That's when the second Alberta position opened in Edmonton. I interviewed for it then. I'd just started a business with my youngest son, and I thought I could do both. The first parole officer who told me about the program was way off base. He said it was a thirty-seven-and-a-half-hour week kind of thing. That just didn't jibe with what two in-reach workers told me. It can't be done in thirty-seven and a half hours, not if you want to work at it."

I'd talked to Steve and Rob, his predecessor, about their work, and I remember tales of sixteen- and twenty-hour days, long drives across northern Alberta in blizzard conditions, tens of thousands of kilometres of mileage claims, which became a serious issue when budgets got tighter.

"How many hours does it take you?" I ask. "Do you even count?"

Steve says he doesn't log the time any more. He used to average sixty to seventy hours a week, but he's cutting back. He tells me he works "something over two hundred hours a month," not counting between 7:00 and 10:00 p.m. every night when he's on call, open to phone calls from lifers on his caseload. Like most nonprofit staff, Steve isn't in it for the money.

Steve chuckles that a unit manager in Drumheller told him he couldn't figure out why Steve would give up a successful construction company and go back into prison. "So I said to this chap I simply couldn't think of a better way to finish out my working life than doing something of value. This probably has more value than anything I've ever done, other than take care of myself and my family."

I'm not clear what's in it for him, so I ask, "Why do you do it, though? Do you have some sense of a life's mission maybe?"

He takes another puff. "I don't know if I have a mission in life. I've never thought of it in that light. I guess just don't do any harm."

"That sounds like the Hippocratic oath," I say, "the oath all doctors take when they enter the medical profession. But it seems to me you're doing way more than not harming anybody. How would you describe what you do?"

His eyes light up. He scrunches his cigarette butt into the ashtray and muses some more. "Reaching out to help people is part of my nature. When I was in the workforce, I taught and trained many people in how to build, simply with the desire to make their lives a little better. No other reason. It made them more useful to me as employees too."

He takes another cigarette out of the package, puts it between his lips, and keeps talking. I watch the unlit cigarette flip up and down as he speaks, like a broken high-voltage wire jumping and sparking all over the ground. "Even when I was up in Resolute Bay, I took a situation with the government where I trained locals to do my job so they didn't have to hire people from the south."

"In LifeLine," he says, "I work with a lot of families. That's one of the beauties of it. I had a lot of family support. Some people do and some don't. That's the sad thing, but that's the way it is. Some have no family support whatever." Back when he got out of Dorchester prison in the 1970s, he says, "We had none of the stuff for guys coming out that they have now. John Howard[6] was there. I heard about them but never saw their office. I had no idea what that was when I got out."

He says he didn't need anything. He was a young man quite capable of working. "A day and a half after I was out into the halfway house, I was working in an oil refinery as a construction worker, a union carpenter. It just grew from there. We came west in '78. We've been back and forth all over the country since: the high Arctic, back east, out here again."

"But let's get back to LifeLine," I say. I've chaired lots of meetings at work and as a volunteer; usually people get back on topic when the chair intervenes, but Steve resists everything I try to keep him on topic. "Your heart is really in this, Steve. I can see that. I'm trying to figure out where that comes from."

"LifeLine works," he says. He flicks his cigarette lighter into flame, and sucks in a lungful of smoke. His eyes sparkle. "To some degree. It works as far as the individual working the job has the ability to communicate and gets other people to communicate and cooperate." He smiles. "I mean within the system: the parole officers, the program people, the wardens, the deputy wardens. When I sit down in people's offices to work with them, there's nothing

---

6   The John Howard Society of Canada has been supporting prisoners and advocating for reforms to the criminal justice system since 1871.

more thrilling. All I get at first is walls. I run into walls big time. There's all kinds of opposition to the old ex-offender coming into an institution and working. You know that. You've seen it."

I recall the time, five years ago, when Steve started with LifeLine. I'd been going into the Max for three years. People there knew who I was and let me go anywhere I wanted to, talk to anybody I asked for. I couldn't figure out what their problem was with Steve. His name had been in CSC's system since the 1960s. He's still serving his life sentence in the community. In fact, Corrections Canada insisted that every LifeLine in-reach worker be a lifer who successfully reintegrated into the community for at least five years. Even so, it took them six months to process his security clearance so he could get into the Max and do his job.

The cogs of the bureaucracy grind slowly for everyone, though, not just lifers. Once, an M2W2 volunteer applied for security clearance at the Max. He got a call saying that he had to come in and submit fingerprints. He phoned me to ask why. I didn't know, and so I asked the person who handled the forms. She said there are two possible reasons: he has the same name as somebody with an arrest warrant out on him or he has the same name as a person with a criminal record. That's assuming he doesn't fit one of those categories himself. A couple of months later, the man withdrew from M2W2 before participating in a visit. Something changed in his life, and he couldn't spare the time any more. I didn't tell the clearance person at the Max he withdrew, because I wanted to see what would happen with his clearance. Nine years later, he still wasn't cleared.

Suddenly Steve gains momentum like a locomotive that's just climbed Rogers Pass and is heading downhill. "It's thrilling when you sit in on a parole hearing with an individual you believe has a chance of making it. There's no guarantee anybody's going to make it. The parole board knows that. We know that. But they have a shot. To be able to help a person get their life in order, what more good can a fellow do? You can't feel any better. The adrenaline rush from seeing somebody succeed is pretty amazing. It's probably something a drug addict goes through when he gets high."

"So you're doing this because you want a fix?" I say.

Steve keeps on rolling. "I guess. It's a whole combination of things. I like the work. I love communicating with people. I'm very comfortable dealing with staff. I was apprehensive when I started. I can walk into anybody's office now, sit down and talk with them, and in short order get a sense of whether this person's going to work with me or whether [he thinks] I'm just a pain in the tush."

He tells me about going to Grande Cache, a minimum-security prison at the time, five hours' drive northwest of Edmonton. His truck breaks down seventy-five kilometres short of his destination. Two prison staff, one the deputy warden, come out to help him fix it. "There wasn't a hotel room available. There was a lot of construction, a pipeline coming through, drilling rigs all over the place. Not only did they have camps; every bed in town was filled. So a staff member puts me up in his home. When I go to Grande Cache now, he says, 'Don't stay in a hotel. We've got a room. Come and stay at the house.'" Steve puts out his cigarette and exhales another lungful of smoke. "Super guy. We have a lot in common. Both in the construction industry, him a painter and me a carpenter. We'd sit up for hours. His wife'd go to bed and we'd be there yakking away. I remember him saying 'I had three or four guys every year that went through my shop that I was able to teach something to give them a better shot at going out there and taking care of themselves.' And he treats prisoners like he treats everybody else."

"That's great," I say, "but where did *your* desire to help *lifers* come from? When you got out thirty-five years ago, what help was there for you? Did anybody help you?"

"I don't recall anybody, not an individual," he says. "But there were people who helped all the way along. Sometimes I didn't even know about it. Years later I realized that a person was in my corner, and I never even thanked him for it. When I came out, I went to a halfway house in St. John, New Brunswick, Parr Town Centre. The director was an ex-assistant deputy warden out of Dorchester, Vince Thomas. He stopped me one day. He was always very supportive at board meetings and hearings. He was in charge of work placements within the institution. You could take trades and that sort of thing. That's all there was for programs.

"He stopped me one day in Dorchester and asked if I knew Pat Jones. I said, 'Yeah, I know him very well. He happens to be my father.' My father had taken this chap under his wing on the waterfront in St. John when he was going to university, taught him how to do stevedoring back in the day when it was all done manually, during and after the war. I later mentioned that to my brother, who was connected with the system way back then, and he said, 'Oh, yeah. He was the guy who got me into the plumbing trade when I was there.'"

Steve lights up the cigarette he's been holding. "I was telling somebody this just the other day. I probably wrote the first correctional plan they'd ever seen." Parole officers do correctional plans now, but in the sixties, there was no such thing. Parole officers now assess the prisoner's history and make a schedule of programs — on subjects like substance abuse, domestic violence, education, training, work possibilities inside the prison — and outline for the prisoner what he or she needs to do to increase the chance of success outside. The prisoner's ability to follow through on the plan is one of the most important pieces of evidence parole boards look at when they're considering a prisoner for release. In the late sixties, they had no correctional plans and no parole officers.

Steve says he simply sat down and wrote up a proposal for how he thought he should spend the rest of his time in prison. When he talks about this, he puckers his lips and blows a pencil-thin line of smoke into the room, calm and proud as the Cheshire cat in *Alice in Wonderland*. "This was after I tried to escape and didn't make it. And after many months of being locked in what we called the secure shop, a shop manned with gun towers. I thought, 'I'm not fast enough, smart enough, or big enough to get over the wall. So I guess I'll have to go out the front door.'"

By that time, Steve had been in prison over six years. His plan involved working hard, being on time, and earning a spot in a minimum-security prison and then parole in eighteen months. In those days, they didn't have the national parole board visiting federal prisons and having hearings on site, as we do now. Dorchester prison had a staff committee that made parole decisions for its own prisoners. Steve apparently impressed them with his plan. Here was a young man, a lifer, who hadn't finished grade eight — he still hasn't — who had written nothing before, and who decided to take control of his own future. He'd attempted so many escapes before that they didn't trust him. They were sure he'd run away again as soon as he got the chance. By sheer willpower, Steve earned their trust and stuck to his plan and got parole. I've heard lots of prisoners tell me they've had it with prison, that they will never come back, yet even those with the best intentions keep coming back anyway. They so often revert to what they know and reconnect with the kind of people they knew before. I wonder, "What's so different about Steve?" I ask him, "Why did you make it when so many others don't?"

"Work was my salvation," he puffs, chugging ahead without pausing to think. "Work has been my nemesis too. I'm a workaholic, which has injured my family relationships at times. I've had to pull back. You really have to have a strong desire to do well. For me the way to do that is work. I don't think so much of personal relationships. Most of my relationships come from work. I have made those connections through work. Back in those days, there wasn't anybody to help you when you got out."

For most prisoners I know, the biggest problem when they get out is how to avoid situations that got them in trouble in the first place: gangs, drug dealers, abusive or alcoholic parents, poverty. I wonder what Steve needed to avoid when he got out, what obstacles in his background could have sucked him back into prison.

I've known Steve for five years. I've never talked to him about the crime that got him a life sentence. That's his business. In M2W2 I tell volunteers we only talk about a prisoner's crime if he brings it up. On the inside, prisoners carry their crimes around like a brand burnt onto their foreheads. The system, guards, parole officers, program staff, administrators, and the courts label each one of them by crime and sentence. The best way for us to show them respect is not even to bring it up, to empower each prisoner to move beyond that label. But Steve had already agreed to talk to me about his life story, and so I ask, "How did you end up in prison in the first place?"

He doesn't even blink. "I didn't come from an abusive family. Back in the day, I had lots of time sitting in a cell. I went into my own head and decided what the hell I was doing there. It got to a point where I could live with myself. Because no human being is comfortable having killed another human being. That's the great- est taboo we have in society. We all grow up in society, whether good, bad, or somewhere in the middle. Some of these stories are so terrible. So much abuse, alcohol abuse, all of that back in my day. Now there's drugs and everything else to go with it. That wasn't in my household. My family had pretty decent values for the 1940s, fifties, and sixties."

For nine years, he says, he was the youngest child in his family and "spoiled rotten." Before Steve was born, his mother had two children who died of pneumonia before they were a year old. Steve's father was a simple man with a grade four education, a hard worker, and he was concerned that his wife was sad and low on energy. His solution to her grief for those lost children was that she needed more work to keep her busy. How to keep her busy? Give her another child! That child was Steve. And for nine years he was the centre of attention for his mother and his older siblings. Then, suddenly, two more children came along. When that happened, he became "a pain-in-the-ass kid looking for attention." He started running away from home, breaking and entering, stealing cars. When he was fourteen, he and his brother did a break-in, stole a car, and got caught. The older brother went to prison, Steve to a juvenile detention centre.

Not long after being locked up, he escapes, gets caught, spends some time in the hole—solitary confinement—and has a meeting with the director. They make a deal. The director says he'll be out in six months if he behaves. Steve agrees. He joins the Army Cadets, does survival training, becomes sergeant of the troop, gets a pass to visit his family, and comes back to the director in six months to get his reward. The director hems and haws and apologizes and cancels the deal. So Steve walks out of the office and keeps on going through the back door and out again into the community. He gets an extra year for that escape. He serves every day of that, not in juvenile detention but in the county jail. When he gets out, he's sixteen. Six weeks later he goes out drinking, gets in a fight, passes out. He comes to, and they tell him he's smashed up two businesses. He gets eighteen more months. But the jailers can't control him. The magistrate gives him three months for escaping and tells him, "If we can't hold you here, I know a place that can." He sends him to the maximum-security federal prison at Dorchester. Steve is seventeen.

Steve asks me to pause the tape recorder so he can let out Silky, his little dog. He goes out the door into the yard carrying the dog and returns carrying Jasper, the Jack Russell terrier who's been outside tethered to a post. He locks him up in a cage in the kitchen, about four feet away from where we're sitting.

"Don't you feel like a jailer, putting him in that thing?" I ask.

"No shit," Steve shrugs. "I don't like the cage, but he's accustomed to it. Ever since my son Ricky drove him out here from Ontario with a U-Haul."

Jasper has a pointed, scruffy gray beard just like Steve's. He's so full of energy he shuffles and scratches around the inside of the cage, yips and whines nonstop. He may be used to the cage, but he sure doesn't like it.

"I served nine months. Survived that quite nicely. I was scared to death going in there, but I wasn't about to show it. I had to survive." Steve walks over and lets Jasper out. Jasper jumps up on us, scampers back and forth across the linoleum, yips and whines.

"Jasper! Stop! No! Down! Sit, Jasper. All the way. Stay. Stay."

Steve holds up what looks like a small tennis racket. "Is that to whack him with?" I ask.

"No. I never touch him with it," Steve chuckles. "But he seems to be petrified of it when I have it in my hand. It's an electric fly killer."

"Jasper! Get over here!" he demands. "Come. Down! Down! Settle down!"

"I remember being petrified," he says of his first days in Dorchester. "They had what we now call the fish tank, for newcomers. They called it the newcomers' gang in my day." Jasper puts his front paws on Steve's knees and whimpers. Steve stands up and walks over to the cage.

"Hey! Get over here! In your room!" Steve wrestles Jasper back into the cage. Jasper barks and scratches the cage door. "No noise!" Steve insists.

"I got released from Dorchester in 1964. I was out all of thirteen weeks."

Jasper barks and barks.

"Hey!" Steve yells. He waves the fly killer at Jasper as if he really means it this time.

"Various things were going on. I stayed with brothers. Headed for Toronto. I got mixed up with this woman on the way and ended up committing homicide in Toronto and going to Kingston."

"Whoa!" I say. "Slow down a little. How did all that happen?"

Steve says he drove away from New Brunswick, heading west to make a new start. Along the way he picks up three hitchhikers. One is a woman he takes all the way to Toronto, Clara. He moves in with her. He's eighteen; she's twenty-seven. They share a third-floor apartment with her male cousin and the cousin's wife in Cabbagetown, a working class district east of downtown. Steve gets a job at the demolition company where the cousin works. Not long afterwards, Clara starts dating someone else, a twenty-two-year-old with a wife and two kids. Steve gets upset about that, and he and Clara argue. Steve feels trapped. He knows he can't do anything about the other man. He also knows he can't move out, because he can't afford to live anywhere else.

For a week he hears that the new boyfriend is spitting mad, threatening to come over to beat him up and throw him out of the apartment. One night the cousin decides Steve needs a little comfort. He takes Steve out to a bar. When they stagger home well after midnight, Clara is there with her new boyfriend. Steve detours into the kitchen to avoid a fight. The boyfriend comes after him. Steve is packing a knife, and the boyfriend knows it. But the boyfriend swaggers right up to Steve anyway, chest to chest. He tells Steve, "You get out of this house or I'll throw you out!"

Steve's heart races, his skin is clammy, his brain shuts down in horror, like when he first entered Dorchester prison as a teenager. But he's had a lot of experience hiding his fear. He stands his ground and looks the man in the eye.

"If you want to go outside," Steve says, "let's go outside. Let's get it over with."

Steve goes out first and waits on the sidewalk. He faces the front door of the building: his knees bent, his body arched forward, the knife in his hand, aimed forward and ready for action. The boyfriend charges at him like a raging bull and knocks Steve into the street. The boyfriend runs away through a broken fence and up the alley next to the house. Steve dashes into the dark after him and stops. He can't see a thing, just shadows. The boyfriend runs at him again, smashes Steve into a brick wall, and dashes out the alley. Steve is stunned momentarily but shakes it off and darts after him.

"Help! Police! Murder!" Steve finds the boyfriend across the street screaming, leaning against a lamppost. The boyfriend is bleeding from a stab wound between his second and third ribs and soon afterward drowns in his own blood. But Steve doesn't know any of that at the time.

Steve stops, pockets the knife, and walks up the street. Before he gets two blocks, a police car pulls up, an officer gets out, aims his gun at Steve, and tells him to get in the car.

Steve tries to keep the news from his parents. He's ashamed of himself. He's worried about his father's heart condition. A lawyer Steve talks to in jail tells him if he can raise $3,500 to pay a hotshot defence attorney, he can get him off. Steve's brother Mitchell is a successful businessman in Kingston. Steve hopes he will lend him the money. So he contacts Mitchell, who phones their parents and tells them the whole story. Steve's father is ready to sell the farm and whatever he owns to pay the lawyer, but Steve won't let him. Steve says he'd rather take his chances with a legal aid lawyer than drag his parents into poverty. The legal aid lawyer tells him the Crown has to prove intent, that Steve went into the fight hoping to kill the man. Steve knows he never meant to kill, so he thinks he'll be okay. He says he never even stabbed him; the man simply ran right into Steve's knife.

When the cousin's wife is on the stand, she swears: "Oh, yeah. Steve threatened him. No question. He said 'I'm gonna get 'im.'" Steve's lawyer cross-examines her, challenges her memory, pushes her so far she can't even believe herself, according to Steve. She says, "Well, no. I guess Steve didn't threaten him after all." The Crown attorney objects, and she reverses herself again. Then the judge calls for order in the court. He looks her in the eye and demands: "Make up your mind. Did he threaten or not?" She says, "Your Honour, he did, but the lawyers had me mixed up." When the judge accepts her testimony, Steve realizes he can't win. His mother and father are sitting right behind him in agony, and he refuses to make them suffer through any more trial. Steve changes his plea to guilty of non-capital murder.

Steve comes back to court for sentencing, gets life-seven, and leaves the courtroom flanked by two armed guards. In the hallway he sees the victim standing there, a corpse staring at him, his colourless eyes blank and empty, his skin gray as a rain cloud. Steve's hair stands up on end, his skin tingles, his fingers twitch. "What the hell am I going to prison for if the guy's still alive?" Steve says to himself. Then his heart flutters and his knees buckle under him. Later somebody tells him the victim's brother came to court that day. He looked so much like the victim they could've been twins.

"It took me years to get to a place where I could live with myself," Steve says. He pauses, lights up another cigarette, takes a deep breath. He holds it in for what seems like at least a minute and lets the smoke drift lazily out of his mouth. "The day they sentenced me, you could've hung me, and I wouldn't have given a shit. The only thing that would've made me want to stop it would've been how it affected my family. Because of how I was brought up, I believed I deserved death. I was actually in favour of capital punishment at the time."

He stops again. After another puff of smoke, he adds, "I was sentenced to life in prison on my nineteenth birthday, October 16, 1965. Even life-seven—for a nineteen-year-old, seven years is almost half a lifetime. You can't see the end of it. And you don't know anything about how the system works or how you're gonna get out. Eventually you find out. You have to decide either to work with it or against it. If you work against it, you're going to be there a long time. Some guys serve over thirty years on a life-ten or a life-seven. Why would you do this to yourself?"

Steve himself now works with lifers, convinces them they have to work with the system as he did or else they may never get out. He goes into prisons and talks to new lifers, shows them how to cope with their new reality. He visits lifers in the middle of their prison time, listens to their beefs, their struggles, their plans, and he journeys with them through their lowest moments. He talks to lifers as they near parole eligibility, shows them it really is possible to make it on the outside, and helps them get through the anxiety and find their way during those critical first months on the outside. Part of that involves Steve serving as an escort for prisoners who get temporary absences. He takes them to meetings and speaking engagements and introduces them to other lifers and to people in the community.

In Edmonton, Steve puts on a monthly LifeLine meeting for lifers out in the community and for lifers who can get out on a pass for a few hours. Twice he's invited people from the Edmonton Victims of Homicide organization to come. "The first time I did it, I was petrified," he smiles. "I was every bit as scared as I was going through the door of Dorchester in the old days. I had more people than normal come to that meeting. One of the victims brought a little stone they passed around, a healing stone, a speaking stone. Whoever has the stone speaks; nobody else."

A lot of healing went on that night, he says. Victims tell lifers what their lives have been like after the murder of a loved one, and lifers talk about their own pain and struggle. Steve tells me of a woman whose sister's husband was serving a life sentence for killing her sister. She'd been writing to the man to try to figure out what happened. She thought they'd had a happy life together. The brother-in-law didn't respond. The woman doesn't understand what's happening and doesn't know what to do. Steve tells her, "The guy can't even stand himself right now. I don't even know the individual, but if he's human at all, not a sociopath or a psychopath, he is in no place emotionally to write a letter. He has no idea what to say. It could take up to five years before he has his own head straight."

"But what about your case, Steve?" I ask. "Have you ever reached out to your victim's family, the wife and two kids he left?"

"No," he says. "That sort of thing wasn't even done in my day. I never heard of victim mediation or anything else. Restorative justice is a fairly new concept. None of it in the 1960s." He pauses and looks over at Jasper in his cage. Jasper has been uncharacteristically quiet for a long time, but I see one sad eye peering through the small window on the side of his cage. Steve goes on. "I thought: would it be productive? That was even before I heard of LifeLine. Wouldn't it be nice to go back to find his wife and children and apologize to them? Or would they try to shoot me if I came to town? That's not something I could fault them for. And after I took this job I thought: Now? Over forty years later? There's no point."

Even so, after all that time, Steve carries it around with him every moment of his life. It's always on his mind, he says, night and day. In a profound way, it's affected the whole course of his life since that night. He says he can go a year or more without thinking of the victim's name, but it always comes back: the memory of the night it happened, the remorse, the shame, the suffering he caused his own family and the victim's family. I've seen this same phenomenon so many times before that I start to wonder: What is there about human blood that leaves a permanent mark on the spirit whenever someone takes another person's life?

After our conversation, Steve walks out the door with me into the yard and over to my car. The sun is almost straight overhead, the sky is clear, the air transparent and still, and in the half minute it takes us to get next to the car, I can already feel the sweat dampening my armpits. It's going to be another warm day, this time with humidity. I ask Steve about all those cars and pickups in the yard. He tells me they belong to some of the lifers he works with. This is where they park when they violate parole conditions and have to go back inside to do more time. They know Steve will look after them until they get out again.

I shake Steve's hand, thank him, and head up Highway 2 toward the Max. This is Tuesday, my day to spend the afternoon with prisoners. I know there won't be much sunshine in there, certainly not enough to burn off any shame or remorse. The sun will shine on the cemeteries nearby, and the grass there will be greener after the rain. The murder victims there will still be dead, their loved ones' lives scarred forever by violence.

CHAPTER 5

VICTIM IMPACT: CRACKING THE SHELL

I escaped the early days of shock and re-entered the world, where I was reminded and was a reminder. As though this is who I am. Sister of Murdered Woman. I have been introduced accidentally by your name, and one woman asked if I had been busy healing, as though this is my project, my responsibility, my duty.

— Lorie Miseck, *A Promise of Salt*

On a sunny, warm spring day in Pueblo, Colorado, in 1954, a five-year-old boy walks down an alley with his big brother. His shoes crunch, crunch, crunch the loose limestone pebbles. Like on the cinder track around the Pueblo Dodgers Class A baseball diamond where he went to a night game with his dad last summer.

He remembers the smell of fresh popcorn, the towers of glittering star clusters backlighting the grass, transforming it into a magic emerald-green carpet where anything might happen. His skin tingles. He stands tall in the batter's box, his Louisville Slugger cocked, his whole body corkscrewed tight to smack the next fastball over the right-field fence. There's a loud crack when the bat and ball collide. The impact resonates up and down his spine. His spikes bite the freshly raked brown soil. His legs pump faster and faster as he nears first base. The ball soars past the leaping fielder's extended glove. The boy raises his arms and punches the air with his fists as the ball clears the fence. He relaxes into a trot. The crowd leaps to its feet and roars.

But in his backyard now, alone, he notices a box turtle, its bald yellow and brown head parting the tall grass as it advances, its jaw locked in grim determination, its beady black eyes focused on the next grass blade and the few inches it can see ahead in the unmowed jungle. The turtle comes to the grass's edge. A broad causeway of loose gravel stretches ahead as far as it can see. Suddenly, the earth, which had been trembling and crunching around him, becomes quiet. A giant blocks the sun. The turtle retracts its head, feet, tail, and becomes a yellow-mottled, chocolate-brown rock.

But the boy knows better. He's seen these animals before. His older brother captured a few of them in local parks and brought them home, fed them wilted lettuce leaves and carrot tops. The boy held one in his hand once, stroked its slick, shoe-sole-hard underbelly, felt its shell's bony edge, the backbone ridge, the lines where the shield-shaped segments meld together, the nicks and cracks at various angles across the mosaic-like yellow-and-brown patterns.

This turtle in the alley, though, is different. He found it himself. It belongs to him. He picks it up, holds it in front of his face, turns it over, examines its underbelly, the frontal flap so tight against the shell he couldn't wedge a dime in there. It's not as heavy as the one his brother let him hold, and it's a little smaller, about five inches front to back. He examines the shell. Not a mark on it, as if it had come to him straight from a factory: molded, painted, clean, and shiny. The yellow markings on its brown back, the brown markings on its yellow belly as symmetrical and pure as the mosaic of Our Lady of Guadalupe on the wall of the parish church: her sky-blue cloak, her golden halo, an arc of white stars above her, an arc of red roses below.

The boy was hoping to find a playmate, but none of the kids in the neighbourhood is outside. He's alone with the turtle. He picks up a stick and pokes its rear end, the thin line between shell and underside. The line clenches even tighter. The turtle won't come out. He faces the front of the shell and knocks on the top with his fist. "Come out and play!" he yells. The turtle is still as a stone. He puts it down on the gravel, nudges it with his shoe. He rolls it over onto its back and then right-side up again.

He finds a chunk of red granite next to the garage. It's the size of a football but much heavier. "I wonder how hard that shell is?" the boy says to himself. He picks the rock up, chest high, and drops it on the middle of the perfect turtle-shell ridge. The rock rolls off. The shell is cracked and cratered at the point of impact. The boy takes a few steps toward the house, stops, and waits to see what happens. He's shocked to see red blood oozing out of the cracks. He knows turtles are cold-blooded and assumed they'd have green or blue blood, like monsters in the movies.

In a few minutes, horny claws and scaly legs emerge. The neck cranes right, left; eyes warily scan the yard. The legs stretch out, push off against the gravel, and the turtle lurches forward. The legs on the more damaged left side are visibly weaker than the right legs. The turtle advances in a broad leftward arc. When it reaches the opposite side of the driveway, it stops to rest. Or could it be dead?

"Gary! Time for supper!" The boy's mother shouts out the kitchen window, and the boy salivates. He remembers how hungry he is. He turns, trots in the back door of the house, into a steaming kitchen smelling of pot roast and potatoes.

The boy doesn't care. He's forgotten the turtle and moved on to his supper, his school work, and the prospect of baseball with friends. Sixty years later, after thirty-two years of marriage and raising three children to adulthood, he remembers the day he dropped that rock just to see what would happen. He regrets that he injured the turtle, maybe even killed it. But it's so long ago now, so far away. How could he atone for what he did?

I was that boy. I still am that boy. I've learned from experience that one thing a person can do, what I have done all too often, is let that feeling of remorse get deep in my gut. My bowel twists in on itself, aches, burns, and clenches. I suffer heartburn, gas, hemorrhoids, and diarrhea. My midsection a granite chunk that tortures me in bed and all day long makes each step a weightlifting exercise, each thought a wrestling match with a sticky ball of tar.

It took me many years to realize I have a choice. When I do something wrong, I can choose to accept that I made a mistake, forgive myself, and get on with my life. Or I can conclude that I am a vile and disgusting human being, swallow a shovelful of shame, and wear it as if I were a turtle and it were my shell.

I don't know for sure that I killed that turtle. It was seriously injured, but it was well enough to stagger away. What if I'd done the equivalent to a human being? What if I'd dropped a rock on my little sister's head just to see what would happen? What if I got into an argument with a bigger boy and decided I could win the argument with a knife or a baseball bat? What if, when I was an adolescent, I got turned on by the sight of a pretty girl and raped her? What if I were a man who got turned on by a woman/man/boy/girl and let the urge take me wherever it would?

What if I were out of work and hungry and I saw well-dressed, well-fed people coming and going from a bank and I went in and took money for myself? What if, like Raskolnikov in Dostoyevsky's *Crime and Punishment*, I decided to kill someone, anyone, simply to find out what it felt like, or simply because I could?

I've carried a lot of shame around my whole life, and it's been a constant struggle to break out of that shell. But all the regrets of my sixty-five years added together are trivial compared to what prisoners I've visited carry on their backs all day, every day. Drunk driving causing death. Break and enter. Serial rape. Pedophilia. Multiple murder. Aggravated assault. Armed robbery. Drug trafficking. Mutilating a dead body.

I should explain what I mean by shame. It's a word that gets tossed around a lot and means different things to different people. The definition of it that works for me is: a painful emotion that results from a person's awareness of his or her worthlessness and depravity. For me there is an essential difference between guilt and shame, based on life experience. Guilt is about violating a law or code of conduct and feeling remorse about it; shame is about putting down a person, trying to make the person feel he or she is not only guilty of an offence but in fact is less than human and deserves to be treated like an animal in a zoo or worse.

Some prisoners have told me that going to prison was the best thing that could have happened to them. They were caught in a gang and couldn't get out. They were addicted to heroin or cocaine or crystal meth and had actually left the human race. They were addicted to the lifestyle drug trafficking bought them and didn't care whom they killed or destroyed as long as they got their money. They've told me prison saved their lives. It took armed police officers, guards, iron bars, concrete walls, and round-the-clock confinement to get them out of their shells so they could look at themselves in the mirror. In every case, prisoners who wanted to move on with their lives decided to own up to the harm they caused to real people and forgive themselves.

One prisoner told me he used to be proud to be a notorious bank robber, like Clyde Barrow and Bonnie Parker, who had fans across North America during the Great Depression because many ordinary people saw the banks they robbed as the enemy. After all, the banks foreclosed on homes and farms and forced people to travel the countryside and grovel just to survive. This prisoner told me he thought bank robbery was a victimless crime. He believed a bank was a corporation as cold and heartless as the glass and stone that housed the vault.

Then, at his sentencing, a victim confronted him, in tears. She said her life was in ruins. Years after the robbery, she still couldn't sleep. She was constantly on edge. Every knock on her door made her knees buckle and her stomach turn inside out. She could not escape the memory of the day the robber came in and threatened to kill her unless she filled his bag with cash: the steely, cold voice, the face masked in light-brown pantyhose, the black pistol barrel glaring at her, the threat of hot lead and death in its dark centre.

She had been happily married until that day, but afterwards, she said, she recoiled from her husband's slightest touch. In the meantime, he left her because she had become someone else. Not only was she unable to work; she was alone and couldn't even live with herself.

The prisoner I met had been behind bars for more than five years and would be up for parole in about a year. He was clearly sorry for the harm he'd caused and was determined to make a new life for himself. He was determined to remember the look on that woman's face and what he did to her, to accept that his crimes hurt many others too. Since his eyes were opened, his greater struggle has been to avoid wallowing in shame and, instead, to move on with his life.

Victims too receive life sentences, even though they didn't do anything to deserve them. In every case, crime causes permanent damage. Even if the crime is "only" break and enter and nobody is home at the time, the feeling of violation can shred the fabric of the victim's life, and the memory of it can surface at 3:00 a.m. as a nightmare. The Canadian legal system now provides victims a chance, at sentencing and parole hearings, to make formal victim impact statements. The murder of Stefanie Rengel had a particularly profound impact that was felt across the country.

January 1, 2008. Near the intersection of Northline Road and Bermondsey Road in northeastern Toronto. A seventeen-year-old boy, four days short of his eighteenth birthday, speaks with his girlfriend three times from outside fourteen-year-old Stefanie Rengel's residence and then phones Stefanie. He asks her to come outside to talk. The boy, David Bagshaw, was involved in a brief friendship with Stefanie two years before. Now Bagshaw and Melissa Todorovic are lovers. Melissa is a fifteen-year-old student at East York Collegiate Institute, which Bagshaw also attends. Bagshaw has called or texted Melissa more than 3,300 times in the previous four months. Since October, Melissa has been so jealous of Stefanie that she has repeatedly pressured Bagshaw to kill her. The boy has a knife in his hand, a long butcher knife he took from his family's kitchen.

Stefanie tells her little brother, Ian, she'll only be gone a minute. She runs outside without a coat. The snow is piled four feet high beside the sidewalk. Bagshaw stabs her six times and runs away before she falls to the snow. Gavin Shoebottom drives by and finds her, calls 911 for help, tries to staunch the bleeding, and holds her in his lap to comfort her, while Stefanie drowns in her own blood.

Stefanie's mother, Patricia Hung, is a Toronto city police officer at the time. Patricia's husband, Sgt. James Hung, is a Toronto police officer too. On July 13, Ms. Hung reads her victim impact statement to the court preparing to sentence Melissa Todorovic after she is found guilty of first-degree murder.

"I am afraid....I am forever changed....At times I'm paralyzed with fear. I wake each night, at least once, in the most indescribable state of terror....I have constant nightmares of horrible acts committed against Stefanie and the boys. I am unable to sleep properly and too scared to take medication to sleep for fear someone will break into our house and I'll be too medicated to protect my family....I am unable to go out at night alone....

"How could I ever explain the ramifications of this on my career. Simply, I don't have one, and that also has been stolen from me. I used to love my job and was proud of my work, and now I don't know how I'm ever going to do it again because simply, I'm afraid....

"The trial process has been unbelievably difficult, an emotional roller coaster that has yet to end. And to make matters worse, I was subjected to the unbelievable insensitivity of a defence attorney who boasted about 'just loving an audience' when I was on the stand waiting for the jury to come in and cross-examination to begin. As if sitting only feet away from the person who killed my daughter and having to be civilized wasn't asking enough, I guess he thought he would have a little fun at my expense.

"I want inner peace, which is believed to come from forgiveness, but I am unable to forgive someone who has shown no remorse. [Melissa Todorovic] insists that she didn't think that [David Bagshaw] would actually kill Stefanie, but instead of being horrified when he did, she asked him to re-enact the crime, then have a little sex and then call her mummy for a celebratory latte. This is the most revealing glimpse into who she is and the danger she poses. How does one forgive that?"

Stefanie's thirteen-year-old brother, Ian, says, "I go to high school in September and I don't know who to trust, who to fear, who to make friends with, so I probably just won't. I can't trust anybody."

On June 17, 2010, I'm driving north on the Highway 2 from Didsbury, Alberta. It's 9:00 a.m., and I'm going home to Edmonton after an M2W2 visit to Bowden the night before. I spent the night with a friend instead of driving in the dark and getting to bed after midnight. I tune in to CBC radio. *The Current* features an interview with Zofia Cisowski, the mother of Robert Dziekanski. On October 14, 2007, her son was tasered by four RCMP officers at the Vancouver International Airport and died at the scene. Ms. Cisowski has suffered for nearly three years, through the loss of her son and the life they would have had together, relentless media attention, the very public posting on YouTube of the video of her son being tasered, conflicting accounts of the incident by the officers involved, the provincial Braidwood Inquiry, and the lawsuit she'd filed against the RCMP officers, the airport, the BC government, and the government of Canada. She speaks with a heavy Polish accent, but the message she conveys is in her voice breaking repeatedly, her tears, and the audible heaving of her chest as she speaks.

As I drive, I wonder what life is like for the four officers and whether they are listening to this interview. I wonder what the toll was on them and their families as they attempted to defend their actions and to maintain the confidence of Canadians in the RCMP. I wonder if they have been able to take personal responsibility for their actions and to forgive themselves so they can move on. I do know that this incident has profoundly damaged the reputation of our national police force.

If not for the video Robert Pritchard shot on his cellphone, if not for Zofia Cisowski's relentless demands for justice, if not for the public outrage over the incident and extensive media coverage, there never would have been an inquiry, an out-of-court settlement, or an apology from the RCMP. That's what it took to crack the culture of self-protection and denial.

That same culture in the Roman Catholic Church, the Boy Scouts, residential schools, and elsewhere has delayed healing for many on the receiving end of sexual abuse by those in authority. Those people have endured decades of suffering, and some have received apologies and compensation. And although they are indeed "victims," that very word has too often implied helplessness. Just as criminals are more than their crime, victims of sexual assault—and other crimes as well—are more than mere victims.

Retired NHL star Theo Fleury, a victim of abuse by junior hockey coach Graham James, recently coined a new term. He calls himself a victor over childhood sexual abuse. On the victorwalk.com website, he talks about how a frog can look all around but can only jump forward, never backward. Although she doesn't use that term, Sarah Salter-Kelly is also a victor, a victor over a crime of a different sort: her mother's murder. She found a way to love her mother's murderer even though he was dead.

CHAPTER 6

HOW TO LOVE A DEAD MURDERER

The thing with trauma is that it can creep up on you. Until you come to that place of peace and liberation, it can creep up on you at any minute, any time of the day, and all of a sudden [you] just feel this great sense of loss inside of yourself that can bring you to the ground.
—Sarah Salter-Kelly, whose mother, Sheila Salter, was murdered in 1995

Thelma and Louise is a movie about two women who've had it with all the abuse the world has heaped on them. After an evening in a bar, they go to the parking lot, where a stranger tries to rape Thelma, and Louise kills him in an outburst of long-festering feminist rage. They drive across the U.S. southwest wreaking havoc and having fun. Soon there's a massive police chase. They're wanted for murder, assaulting and kidnapping a police officer, destruction of property, and a variety of other crimes. They're in a remote part of the U.S. southwest, driving full speed with the top of their convertible down, their hair streaming out wildly behind them. They realize there's no way out. Thelma says to Louise, "I don't ever remember feeling this awake." At a dead end near the Grand Canyon, Thelma says to Louise, "Let's not get caught....Let's keep goin'." Louise agrees. She steps on the gas, the car flies off the edge of the canyon, and the movie ends with the car frozen in the air a mile above the canyon floor.

The movie should come with one of those disclaimers in ads for trampolines and high-performance vehicles that says, "Do not attempt this at home." The movie came out twenty years ago, and Thelma and Louise are still in that car suspended in the air over the canyon. They are still evading the hordes of police who have them cornered. They are still free, empowered, self-possessed, defiant women. Their story still resonates as a feminist outcry against sexism. And they are still fictitious characters, not real people. For real people, suicide is one sure way to escape time — and to escape doing time. It's an option many people in prison wrestle with every day. Peter Brighteyes was one such person.

On Tuesday, April 8, 1997, Alberta Court of Queen's Bench Justice Alec Murray gave Peter John Brighteyes, thirty-five, a life sentence for the first-degree murder of Sheila Salter. Brighteyes would not be eligible for parole until April 2022. On April 25, 1997, the day after he arrived at Edmonton Institution to begin his sentence, Brighteyes hanged himself with his shoelaces. This ended one chapter for the Salter family and opened another.

||||||||

At 8:30 a.m. on Thursday, December 7, 1995, Sheila Salter was in the parkade near her office, about to begin a day of work. A man waiting for a haircut at 12406 112th Avenue heard what he thought was a woman's scream. Then Sheila Salter disappeared. For the next ten days her disappearance was the top story in all Edmonton news media. The front page of the *Edmonton Sun* of December 8, 1995, featured a banner headline in two-inch type: "IN COLD BLOOD!" "Violent abduction" was the subheading. Below and beside these words were two colour photographs. One, a two-and-a-quarter-by-two-and-a-half-inch snapshot of a smiling Sheila Salter. The other, an eight-by-seven-inch picture of her Chevrolet Blazer with five police officers in and around it. Page three headlines roared: "MEN

SNATCH MOM OF 3: Police fear woman kidnapped from parkade may have been murdered," "Friends, neighbors in shock," and "Abduction chronology." The main story noted that police found "a substantial amount" of blood inside the vehicle and splashed on the outside. The next day the *Sun*'s front page featured a policeman lifting the lid of a Dumpster and looking inside: "COPS HUNT BODY," "Abducted mother likely slain: Police."

For the next nine days both the *Sun* and the *Edmonton Journal* featured large photos of Sheila Salter and her husband, Ted, in happier times, of Ted and Sheila's parents, Agnes and Harry, weeping. The *Journal*'s coverage was matter of fact and balanced compared to the *Sun*'s trademark sensationalism, but the underlying message was clear: our community is not safe, especially our women, even in daytime in the city centre. Two days after the abduction, "TRAIL HAS GONE COLD: Police suspend search for missing mom, ask public for assistance." On December 11, "Snowfall freezing search for mom." December 14, "HUSBAND CLINGS TO HOPE." Later in the week, "Family prays for a miracle."

On Sunday, December 17, 1995, Edward Bork goes to his brother's farm to salvage an old stove and nearly trips over Sheila Salter's frozen, naked body in the uninhabited farmhouse near Chipman, forty-five kilometres east of Edmonton. On Tuesday, December 19, the *Sun* announces: "MANHUNT! Canada-wide warrant issued for suspect after body of city woman found." Beside a large picture of five policemen trudging through snow away from a weather-worn, unpainted brown wood farmhouse is a three-by-four-inch mug shot of Peter Brighteyes.

As I flip through the pages of the scrapbook Sarah Salter-Kelly loaned to me, I recall my own feelings during that time over fifteen years ago. I had a wife and two daughters, seventeen and fifteen. I knew I couldn't protect them from the men out there who rape, kill, and brutalize women, from the ancient patriarchal systems that still put women down. I carried a lot of shame too, as if my Y chromosome and my penis, testicles, facial hair, and deep voice made me an accomplice to every violent act against women everywhere, every day. Over the years, my wife reminded me many times that she didn't feel safe even walking alone in our own neighbourhood after dark; the Sheila Salter rape-abduction-murder made her fear the daytime too.

A friend of a friend who knows I'm working on a book about my prison experiences says she thinks Sarah Salter-Kelly might be open to talking to me about her mother's murder and how it changed her life. In November 2010, we meet at the Second Cup at the Stanley A. Milner branch of the Edmonton Public Library. It's a preliminary get-acquainted meeting where we can size each other up and she can let her gut decide whether she should get involved in my book project or not. After several months of scheduling changes, sick kids, and snowstorms, we manage to get together again.

On May 16, 2011, I drive forty-five minutes southwest of Edmonton to her acreage west of Pigeon Lake and pull into the driveway. The sign in the front yard says "Medicine Spirit Center." Sadie, her dog, barks ferociously, and I hesitate before I open the car door. How serious a guard dog is this, I wonder. When Sarah comes to the door of the house to wave, Sadie wags her tail and stops barking. Sarah offers me a cup of tea and a seat on her front patio, a protected area away from the swarming mosquitoes.

A fierce wind has been blowing in north-central Alberta non-stop for a week and a half, but it lets up this morning. Hundreds of Alberta forest fires are still out of control, including the one that forced everybody in Slave Lake to evacuate without notice and destroyed nearly half the buildings in town. I comment on the connection between the "spirit" on her sign and the wind, how closely related the two concepts are. In Greek the same word fits them both.

Sarah sips on her tea and says, "Sometimes we need those fierce winds. Yeah, metaphorically, they teach us about surrender, flexibility. Lots of stuff. How as a human, there's a part of me that says, after a week and a half of wind, 'I don't care what you're gonna teach me. Right now I just want it to be calm for a little bit.' I just want to go outside without a hair tie and get some work done."

So I ask her about the fierce wind that changed her life fifteen years ago. She told me when we first met over coffee in downtown Edmonton that she refused to accept that she and her family, even her mother, are victims of homicide. So I ask her where that comes from, and if her mother isn't a victim of homicide, how would she describe what happened to them all?

Sarah leans back in her chair and cradles her teacup in her hands. "I grew up in a household where we weren't allowed to use the word victim," she says. "My mom was a life skills coach, so there was a lot of mindfulness around language from the age of ten. We couldn't use words like try, should, would, could, victim. The idea of blame wasn't part of my vocabulary. I was taught that we choose everything. I remember at eight years old having some sort of complaint about my brother. I remember my mother saying, 'Well, don't blame me. He's your brother. You chose him.' I said, 'What're you talking about?' 'You chose him before you came here.' I had to think. As I sat with it, I realized, that's really power, to think that we can choose anything, including the people in our lives, our experiences whether good or bad."

I think, "What the heck is she talking about? Is she nuts?" I know from personal experience how a victim mentality can totally disempower a person, how it can feed rage against the perpetrator and in effect leave the perpetrator in control for years, maybe for a lifetime. I know that grieving, suffering people need empathy and compassion, but at some point a person has to move on and live her own life. Well-intentioned compassion for a person, when taken too far, turns into poison. But how could an eight-year-old girl choose her younger brother? What the hell?

I try to mask the skepticism in my voice. "And he chose you too, I suppose?"

"Yeah," Sarah says. "And I chose her and I chose my dad. So as a kid I was never able to get into that place of blaming my parents. That drama was just not engaged in any shape or form for my parents. So when my mom was murdered, this whole sense of victim as somebody who's experiencing homicide—I didn't know what to do with it. I struggled with it.

"This just didn't make any sense to me. My mom was just murdered. She always taught me we choose everything, that there are no accidents, that there's no such thing as a victim. Ever. The duality of those two concepts took a few years to come together in my mind. Also, I was only twenty when she died. Throughout my twenties I was able to bring those into balance."

Sarah turns her attention to her cup of tea and, with her eyes closed, inhales the steam rising from it. "You know, one of my somewhat revolutionary concepts on that is that we choose our deaths, regardless of how they come about. That doesn't mean it's okay to murder. However, I think if we're able to look down on earth from a somewhat metaphysical perspective, we can recognize we come here to learn certain lessons. Not from a place of good or bad, just that we come here to learn certain lessons that are part of our own personal evolution. And sometimes those horribly traumatic experiences are part of that.

"So I'd say probably it was about ten years before I was at peace with Mom dying. As far as the victim aspect, only the first couple of years. It wasn't that I necessarily felt I was a victim.

"I also recognized that Peter Brighteyes was a survivor of residential schooling and colonization and everything that's impacted the Aboriginal community. So he was what he was in some ways because of that, yet he also chose not to take a different path. He didn't have to become a murderer. I just recognized that was part of what influenced who he became in this world.

"I never called myself a victim. I never joined any victims groups. At the same time, if I met somebody who had experienced trauma—and I think there were very few—what was nice was that there'd be some sort of kinship, and somebody would understand a little bit of my experience. Because there's such little information out there about how people can come into a place of healing or resolution when they've experienced trauma. Which is in part why I do what I do."

Sarah's mother, Sheila, was a life skills coach, she tells me, but I have no idea what that means. Sarah says in 1990s Alberta, Premier Ralph Klein was busy laying off provincial employees. Private businesses were cutting back. A lot of people who'd been in good jobs for a long time needed help to see how they could transfer their skills into other areas, start new careers, and find new ways to earn a living. Sarah's mother set up Salter and Associates to support those people, to help them look inside themselves and find new ways to move beyond self-pity and powerlessness. Sarah herself took a number of formal life skills courses, beyond what she absorbed from her mother and father every day at home. It seems to me Sarah's childhood must've been one long course in life skills and empowerment.

I wonder what that would have been like. The underlying, constant principle I remember from my childhood is the Catholic doctrine that every human being is conceived in sin. Thanks to Adam and Eve, sin is central to human nature. I have free will and make choices, but I'm programmed to make sinful choices. The church, my teachers, and my parents convinced me that if Jesus hadn't suffered and died for me and if I hadn't been baptized into the one true faith, I'd have to burn in hell for eternity. They also taught me I'd end up in hell anyway if I made sinful choices and didn't get a priest to forgive my mortal sins. For much of my adult life I struggled under a heavy load of shame and guilt and fear of hell.

Yet Sarah Salter-Kelly tells me her mother chose her own death and that Peter Brighteyes was somehow teaching her something she needed to learn! In her I sense only positive feelings for Peter Brighteyes. She seems to think even he doesn't belong in hell, since she doesn't believe there is a hell, and her world has no room for shame, guilt, or victims. If I'd met her a few years ago, when I was still immersed in traditional Catholic theology, I would have had nothing in common with her. I would have thought she was one of the reasons the whole world was going to hell; after all, C. S. Lewis claimed that Satan's greatest victory in our time is that so many people believe he doesn't exist, even though he, like Harry Potter's Voldemort, is everywhere. I've left traditional Catholic beliefs behind, but I still have a hard time understanding Sarah's world view.

I ask her, "Say your brother turned out to be a sexual predator and he raped you. If you were raised to think it was your choice to have him as your brother, are you saying there'd be no feeling of guilt, that if you made this choice, it was something *you* did.... How do you deal with things like culpability, for example, his for raping you and yours for choosing him?"

Sarah wonders out loud how this might look in print, turns to watch Sadie run around in the yard, then faces me again. "The thing is, there's no blame or shame involved. No matter what. If somebody's misusing their power, raping the innocent or whatever, I still believe the innocent chose for whatever reason to learn certain lessons from that struggle, from that victimization. As an adult they can learn how to put all those pieces together and find out whatever medicine exists in their wounds. From the perspective up here of sitting down, chatting with God, saying 'What do I need to learn in this lifetime?', there was choice. Down here, as an eight-year-old who's getting raped by her father or sibling or whatever, they're not in a position to exercise choice, do you know what I mean?

"As an adult, when someone looks down and goes, okay, just a second here, am I gonna run away from that wound when I was eight years old and somebody raped me? Am I gonna let it hold a shadow of shame over my life and not talk about it, not be willing to share it, not go there? Then that person is bound by that wound. So that person, as an adult, has a choice to feel that. I'm thinking about a good friend who was raped by her father growing up. She believes she needed to experience that in order to bring that understanding of a woman's power into the work she does now.

"The problem is it's taken so long for women especially to trust in their own power and to allow for the rest of the world...to recognize that they have power and they're not to be pushed around, slapped around, violated in whatever way, shape, or form. So if we were to take that concept of choice—and it's already out there in a lot of different New Age writings—and say to a woman who's just been raped that you chose to be raped, right away you bring in that shame and that guilt, 'Maybe I was dressed the wrong way, maybe I did this....' Which is a bunch of fucking bullshit.... If somebody had said to me in the first couple of years after my mom died that my mom chose to be murdered, I would've reacted with a lot of rage. It took her telling me and it took me sitting with it for about ten years to know it was really true. It took me hearing her. And I have a pretty infinite ability to connect with the world of spirit and trust what I'm hearing."

Sarah pauses and waits for my next question. I'm trying to figure out where to start. There's so much in what she just said that contradicts my own understanding of reality. An eight-year-old can choose her own parents and brother and even choose to be raped by a family member, yet this choice isn't really possible until she's an adult? Sarah's dead mother talks to her? Her mother "chose" to be murdered? I ask, "What does it mean that she chose to be murdered? How would you explain that?"

"How we die may act as a vehicle for light and healing to come into our planet," Sarah begins. "If we're willing to look at some of these experiences somewhat in the way I'm doing my best to do and recognize the transformational opportunities in all of our wounds, then we're not stuck anymore." She relates this principle to the point I made to her during our first meeting about our dehumanizing prison system, one of the main points of this book. She says that by denying prisoners the opportunity to participate in our communities, we are negating our own potential as a society to grow, to "evolve collectively." She says each victim has to have a conversation about his or her experience with others so he or she can move on. Sometimes that means talking with the perpetrator. She says the perpetrator has to take responsibility for what he's done, and he has to share his story with others too.

I still don't get it. Sounds like she's avoiding the question. Then I get a glimmer of something. I think of the Gospel stories of Jesus in the Garden of Gethsemane praying and then deliberately and consciously choosing to die. I say, "When you talk about your mother's death as an opportunity for transformation and healing, it sounds to me a lot like the Jesus myth."

Sarah's eyes light up, she smiles, and she says, "Yeah! There's tremendous beauty. If you can take all the crap out of Christianity that was put in there for political agendas and find the beauty in it, there's huge beauty in Jesus's story. Huge beauty in him recognizing when he was on the cross that he'd been pretty much betrayed by everybody he knew and still came to a place of forgiveness. He recognized they weren't getting it. And didn't he say, 'Father, forgive them for they know not what they do?' So forgiveness is also a vehicle for transformation."

I'm tempted to cut in and say, "Whoa! There you go avoiding the question again," but I realize this is her answer. After all, is it any more far-fetched to say Jesus chose his death than to say Sheila Salter chose hers? Besides, while I'm thinking this through, she's already moved on.

"When I came into a place of forgiveness with Peter Brighteyes, my intention wasn't necessarily forgiveness at the time." In Sarah's mind all of these things are interwoven, and they have a logical connection, but it's not the kind of logic I expect when I ask direct questions. She says, "My intent was to create a ceremony and sit with him. I knew at the ten-year mark that I needed to talk to him. I didn't know any other way to talk to him aside from sitting down and creating sacred space and having a conversation. So my plan was to have a conversation and in my own prayer and ego at the time, make sure that the powers that be knew what he did. I needed to articulate it myself. That was part of my own healing process."

Sarah seems to know I haven't had much experience sitting down and talking to dead people. So she switches into teacher mode. "There's something called journeying, which is similar to when someone's led on a meditation, but when you get used to it, you just go on your own." She tells me she had some of these journeys where she saw him for who he is, "separate from who he was in this lifetime." She adds, "If that makes any sense. Or who he is aside from the actions he chose to take in this lifetime." She says she recognized he wasn't really any different from her, just that he made "really crappy choices." She says she realized she was in a place where she judged him, was angry with him, frustrated and hurt by him, and that kept her bound to him. When she learned to see who he was, she says, she found compassion and forgiveness, and that shifted the energy in her relationship with him.

She looks at me again and says, "I think this happens to anybody who goes through trauma. It could be childhood trauma. It could be somebody did something nasty to you on the playground. When you feel that in your gut or in your body and you carry that into adulthood, you're energetically bound to that person until you learn how to release it." She says, if there's anything you have a hard time talking about, something that feels raw and upsets you when you do discuss it, you're not free. "And I hate not being free. I don't like being bound by anything at any time. Once I realized it was up to me to change that, once I remembered, I started actively pursuing it."

She tells me how her working to release herself from Peter Brighteyes got her involved in the Inca medicine wheel and how she ended up not merely forgiving him but actually loving him! I expect she senses I'm deeply shocked even though I'm trying my best to hide it. She laughs and admits this is "crazy shit," "froofy stuff," "flaky." She says that in 2006 she created a ceremony with Peter Brighteyes and spent about eight months with it. She set up an altar and prayed before each direction, sat in each direction, focused on what each direction meant to her, centred herself, talked to Peter about how she felt about what happened to her mother. She said it was a lot like what psychologists suggest people do to work through grief: write to the dead person, put raw emotion on the page, and work through it bit by bit. After two months of calling on Peter's spirit and talking to him, she says, he actually showed up!

"I would drum and sing and just lie down or sit. I let myself be guided to where I needed to go," Sarah says. "I was sitting on this sand wall in my vision. I was holding onto this young boy and talking to him. He was telling me he was really worried about something he had to take responsibility for. I was encouraging him to do what he needed to do." Suddenly she saw that she was the mom and Peter was her son. She felt an overwhelming sense of love and compassion for him. And she was disgusted with what she saw and felt. So she pulled herself out of the vision and went into a cursing rant. None of it made any sense to her. Still, she pushed herself, continued the process for six more months, because she knew she had to work through this somehow even though she didn't understand it. She took some advice from one of her mentors and finally conducted a fire ceremony to release Peter under the full moon in November 2006. For nearly a year, she says, she didn't see Peter again, but then he came to warn her about a man in a course she was taking. She told Peter to go away, said "we're done, we don't need to talk to each other anymore." But he was persistent, and she realized this and other warnings from him were "always dead on."

As we're talking, a large raven circles her yard just beyond the porch. Sarah says, "That raven's been around all day, especially this morning. Around the hill and some of the trees." I ask her if the raven means something special to her. "Yeah," she says, "the raven is deeply connected with my work with Peter. Raven medicine is about learning to go into the shadow and bring the medicine of the shadow into the light." She says she's not surprised to see it appear while we talk about Peter and her mother's murder. She tells me her relationship with Peter Brighteyes led her to connect with Aboriginal issues, to try to understand the impact of residential schools, colonization, and reserves. She tells me that just this year she spent a day with a former chief at Saddle Lake, where Peter was born. She says she talked to Peter's sister and in February went to Saddle Lake to do a presentation as part of a residential schools healing process.

A phrase from the Watergate days in the United States comes to mind: "follow the money." Woodward and Bernstein helped bring down President Nixon by tracing to its source the money that paid for the Watergate burglary. In the spiritual direction work I've done, the central principle is similar: follow the energy. When I listen to a person talk about his or her life, I encourage him or her to dig where there's some emotional heat (or cold) and see what's down there. When I talk to patients at the University of Alberta Hospital, I encourage them to take me with them wherever they've got emotional energy to go that day. When I make decisions in my own life, it's been the same process: whether to retire from M2W2, whether to move in with my new life partner and help raise her grandkids, or what to write my next poem about. In Sarah's story I see the same pattern, the same process. Who am I—who is anybody—to say her experiences with Peter aren't real? That her love for Peter, his messages, and her visions of him are hallucinations or projections? Good sure seems to be coming out of them.

So I finally get it. I get what she means when she says she loves Peter Brighteyes and that they have a life-giving relationship, even though he's been dead fifteen years. I also get that she couldn't have that relationship unless Sheila Salter herself laid the foundation for it. In our conversation, we followed Sarah's energy into the ceremonies and warnings and the love for Peter Brighteyes, but then I realize we've been wandering off down a side trail. So I bring us back to the main line: Sheila Salter.

I tell Sarah I've known people who've lost a child. I lost one of my own daughters for eight years. She simply cut me out of her life. I tell Sarah I've lived with grandchildren for a year now, a year of virtually no contact with the children's mother, a year when four-year-old Lily wakes up repeatedly in the night screaming "MOMMY!" as if she's watching her mother being chopped into small pieces by an axe murderer. I tell her how often I've heard people say that when you lose a child, it's a wound that never heals. I tell her I've heard when you're abandoned by a parent or the parent dies suddenly or prematurely, you never get over it. I remind her that we've just spent forty-five minutes talking about Peter Brighteyes and his presence in her life, but I'm not getting a sense of where Sheila Salter is in Sarah's life right now, fifteen years later. Or whether she still has that emptiness inside, that hole that only her mother can fill.

"I think sometimes with our parents it's more of a craving for the Great Father or the Great Mother," she says. I've heard Catholic priests and others talk like this about a general hunger for God in our secular society; Sarah says she hungered for her mother that way until she became a mother herself. She admits it's an irrational, insatiable hunger, and no human being alive or dead could possibly satisfy it. About eleven years ago, when her twin daughters were born, she says, "I just started letting go of that stuff. I learned what it meant to be a mom. I started letting go of some of my craving for her."

She tells me she's always running into absolute statements about mother loss and child loss, that you never can get over it, that you'll always be grieving. "That felt like a sentence to me," she says. "A prison sentence. Damnation. 'Here you go; you're screwed now for the rest of your life. You'll feel a little better after a couple of years; however, pretty much you're fucked for this lifetime.'" She says, "There has to be another way. Think about water moving through a course in a stream. When it comes up against forks, water always finds another way to move around something. Always. I believe that's possible for all of us in our healing. It's about shifting perspective."

I think about Sam, my twenty-eight-year-old son. He had heart surgery when he was a year old. The surgeon made a slice around his left shoulder blade, and he's still got the scar. In fact, it's way bigger than it was. He's six foot three and weighs 225 pounds. I tell Sarah about him and I say, "He's always gonna have that scar."

"Well, that's part of who he is," Sarah says.

And I say, "You still have a scar too."

"Exactly," she says. "I'm definitely marked by Mom being murdered."

But what does that mean? How does that scar show up now? Sarah doesn't give me a direct answer. She tells me a story.

At the three-month mark, she says, an employer told her she should be done with healing from her mother's murder. At six months she got a letter from Employment Insurance saying her benefits were being cut off in a few weeks. "I wrote them a letter," she says, "that I would let them know when I was finished with my healing, but it wasn't yet." She pauses for a second. "The thing with trauma is that it can creep up on you. Until you come to that place of peace and liberation, it can creep up on you at any minute, any time of the day, and all of a sudden [you] just feel this great sense of loss inside of yourself that can bring you to the ground."

I ask her, "Do you still get that feeling?" She shakes her head. I say, "Not even a twinge or a memory comes up? Nothing like that?" She shakes her head again.

"No. Nothing that I'd have to respond to for more than a minute or two." She pauses as if to check whether anything like that is coming up right now. "No. It hasn't for a couple of years. Maybe even a little bit longer than that. In those first ten years—it sounds like a long time. That's just how it was for me. It would happen less and less often. However, there'd be moments of absolute grief. It doesn't mean that I don't go through grief or emotion in the day-to-day human learning experience."

"I know that before I had come to that place of peace," she adds, "I had this irrational sense of fear that my daughters would just be taken. Probably until they were about four or five....I didn't entertain it regularly. I just noticed it. You know, with twins, you go out somewhere and they both go running in different directions. People said we should get harnesses for them, but of course I would not tie my children! And so we'd always be watching. We lived in Westmount and northwest, in Wellington. So Westmount Mall is somewhere I might've gone to run a few errands. Or if we were out walking in the river valley, I'd just be watching. I remember teaching them about strangers. I don't think I've ever even taught my son. He's almost six. Granted, he's grown up out here."

"I remember having conversations with them. Not from a fear-based place, just 'don't get into cars with strangers, even if somebody offers you candy or a puppy.' I made sure I had those conversations. I do believe I projected some of that fear onto them. I think they were more cautious than maybe necessary. I think some of that came from my having gone through that experience of my mom being taken. That was maybe a natural progression of events. However, when I became conscious of doing it, I thought, wow, I've gotta stop holding this fear in my life. As long as I hold this fear it's gonna affect the kids. I believe that we generationally pass down our patterns. So if we don't heal our patterns, they get carried down to the next generation and the next."

I'm getting ready to turn off the recorder, but I look around again at the greenery, the trees, the grass, the wide open spaces, her dog Sadie running around free in the seven-acre yard. "How much of your healing," I ask, "comes from your being out in nature?"

"Huge," she says. "Not just here. That's always where I feel my soul is most at peace. As a kid, we'd go camping in the far remote areas of Willmore Wilderness Park where there often weren't other campers." I tell her I know where it is, northwest of Hinton, but that I've never been there. "Some pretty beautiful sacred places that are kind of untouched by people. Really magical. We hiked. We had a canoe. We camped a lot at a place called Rock Lake. There were other places too, further up the highway towards Grande Cache. Rock Lake is one of the places, the mountain at Rock Lake, where we put Mom's ashes. It's just a magical place. That's where I always found my own sense of power."

"Not just in nature," she continues. "I moved to Vancouver when I was seventeen. I lived in Surrey and managed to find any ravine, anything I could find to connect with nature. In my times living in Edmonton, the river valley saved me. I lived in the Mill Creek area before. I grew up in Lessard from when I was eight until I was fifteen. That's just a couple of blocks from the river. Although we were not allowed to play in the river, I grew up with the river. That's where we spent all our time. That's where I felt I could be me and I could source that connection with nature. And that brings me closer to god, my connection with Mother Earth. That's where I find that balance in myself."

It makes sense to me. I've been to the Grand Canyon, Jasper, Banff, Zion, Death Valley, Yosemite, Yellowstone, Long Beach (Vancouver

Island), Uluru (Australia), Edmonton's river valley parks. I've climbed and hiked and paddled and swum and photographed. I've been there alone and simply touched the stones, stared up at the clouds, inhaled the sage and pine and the desert dust. I've taken long walks to work through conflicts and to be with the anger, the sadness, the fear from my marriage breakup and the separation from my kids.

I get up to leave, but first Sarah invites me to tour her healing centre, the big room where she works with groups and the smaller room where she does one-on-ones. She tells me this place is really in between wilderness and what she calls "consensual reality," the normal world where people go to churches, where people don't do drum and smudge and fire ceremonies, where people don't get visits from dead murderers.

Sarah walks me to my car, and I thank her for the tour and the conversation. The drive home is only forty-five minutes, but it's a journey far longer than a lot of murderers, prisoners, prison volunteers, and regular churchgoers like my mother could ever make. And for some people alcohol, crack cocaine, heroin, hanging in a cell with shoelaces around their necks, or driving off a cliff seem like better choices. But I'm glad Sarah Salter-Kelly has chosen this path and invited others to see how it might work for them too.

As for me, I know my path ahead passes through several prisons. Every time I go into one, it feels like a journey to the underworld, that standard component in epic and legend for millennia. The first time I spent a whole weekend at the Max I ran head-on into a part of myself I was sure did not exist: the underworld I entered was my own shadow. Before that weekend, if somebody had told me about that part of myself, I would not have believed that Peter Brighteyes and I had anything in common.

CHAPTER 7

THE ROLE PLAY'S THE THING TO OUT MY INNER THUG

All the world's a stage.
— William Shakespeare, *As You Like It*

"Dangerous G" is six feet tall, thin and wiry, 180 pounds of ravenous mountain lion ready to pounce. The hair on his temples is graying and sticks up like blunt horns on both sides of his shiny bald scalp. His piercing, dark-brown eyes could burn a hole through the steel door of a bank vault. Beside him struts Pappy, five feet two inches tall, with a doughy white paunch so he looks seven months pregnant; he sports a full head of sleek, silver, fox-like fur. They glide up the aisle of a nearly empty subway car. G's gaze locks onto a black man in a green canvas coat who is staring out the window. Orange mercury vapour lights from a nearby avenue flash across the glass in a fury of empty lots, broken bricks, fragments of demolished concrete foundations. A lonely red brick smokestack pokes up through the rubble like a rigid middle finger.

G steps in front of the man and shouts, "Get outta my seat!"

The man keeps staring toward the window, even though the reflection of G's back has already gobbled up half the glass.

"Are you deaf or what, boy?" G breathes in short, quick pants, like a sprinter in a race. "YOU. ARE. IN. MY. SEAT!"

The man jerks his head around. G towers over him. Their knees nearly touch. Pappy is on G's left, his hands limp at his sides, like a gunslinger itching to draw his six-gun and show skeptics how quick he really is. Pappy looks straight at the top of the man's head and smirks.

The man takes a deep breath and raises his head. "But there's lots of empty seats." He raises his left hand and waves at the vacant rows of padded blue vinyl benches. Except for him and the two newcomers, the subway car has only one other person in it, a Hispanic man in coveralls splattered with white and blue paint. At the first sound of raised voices, the Hispanic man bends lower and buries his face inside his faded blue denim jacket.

"Maybe you didn't hear me," G grins. He's not shouting any more. His voice is cold and hard as a glacier. *"I said get outta my seat!"*

The man sighs. "I have this seat," he says. "Find yourself another one."

G's face glows red. He grits his teeth and hisses, "You *will* give me that seat."

The man blinks but doesn't move. Pappy's right index finger twitches. G's heart races. His hand reaches inside his jacket, under his left arm where his hunting knife's sheath lies warm and smooth against his chest. He clutches the handle and starts to draw it out.

"CUT! CUT!" a woman shouts from the audience. "That's enough! Hold it right there. All four of you, move those chairs around to face the rest of us and have a seat."

Suddenly I'm back in the Max's program room with thirteen other people. My pulse is pounding, my chest full of G as I sit down. I wonder who I am now: G or me? My skin tingles. My biceps, quads, pecs flex and twitch with adrenaline. I wonder: If I'd really had that imaginary knife, if I'd really been G instead of somebody pretending to be G, could I have used it? Would I have used it?

The woman turns to me and says, "G, what were you feeling just then? Did you even think about taking one of those empty seats?"

"I was pumped. I was ready to bring it on." My teeth are still clenched tight as a vise. "That seat was mine, and I was gonna take it."

A second man says, "G, did you ever think that maybe Peaceful Pete had a point? That you had your choice of dozens of other seats in the subway car?"

"That didn't matter. He didn't matter," I say, speaking for G but hovering between him and me. "As far as I was concerned, he was only an empty pile of clothes. I could brush him off that seat like a crumpled Big Mac wrapper or a dead bug."

A second woman asks, "Bystander Benny, you were just sitting over there watching all this happen. Did you ever think that maybe you should step in and try to cool things down a little?"

Benny says, "I was scared. When G got mad and wanted that seat, I knew a shiv was comin' out. Peaceful Pete was gettin' stabbed up. I gotta keep my head down. If I didn't, I'd get it too. Sure, it was wrong for two of 'em to jump the guy. But I couldn't do nothin'.'"

She turns to the silver-haired man. "What about you, Pappy? How did you feel about G picking a fight with Pete over nothing?"

"Well," Pappy shakes his head, "I've known G for a long time. We were in prison together. In a gang before that. When he wants something, he just takes it. I get outta the way."

"Is there anything you could've done to help resolve this conflict in a non-violent way?"

Pappy pauses. "I dunno. Maybe. But I tried stoppin' him before. Got scars to prove it."

"How would you four like to start this episode over again?" the first woman suggests. "How about if this time you try to find some way you can use the AVP principles we've been learning about to deal with this conflict in a better way?"

She points to a poster on the wall. The Alternatives to Violence Project (AVP) logo. It has three concentric circles on it: "Transforming Power" in the centre, "Caring for Self" and "Respect for Others" around that, and in the outer circle "Think before Reacting," "Ask for a Nonviolent Solution," and "Expect the Best."

The role play is happening on Sunday morning. Fourteen of us have been in the program room at the Max from 6:00 to 9:00 Friday night and from 9:00 a.m. to 9:00 p.m. Saturday doing exercises to help us solve conflicts non-violently. Seven prisoners, three of us from the community, and four volunteer facilitators from Olds, Blackfalds, Wetaskiwin, and Edmonton. In the role play part of the workshop, every participant has the chance to let his defences down and step into another person's skin. It's an exercise in empathy where anything might happen. The facilitators' job is to keep everybody safe and look for teachable moments.

The four of us put the chairs back where they were at the start of the scene, and we begin again. My heart's still racing. I'm full of adrenaline, still determined to get Peaceful Pete's seat on the subway. I hear the facilitator's words about non-violent solutions, but they might as well be in Japanese, Greek, or Martian.

Now I'm back with Pappy again. We strut down the aisle in the subway car. We approach Peaceful Pete. I stop in front of him. Before I can say even a word, Pappy sits down next to Pete and says, all smooth and slick and sweet like a used car salesman reeling in a mark, "Sorry to bother you. Would you mind moving to one of those empty seats? My friend here really wants your seat."

Pete jerks out of his daze at Pappy's friendly voice, and before Pete sees G's glaring eyes and clenched fists, he gets up and moves to the empty seat near Bystander Benny.

"Cut," says a facilitator. "Now I'd like all of you to sit down again and face the rest of us."

I think—or G thinks—"What the hell? This new scene can't be over already! I didn't do anything!"

The facilitator looks at me and says, "G, what was going through your mind this time? How did you feel about how Pappy resolved the conflict?"

"It happened so fast. I didn't have time to think. I've still got that anger pumping through me. I still don't care about Peaceful Pete. I wasn't interested in any wimpy non-violent solution. I was ready to give it to him." I look at the other participants, prisoners at Edmonton Institution I've known for a year or more, men serving sentences for murder, assault, armed robbery, rape, and other serious crimes. The giggles and playfulness that were such a big part of the weekend are gone. They're looking down at the dirty red carpet. Most of them have their elbows on their knees. Not one of them says a thing. It looks like they're all trying to hide.

"Pappy cut in front of me," I say. "It was like my anger was a balloon, and he popped it. My gut's still tight and churning. I was ready to fight. Now I feel lost, empty."

The four facilitators take turns asking the other three characters how they felt, why they did what they did, what else they might have done to solve the conflict, what thoughts went through their minds. One asks Pappy if he's ready to step out of his role. He says yes, and he's asked to stand up, take off the masking tape on his shirt that says "Pappy" and put it on his chair's backrest. "Who are you now?" "I'm Jovial John," he says. The facilitator shakes his hand and says, "Welcome back, Jovial John. Do you have anything to say to Pappy or to these other guys?"

John says, "Pappy, you did the right thing at the end there. Somebody could've got killed. But you gotta be more careful about choosing your friends. You're gonna end up dead if you keep hangin' around with G." He walks over in front of me and shakes his head. "G, you are bad news. I wish I'd never met you."

A facilitator interrupts. "Who are you now?"

John looks at the facilitator, puzzled.

She says, "Remember, you're not Pappy any more. You're Jovial John. *You* were never involved with G. *Pappy* was."

"Oh, yeah." John starts over. "G, you are bad news. Pappy should stay away from you. You gotta manage that anger. Somebody'll end up dead if you don't." John sits down with the group, offstage, facing me, the other two role players, and the chair with Pappy's name on it.

Facilitators lead Peaceful Pete and Bystander Benny through the same de-roling process. Finally, a facilitator comes to me. "G, are you ready to come out of your role?"

"Am I ever!" I say. I jump up off the chair, rip the masking tape off my shirt, and stick it on the chair back.

"Who are you now?"

"I'm Gregarious Gary."

"Welcome back, Gregarious Gary. What do you have to say to all these characters?"

"Bystander Benny, I don't know what more you could've done. Maybe get off the train. Peaceful Pete, you were just in the wrong place at the wrong time. Pappy, you seemed like two different characters, one the first time and then somebody totally different. I bet if this scene happened in real life, after you and G got where you were going, G would beat the crap out of you. G might stab you up instead of Peaceful Pete." I turn to the chair with "Dangerous G" on it. "You are a menace. I'm so glad I'm not you. I'm glad this was only a role play. I—I mean you...you could've killed somebody."

I sit down with the audience, facing the four empty chairs. The rest of the participants ask questions and talk about what they saw. I let all of that wash over me. I try to figure out who I am. I thought I knew, but now?....

Before the role play, the facilitators told us not to plan anything. They told us to imagine the character we play and step inside. They told us to pick roles as different as possible from who we are in real life. My group got a slip of paper with minimal information on it, and they told us to decide who would play which role, pick character names, and then let it roll. The paper said: two tough guys get on a nearly empty subway car and pick a fight with one of the men sitting there. John and I, the two prison visitors, chose to be tough guys on the prowl; the two men in our group serving life sentences for murder played the non-violent characters.

It's March 2003, and I'm nine months into the job of coordinating the M2W2 prison visitation program at the Max. In July 1970 I came to Canada as a draft dodger. I was so viscerally opposed to the violence of the Vietnam War that I left my family and my country behind me instead of joining the army. The only reason I sign up for the Alternatives to Violence workshop is so I can help the men in prison find better ways to live. I've been a non-violent man for over thirty years, and I'm sure that my experience in non-violence will help these violent men change their ways.

During the debriefing process, one of the prisoner participants says, "G was me. When he got all worked up over nothin', itchin' for a fight. When he said Pete wasn't even human, just a pile of clothes..." He stops and takes a deep breath, looks around. "That's why I'm in here. I was a cokehead. A drunk. I didn't care about nobody. I was mad all the time."

At the next break the man who played Peaceful Pete comes up to me. I don't know him very well. We first met two days before, Friday at 6:00 p.m. when the workshop started. He strutted in wearing sunglasses and dared the facilitators to show him something relevant. When he saw I had a photo ID instead of a yellow visitor's tag with a big black V on it, he said I was a CSC informer and that the facilitators' introductory talk about trust and confidentiality was a pile of crap. I explained who I was, but I could tell he wasn't buying it.

He's been wearing sunglasses the whole weekend. When I try to make eye contact, I see my own reflection. He chuckles and smiles at me. "You'd fit right in here, you know, that big violent streak." He looks me up and down and says, "You'll have to bulk up, though. Extra protein. Weightlifting. Lots of push-ups and pull-ups. Even if you had a shiv, if you don't got muscle to go with it, you're nothin' but a pork chop in here."

It's been many years since that day. G is still inside me. I keep him on a short leash. Until I became G, I'd forgotten the angry little boy I was. My father told me over and over when I was six, seven, eight years old that I had to control my temper. My older brother, Paul, did little things to make me mad. I'd swing my arms and fists around and try to hit him. He was six years older than me, his arms much longer than mine. He'd straight-arm me so my arms would hit nothing but air. He laughed and called me "Windmill."

I'm an AVP facilitator now, and I've been in over twenty of these workshops since that first one. In every one I volunteer to do the role-play demo so I can step outside myself and learn something new about me. I've been a young man who gets his girlfriend pregnant and comes home in the middle of the night to find his father waiting with a barrage of vicious name-calling. I've been a wealthy businessman driving home drunk, offering a bribe to the policeman who pulls him over. I've been one of the boys at a singles bar taunting a rival about his erectile dysfunction. I've been a woman driver who smashed the front end of her husband's favourite sports car. I've been a man out on parole who throws a party and loses his temper with a friend.

Every time I learn more about empathy. I see conflicts from somebody else's point of view and experience his or her feelings. I have a piece of each of these other people inside me. In most of the role plays, I've done the replay, so I get two runs at it. Even my bones know now that my life is a series of choices, that I create who I am moment to moment. A saying we often post on the wall during workshops says, "10 percent of my life is what happens to me; 90 percent of it is my attitude." I finally get it.

In *Man's Search for Meaning*, Viktor Frankl talks about his time in a Nazi concentration camp. Nazi soldiers treated him like a rat to be tortured and thrown away. He notes that many prisoners simply withdrew and died. He tells of a man who screamed through a nightmare and woke up all the other prisoners. Under normal conditions, a compassionate person, he says, would wake the man up and relieve his suffering. But Frankl wondered: Could the nightmare be any worse than the camp? Would I be doing him a favour if I woke him up to *this*? He says he survived because he decided not to respond to his Nazi captors in kind but with kindness. He refused to take on the hatred they laid on him. He realized he would probably die a cruel death in the camp; he chose to be himself in the meantime.

On September 9, 1971, in a more recent nightmare, a thousand of the over two thousand prisoners in the Attica Correctional Facility in Attica, New York, took thirty-three prison guards hostage and issued a list of demands to the authorities. Four days later Governor Nelson Rockefeller ordered state police to end the riot. Thirty-nine people died: twenty-nine prisoners and ten state employees. Not long after that, a group of lifers in New York asked the Quakers to help them make prison life less violent. The Alternatives to Violence Project was the result. Since then, AVP has conducted thousands of weekend workshops in prisons and communities in over fifty countries.

It is an unusual organization. I often wonder how it functions at all. A basic principle is that all facilitators and participants must be volunteers. Volunteers organize every workshop, look after prison security clearances for facilitators and community participants, and attend provincial and national meetings. Nobody gets paid. Decisions are made by consensus. That means not many decisions get made and those that do take a lot of time. That's the Quaker way, apparently. Scheduling workshops is a chicken-and-egg process, and it's a minor miracle each time we bring one off, especially at the Max. When I registered for that first one, I got short notice that it was happening, less than six weeks. I've done workshops that clicked into place on two weeks' notice, but most take much longer.

For example, in September 2008 I asked prisoners at the Max if they wanted to sign up. They asked, "When will it be?" I told them, "If I can get at least twelve prisoners signed up, I'll talk to prison staff to see what dates are available. Then I'll ask the facilitators who can come on which weekend. My guess is we could do it late October or early November." Almost immediately, twelve signed up. At that time the Max had some new security issues to deal with, and construction was under way on a new program room. That room was supposed to be done by Christmas. Then by January 31. Then by March 1.

In February, management decided that the program room would become a staff meeting room. They told me we could use the Aboriginal cultural centre instead. I found two other facilitators for April 17–19, 2009. I found four community participants and got them security clearance. By this time, many of the prisoners who signed up in September had transferred out, gone to another unit, were in segregation, or had changed their minds. With the help of the unit representative, I got some new guys to sign up. The final list had fourteen prisoners on it. Seven showed up Friday, one dropped out Saturday morning. Six finished the program.

AVP workshops are like mercury: each piece contracts and expands depending on circumstances, and the whole thing bends and flows around obstacles. Now that I'm into the culture, the process seems magical and virtually effortless. Unplanned things happen. Everything works out. Every workshop has a different dynamic, a different flow, a different sense of time and community.

Sometimes an exercise gets sidetracked. Once, a prisoner suddenly opened up about his crime in graphic, tearful detail. He got a long prison sentence for attacking someone who sexually assaulted a woman in his family, for exacting vengeance on a sex offender, just as the con code dictates. Instead of having his family honour him as a hero, they disowned him. He realized, too, that his actions caused permanent damage to another family, as well as to his victim. He was now alone, and he hated himself for what he'd done. The prisoner was desperate to start a new life but didn't know how. We let him talk, and the exercise took two hours instead of one. We had to cut another exercise out completely, but we all agreed that man's story had more impact than any exercise we could have picked.

I've seen an exercise go flat, where everybody chose to pass—which is their right, since everything is voluntary—and we had to move on to something else. Once, we had a group of General Population (Pop) prisoners. At the time we ran that workshop, the prison had three Pop units, but a problem was that Pop inmates had a reputation for demanding the same programs as Transfer and Release Units (TRU) inmates and not showing up.[7]

This time they are determined to show the warden they mean business. Eight of them sign up, eight come, and all eight stay for

---

7   General Population used to include everybody except the few singled out
    for punishment or protection in Detention and Segregation, what American
    prisons call solitary confinement. The Edmonton Max, when I started there in
    2001, had four General Population (Pop) units, three protective custody units
    (misnamed TRU, Transfer and Release Units), and a mental health unit.

the whole weekend! We're shocked. The first time this has ever happened! During the introductions, we ask them to say something about themselves and say why they came. Each one speaks thoughtfully about hoping to resolve conflicts without bloody noses, black eyes, busted teeth, a shiv in the gut, heads smashed against steel doors, without bullying. Tom, the leader, says they have to show prison staff they will attend programs or they won't get any at all. "We've gotta have programs if we're ever gonna get outta this hell hole."

We move on to outline the history of the program and lay out the rules for the workshop: no putdowns, the right to pass, affirm each other's good points, listen without interrupting, volunteer only yourself, observe confidentiality. We emphasize that this workshop is experiential, that we don't lecture, that we engage everyone in brainstorming, discussing, doing exercises, and playing games.

The first exercise is Adjective Names. The AVP tradition is for each of us to pick an adjective name to affirm something about who he is or who he wants to be. It's a way to get to know each other in a playful and positive way. I say I used to be Gregarious Gary because I am an extrovert and I want to remind myself that I am more alive when I'm around other people. At a later workshop I was Grateful Gary; I am thankful for the opportunities and talents I have. Now I am Generous Gary to remind myself that my talents are a waste unless I share them. Peaceful Paul goes next and then Persistent Nelson.

Nelson notes that he's the exception to the tradition that adjective names should start with the same letter or sound as the first name. And he's kept that name for a lot of years. He invites the prisoners to pick adjective names that suit them, something affirming and maybe something whimsical or funny. He says it may take a while to get names for everyone, but if we all pitch in and have fun with it, it's a great way to build community. The first one passes. Then the next. Then the next. Finally Tom stands up, all six-foot-six, 285 pounds of him. He says, "I've fought a lot of guys for my name. I'd die for my name." He slowly turns to look every person there in the eye. "I won't change my name for anybody." The other prisoners bow their heads and nod.

Adjective names are a key piece of the workshop. I've seen adjective names break down barriers, release tension, and build community throughout the weekend. Often when someone says an adjective name or when someone forgets to say it and has to be reminded, everybody chuckles. It's a good game everybody can play anytime. But these guys are all giving it a pass. Without a pause, without consulting me or Paul, Nelson jumps into the Light & Lively[8], a silly game called Big Wind Blows, musical chairs but without music.

This same group fights Sunday morning's role plays too. They don't want to take on anybody else's conflict, and so they act out real conflicts from their unit, breaking every AVP role-play rule in the process. Sunday afternoon, we often do a quiet, introspective, identity exercise we call "Who Am I?" Usually at least half the participants have a hard time being still and quiet, and we expect the same from these guys. We're shocked when they follow the guided meditation as patiently and silently as nuns meditating in a convent.

Paul, Nelson, and I debrief at a local Tim Hortons late Sunday afternoon. Nelson says, "What was all that about? That was like no workshop I've ever done." After a few chuckles, one of us says, "These guys' whole lives are role plays. All that bravado. All that macho tough guy stuff." "Yeah. If they open up and show any weakness or feelings, they'll get jumped." "And the 'Who Am I?' thing. How often can these guys be themselves? Where else except inside their heads?"

On another weekend, three of us facilitators have the program room set up for the 9:00 a.m. Saturday start: agenda on the flip

---

8   Light & Livelies are brief exercises that get people moving around and laughing after engaging in more serious and sometimes difficult subjects. Light & Livelies maintain the lighthearted mood of AVP, which helps participants feel more comfortable with each other, learn more effectively, and most of all, have fun in the process.

chart, coffee made, chairs in a circle, each of us primed to lead and to follow. No prisoners come. At 9:30 we phone the supervisors. Two uniformed guards come to meet us. They represent the guards' union. They say the room isn't safe for us and the program has to be cancelled. Without cameras and gun ports in the room, they can't guarantee our safety, they say. One talks about a female program staff person a few years ago who was held captive in the washroom across the hall for twenty minutes and sexually assaulted. "We're responsible for your safety," they say. It doesn't matter that program staff had prisoners in this room mere days before, or that prisoner programs have gone on in here for the last twenty years.

The acting warden comes in later, and he says he wants the program to happen. At 2:00 p.m., we relocate to the gym — with its gun ports and security cameras. The prisoners straggle in. For the first hour they vent: We waited months for this program, it's been going great, and now the guards fuck it up! "Will we be able to finish the workshop?" they ask. "Will we still get certificates?" "This is so typical of how the staff jerk us around all the time!" "I want to just yell and scream and beat up one of these stupid fuckin' guards!"

For those five hours they were locked up on the unit, waiting to see if the program would start up again, they were fighting mad. But they told us they talked it over, supported each other, and remembered why they signed up for the program in the first place: to reduce the violence in their lives. They asked each other what good it would do if even one of them beaked off at the staff or started throwing things or acted up in any way. The guards would win.

Paul, Nelson, and I see the answer right there. "Yes, if you finish the rest of the program, you will get a certificate," one of us says, certain the other two will agree. "What you did during those five hours demonstrates how much you are learning. That was tough, but it was a bigger test than any exercise we could've given you." "Trust the process," a senior facilitator told me when I was new to the game. "It works."

A key part of the process is personal, free choice. Every AVP facilitator gives up an entire weekend without pay for every workshop. The participants, too, give up a whole weekend. Corrections Canada, most of its institutions, and many of its staff know about AVP and support it, but the program isn't part of any inmate's correctional plan. I never met a prisoner who wants to take a CSC program that's not required in his correctional plan, the program of steps that caseworkers develop to facilitate the prisoner's progress toward eventual reintegration with the community. In fact, correctional services will not allow prisoners to take a program if it's not "in the plan." Prisoners focus on what they have to do to get out of prison. Usually they go through the motions. They sign up for programs and attend just to play the system and get another tick mark in their files.

The first question I get when I approach an inmate to tell him about AVP is, "Will it help me get parole?" I say we don't work for CSC and we don't give reports to them. We don't tell anybody what a prisoner tells us during a workshop, unless we have the participant's permission. (Reports of sexual abuse of children, of suicide risks, and of threats to the institution are exceptions, of course.) I tell the prisoner if he completes the program, he gets a certificate, and then it's up to him to show it to his parole officer. We don't give any reports to corrections staff on individual inmates. I say his improved behaviour after taking the program is the best possible report he can give his parole officer.

My introduction to AVP came from seventy-year-old Martin Hattersley, a unique hybrid of Edmonton lawyer and Anglican priest. At the time, Martin was a member of the Max's citizens' advisory committee. We had lunch on Sir Winston Churchill Square in the centre of downtown Edmonton, within a block of where his daughter was murdered in a public washroom in 1988. Since then he has been active in a victims support group and a frequent speaker on issues of crime, prisons, parole, and violence.

He was a mere wisp of a man when I met him, and he hobbled along the sidewalk at less than half my normal walking pace.

Even at that time he had severe back problems and his health kept him from facilitating workshops. Despite those obstacles, he has remained a stalwart champion of AVP to this day. Martin asked me if I would like to help get it going at the Max. I'd never heard of the program, but I knew prisoners at the Max needed less violence in their lives. I'd been M2W2 coordinator for only two months. Before that I was on long-term sick leave from my job at the Alberta Legislature. For two years, I was so burnt out I couldn't work at all. I knew I wasn't a violent person and that I didn't need AVP myself, but I did want to help the prisoners.

But I was in the middle of a marriage breakup. I was reconstructing my life. I was in shock from all the change. I moved slower than the hour hand on a clock. Every action I took and any work I did, no matter how small, wore me out. I taught two English courses at the King's University College. I'd been out of the field for twenty years, and so every lesson plan took ten times longer than it should have. Each Tuesday's visit to the Max for M2W2 was like pushing a boulder up a hill. I dragged myself out of bed each morning and pumped myself full of enough air to convince people I was still alive. I had trouble sleeping and needed every hour of every weekend to rest so I could make it through the next week.

I told Martin I couldn't afford to spend a Friday night, twelve hours Saturday, and seven hours Sunday taking a program *I* didn't need. But he was persuasive, and so I signed up anyway. I did it to help the prisoners. On that weekend, out came Dangerous G, an angry, violent, wild man who'd been locked up in a cage for forty years. I'm glad I've never had a problem with alcohol or drugs and that Dangerous G didn't come out when I was high, or I would've been locked up myself.

CHAPTER 8

FORTY-SIX YEARS ON DEATH ROW, MARRIED TO A CORPSE

If they'd given me a choice at the time, I'd have taken the rope. Because you only suffer for five minutes and that's it. This way you suffer for the rest of your life. This happened forty-six years ago and it still bothers the hell out of me. I still dream about it too.

—Roy Chudek, convicted murderer

"That's amazing. You've been married fifty years. What a feat!" The white-haired priest congratulates an elderly member of his parish over a cappuccino at the Tim Hortons six blocks from the church. "You must've survived some really nasty fights." The priest takes a sip and lowers his voice to a whisper. "In all those years, did you ever reach the point where you thought the marriage was over? Did you ever consider divorce?"

The man smiles. "Murder, lots of times. Divorce? Never!"

A marriage can only end one of two ways: death or divorce. A woman I know was living with her third husband when I heard her talk about relationships and how to cope when they end. We were members of a team teaching adult catechism in St. Theresa's Catholic Church. When we talk about matrimony, she notes that she's been divorced once and had the marriage annulled by the church, and she was widowed once. "Both times it was like somebody died. And part of me died too. Both times I went through long periods of crying and grieving. I fought like hell to get going again." She pauses, looks around the room, wondering if there is a polite way to say this: "It was a lot easier when the one died. He was dead. The marriage was over. Period. With the other one, it felt like he was dead—part of me wished he was dead—and then I'd run into him at the grocery store or walking down the street. The first few times it happened, I freaked out, like I was seeing a corpse," she chuckles nervously, "a dead man walking."

When I meet Roy Chudek on June 26, 2004, he's seventy-two years old and nearly dead. He's so emaciated from his battle with pancreatic cancer that his cheekbones are clearly visible through his thin, yellow skin. In his prime, before he did bodybuilding in prison, he only weighed 128 pounds; now he looks less than ninety. But his eyes glisten, his voice sparkles with laughter, and he often smiles as he recounts for me the highlights and lowlights of his long life.

Back in 1958, he was condemned to hang for murdering his wife, Lee. He was thirty-four when he was drunk and shot at her lover as the man ran from the house trailer where Roy and Lee lived in Swan River, Manitoba. He missed the six-foot-seven, three-hundred-pound lover. Three bullets hit his wife and killed her instantly. Roy was convicted and spent two and a half years in Headingley jail waiting to be hanged.

"Three days before they were going to hang me," Roy smiles between puffs on his cigarette, "the secretary comes running in and says, 'Your sentence has been commuted. Have you got anything to say?' I guess they wanted me to say something for the newspapers. I said no, I don't." He looks down at his slippers and the faded yellow carpet. I see his lip quiver and a tear form in his eye. "If they'd given me a choice at the time, I'd have taken the rope. Because you only suffer for five minutes and that's it. This way you suffer for the rest of your life. This happened forty-six years ago and it still bothers the hell out of me. I still dream about it too."

He takes a long, deep drag on his cigarette, sits up straight in his chair, and smiles at me. "Wanna see a picture of her?" I say, "Sure," and he races to the bedroom, grabs a framed eight-by-ten photo off his dresser, and hands it to me, beaming, as if he were a newly engaged man showing off his fiancée. "This was taken in the fifties, and so you've gotta turn the clock back. She's been dead forty-six years. This is a black-and-white picture, but she was a redhead and had blue eyes."

I'm in Roy Chudek's third-floor apartment on 92nd Street in Edmonton, just north of Jasper Avenue. I'd phoned him a couple of weeks before because my boss in the M2W2 program, Ken From, suggested I talk to Roy about his life and write a story up about him for our *Bar None* newsletter. I'd already interviewed half a dozen prisoners at the Max for the book of oral histories I was working on, and when Ken heard Roy was dying of cancer, he thought he might want to talk to me on tape and get in the book himself. Roy, he said, is a lifer, one of the last survivors of the capital punishment era in Canada. On the phone, Roy said he'd be happy to be part of the project.

In June 2004, my separation from my wife is less than two years old, our divorce nine months old. We were married for thirty-two years. I still wake up two, three times in the night — my record is seven, but I can't always keep track. In one of the dreams, my ex-wife removes her blouse and bra to seduce me, tells me she will forgive me and everything will be like it was. In the dream, my three kids are preschoolers, even though the youngest was nineteen when we separated. My son and two daughters sit on the floor and play with a Fisher Price tool kit and Cabbage Patch dolls in another part of the room.

I wake up after each dream, the muscles in my head clenched tight like a fist and my bowels aching and angry. In June of '04 every night is still a wrestling match to move beyond the life I'd constructed for three decades and to erase the future retirement that seemed so real I could taste it: My wife and I gradually grow gray and wrinkled. We celebrate the Christmas holidays with all

three grown kids and their spouses. A couple of preschool grandchildren run around the tree, pick wrapped boxes off the floor,
and shake them. I snuggle my newborn granddaughter as she fin-
ishes her bottle. We are finally free of the daily grind. We're living on pensions. We travel to Newfoundland, Italy, New Zealand,
Nigeria, Australia. We volunteer at an orphanage in Thailand,
teach hygiene and cooking in Burundi, learn to farm with peas-
ants in Mexico. We learn new languages, meet people of all races,
cultures, and creeds, and when we're back home in Edmonton, we
watch our kids' careers grow and blossom.

In my waking life in June 2004, I still can't bear to open the four
heavy loose-leaf binders full of photos from our life together. I
have an eight-by-ten photo of my three kids and son-in-law that I
plaque-mounted so I could reconnect with them when I looked up
from my desk. They were on the other side of the continent from
me, over two thousand miles away, and I wanted them in my life.
But I couldn't sleep with them smiling at me like that, and I had
to hide the picture in a drawer. I prayed that I could move past all
the grief and the tears and make a new life for myself. Every day
I looked into my own eyes in the mirror as I shaved. I wondered
who this fifty-five-year-old man was, this stranger who gave up so
many pieces of himself when he separated from his wife and then
his kids moved away. I wondered how I could love myself when it
seemed that the people I'd loved most in the world didn't love me
anymore.

So I come to Roy Chudek's place with thirty-two years of married history and fragments of unravelled future in my head; Roy
comes to me with a forty-six-year-old corpse, prison, alcoholism,
childhood poverty, and a .22-calibre bullet stuck in his head. In
that condemned cell in Headingley, he tells me, he got "a radio,
the Alcoholics Anonymous book, and the Bible. That's all you were
allowed in those days. So I figured, I'm not gonna have a drinking
problem if they hang me, so I'd better start readin' the Bible. But
it was full of *thees* and *thous*. I couldn't understand it. The sheriff
came in and asked if I was readin' my Bible. I said, 'I can't make

any sense of it.' So he got me one in modern English, and that's when I really got into the Bible. It felt so good. Towards the end, I was just countin' the days. I didn't want to get commuted."

Roy tells me he was never a religious man before. Several times in his life, he says, a higher power intervened to help him. The first was on the day of the murder, December 7, 1957, when he tried to kill himself. On that day, once he realizes Lee is dead, killed by bullets from his revolver, he knows he's going to hang. In those days, capital punishment is automatic, he says, no such thing as manslaughter or second degree. It's black or white, death by hanging or freedom by acquittal.

"I decided I wasn't going to go to jail," Roy chuckles. "So I loaded up the .22 and shot myself in the roof of the mouth. I had a brass plate there, but I took it out so it wouldn't slow the bullet down. I shot myself, and the gun went click. I injected another shell into it, and I pulled the trigger, and it went click. And the third one went click. I thought, 'Holy God! What's the matter? This gun never failed before.' And the fourth one I injected in the gun, put it into my mouth, and it went off. I still say to this day that higher power up there must've been guidin' that gun because the fourth one worked. But I guess the higher power said, 'This isn't gonna kill him, and so I'll let the gun go.'"

Listening to him, I feel like I'm reliving a B-grade movie: young love, betrayed husband, philandering wife, raw sex, murder, drunkenness, a trial judge later convicted of fraud and imprisoned, and even some slapstick and Kafka thrown in. Roy shakes his head in amazement when he talks about what happens next.

"I thought the top of my head was right off. I got up and looked in the mirror on the dresser to see if my head was on top, and it was. My eye came out of my head when I shot myself, and so I'm holdin' this eye in my hand, tryin' to protect it." He pauses for another puff of cigarette, which he politely exhales away from me. "I couldn't believe I was still alive. So I tried to shoot myself again, but I had stiffened up with that bullet in my head. I tried to pick up the gun, but my hand wouldn't bend around it."

"I guess somebody heard the shots and phoned the RCMP." He clenches his fist and bangs it on the table. "You can say whatever you want about the RCMP, but they are far worse than any Gestapo that Adolf Hitler had." He pauses for a breath of fresh air. "He came in and checked her out, and he said, 'You shot her?' I said, 'I guess I must've. I don't know.' So he wrote a statement out, and he said, 'Sign it.' I said, 'I'm not signing nothin'.' He said, 'You'll sign, you son of a bitch.' He grabbed me by the hair, threw me on the floor, and kicked the living hell out of me. His feet were going around me, and I'm hanging onto this eye so he doesn't step on it. He grabbed me by the hair and sat me down in the chair and said, 'Sign.' I said, 'I'm not signing nothin'.' So he threw me back down on the floor and worked me over again. He worked me over three times. The third time I came out of my body. I was up there, and I was watchin' him kick me and beat me. I felt no pain, no resentment, no anger or anything. I just watched. Then I went back into my body, and I felt the pain and the hatred and everything else that goes with it. I thought that my coming out of my body like I did was a sign from God that I should sign, and so I did. Of course, that convicted me."

For the trial, Roy says, he got a state-appointed attorney who shared privileged conversations with the Crown, he got a judge who fell asleep on the bench and was later convicted of fraud, and he got a jury of men he said couldn't even speak English well enough to understand the testimony of the psychiatrists who spoke in his defence. When the judge asked the jury for its verdict, Roy says the foreman of the all-Ukrainian jury, "the brains of the jury," said, "Guilty, just the same like charged, and I think a little bit more."

I'm so caught up in the energy and the flow, the sheer physicality, the lust, the anger, the hatred, the betrayal in Roy's story that I'm jealous. Listening to his passion, his pain, and his lighthearted humour in talking about dramatic and violent events I could barely imagine, I wish I could be like him—except for the terminal cancer. Compared to Roy's life, mine is as boring as cold porridge. The only times I ever fired a gun were in Kansas, rabbit hunting with my dad and shooting at targets with my brother when I was fourteen and fifteen years old. I couldn't hit anything. Maybe it was my bad eyesight. Maybe I simply couldn't hold the .22- calibre rifle steady. I probably jerked the trigger instead of squeezing. Maybe I had some innate fear of guns and killing I hadn't discovered yet. I do remember having a few clear shots at cottontails, one sitting still in a cornfield, another beside a leafless bush. I got the shots off, but I never had a hit.

I had no personal experience of death either until I was in my fifties. I visited the wife of a good friend of mine as she lay dying of cancer in palliative care. I was at her bedside with her son half an hour before she died, watching her chest heave and hearing her lungs rattle. And suicide always revolted me. I had plenty of nightmares about being buried alive, trapped in the dark under six feet of dirt, my body rotting into a stinking blob of meat and maggots. I heard too many Catholic priests and nuns preach about death and eternal hellfire. I grew up with a father who spent most of his later life in sheer terror at the prospect of his own death. I couldn't understand why people would try to inflict death on themselves, end up in hell, their corpses not even allowed in the churchyard.

I grew up in a middle-class, Catholic family in the American Midwest. My father was an officer in the army during World War II, and he worked hard all his life to provide us with good food, adequate clothing, a comfortable home, quality dental and medical care, and a Catholic education, right through high school and beyond. My mother and father stayed married for sixty-six years. He never beat us. She always fed us. They taught all four of us to study hard, work hard, and make the most of our talents. None of us committed any crimes, much less murder. None of us got hooked on drugs or alcohol. None of us did any time in prison.

As I sit on Roy Chudek's vinyl-upholstered kitchen chair listening to him, I wonder if I could have ended up like him. I ask him about his background, his childhood. He was born in 1932, he says, into a dysfunctional family. His father was "a sadistic son of a gun" who "used to beat the heck out of us and out of Mom, especially when she stuck up for us." It was the hungry thirties, he says. "At home we had no food at all. Six girls and six boys. We used to fight for a little piece of bread or anything." Roy says he was brought up in orphanages and foster homes in Alberta. "The orphanage was pretty good, but the foster homes used a lot of beatings. They worked you from daylight until dark. It was child slavery." But at least at the foster homes he got fed. "They took me to my second foster home because I was sick a lot of the time, mostly from malnutrition."

When Roy is eleven, the orphanage sends him to a foster home in the country because they think the fresh air will help him get his health back. "Sure enough, I got sick. The husband was out threshing. My job was to fetch the cows, milk 'em, and do the chores. His wife told me, 'You better go out and get the cows. My husband's gonna be home pretty soon, and if you don't have the cows milked, he's gonna beat the hell out of you.' I couldn't get out of bed. I really tried hard, but I couldn't." Roy says when the man got home he yelled at him, "You lazy little son of a bitch. I'm gonna fix you once and for all." So the man dragged Roy out of bed by the hair and into the pouring rain with nothing but a pair of pants on. He took him to the top of the hill between the house and the barn, threw him down the hill, and said, "Now, you little bastard, you either get back on your own, or you can damn well drown for all I care."

Roy makes it back to bed but is laid up with rheumatic fever and pneumonia. At the end of the summer, the man takes him to the Lacombe train station to send him back to the orphanage. He gives Roy four one-dollar bills to promise he won't tell the orphanage he was sick. "Well," Roy laughs, "four dollars to me was like a million bucks. I never had so much money in my life!" He brags about the money, and the headmistress finds out where and why he got it. She puts him in the hospital for a week to recover.

His next foster home is with a family so poor they can't feed him. He works as a school janitor for fifteen dollars a month, but the family takes all his money to buy food. When he's fifteen and in grade six, he goes to a foster home on a dairy farm. The farmer convinces him to quit school and work for him for wages. He's not there long before he thinks about Leduc No. 1 blowing in and all the money in the oil patch. He thinks to himself, "I'll just follow the light in the sky and I'll get there." He walks forty miles to Calmar with only two sandwiches to eat. The only money he has is fifteen cents to buy a milkshake when he gets there. Despite his age, he makes an impression on the oilmen with his hard work and his desire to learn. "Three years later," he says, "I had the driller's job. I did pretty well. I was the youngest driller in Canada at the time."

When he meets Lee, he's only nineteen. Roy says, "They called me 'pimple-face' because I had pimples all over. So I didn't bother with any girls. Then we moved to Manitoba, and I met this beautiful little girl. Her name was Lee. Everybody tried to date her. She was a waitress in the hotel." The older men on his crew tease Roy about asking her out. He takes that as a challenge. Roy tells me he's so tongue-tied when he meets her after her shift that he can't get any words out. Lee guesses what he wants and agrees to go out with him.

Having been a pimple-faced teenage boy myself, I remember what it's like to feel despair, knowing no girl would go out with me. I remember being so ashamed of my own face that I went on few dates in high school. I had to work up my courage for weeks even to call a girl on the phone. When I did get a good-looking girl to go out with me, I felt like I'd won the Irish Sweepstakes. When I first had sexual intercourse with a girl, I flew so high I wondered why I or anybody else should ever live on the ground again.

Five months after their first date, Roy and Lee get married. When they return from their honeymoon trip to the mountains, Roy crashes to earth. While Lee's unpacking her suitcase, Roy sees photos of her underneath some clothing. In them, Lee and a big black man are naked and having sex. Roy is outraged. He says, "What the hell is going on?" Lee says, "Oh, honey, I've got to tell you something I didn't tell you before. I can't say no to any man. I just can't. I've had black, yellow, white, anything. I cannot say no to anybody." Roy says, "Why didn't you tell me that before we were married?" "Well, you would've never married me."

Roy says the whole six or seven years of their marriage was a roller coaster. They'd have great times together while he was home, but being an oil driller, he was always on the road. He'd come back and find her with another man and throw her out of the house. Her mother would plead for him to take her back. He'd take her back, and the cycle would repeat itself over and over again. All the while he'd medicate his wounds with whiskey and beer. When he finds Lee with a three-hundred-pound lover in December 1957, he's so drunk he can't shoot straight.

Roy spends a year in remand before his trial and two and a half years on death row. When he's taken to Stony Mountain penitentiary the day after his death sentence is commuted, he tells me, "It was a huge, huge surprise to me: the big concrete walls, a guard in each corner. You knew you were in prison."

Roy starts to think about spending the rest of his life in this place, and he's overwhelmed. They put him to work in the prison's tin shop. "This Frenchman was there," he says. "He only had ten years in on a life sentence. He could see I was really down and out, and he says, 'Well, kid, this is as big as the big house gets. You got nothin' to worry about. You'll be looked after for the rest of your life.' And he laughs. So I went to my cell, and I looked to my left and asked, 'How much time have you got in?' He said, 'Thirty-three years.' I turned to the next guy and said, 'How much time have you got in?' He said, 'Forty-two years, punk.'"

But Roy keeps finding people who think he got a bum rap, that Lee's behaviour drove him to it. Roy tells me, "Everybody I was interviewed by—psychologist, psychiatrist, priest, or whoever—said, 'You shouldn't be in here.' I agreed with them totally." After five years, they send him to the prison farm, outside the walls, the place they normally send short-timers to. Everybody there wonders what's going on. He applies for parole, is denied, and three weeks later he gets it anyway. When he gets out, he meets a woman. He says, "You have to have sex when you get out. So we started having sex, and I got her pregnant." His parole officer says he has to marry her or go back to prison, and so he marries her. Before long they have two kids.

Roy is a truck driver for Orange Crush at the time, but he tells me he wasn't making much money at it. He starts looking for a better job, and he finds one: selling oilfield equipment. He's delighted to be back in the oil business. "They gave me a Jeep, good pay, and everything was working out well. But the company said, 'You have to have at least ten cases of whiskey in your office, so that if somebody comes in and buys one hundred thousand or two hundred thousand dollars' worth of equipment, you give them the whole case. That's the way we operate.'" Seeing all that booze every day is too much temptation for him. He starts drinking again, the RCMP find out, and he's back in prison for six more years.

He goes to Drumheller, which "was like a kindergarten compared to what I'd been in. I liked it there." He had only finished grade seven, so in prison he earns his grade twelve through correspondence, and then he gets his fourth-class power engineering ticket. "It came in very handy, because I've been working on that ticket for thirty years, ever since I got out." After getting out of prison for good in 1971, Roy sometimes loses a job, he says, when somebody recognizes him and reports to the boss, "You've got a murderer working here." But he never stays unemployed for long.

When I ask him about his health, Roy lights up another cigarette and draws deeply. "Five or six years ago, I went to see my doctor. I asked the doctor right away if it was cancer, and he said, 'No, it's not cancer. You've just got a bad stomach. Don't worry about that. It's just age.' Then three weeks later they found out I had cancer. It was pancreatic cancer, which is the worst you can get. The doctor said, 'You'd better start thinking death. You'd better get your funeral ready' and stuff like that. So I did. They gave me two and a half months to live. Then the two and a half months came up, and they gave me another two and a half. And it went on and on. I'm still here. I don't know when my time is up."

When our interview is over, I thank him and promise I'll give him a copy of the transcript when I've finished it. He smiles and thanks me. He says his daughter has often talked about writing up his life story but never got around to it. He's glad that I've volunteered to take on the project. A week or two later I come back with the transcript in hand, and Roy's not alone. He's got a woman there to answer the door and let me in. I figure it's not polite to ask who she is. Maybe she's a nurse. A daughter. A friend. When I come in, Roy's sitting on the loveseat. His skin is yellow as mustard powder, his eyelids droop, and he struggles to lift his head to look at me. The smell in the room is different. On top of the stale cigarette smoke is the sickly sweet smell of old meat about to go rancid. I give him the transcript, and he thanks me. But this is very different from the Roy I met before. He mumbles only a few words, then stops and stares at the floor.

A few weeks later I am at Evergreen Funeral Parlor in northeast Edmonton at Roy's memorial service. His parole officer is there, and some other people I know from my prison work. There are maybe thirty people in total.

I look around the chapel, at the flowers, the people in black suits and dresses, the plain brown casket at the front. Afterwards I wander around the cemetery, where the neatly trimmed lawn stands taller than the little brass nameplates on the graves. I wonder, if I'd been beaten by my father, sent off starving to one foster home after another, bullied by other kids in school; if my wife had repeatedly cheated on me, if I'd used alcohol to dull my pain, if I'd had a gun handy when my wife and I had a major fight, am I sure I would've made better choices than Roy did? And would I have made good use of time in prison? Would I have survived all those years in prison without being brutalized by the place, transformed into someone more violent and uglier than the prisoners I lived with?

This is where we all end up, I tell myself. When the time comes, will I be able to face my own death with as much dignity and good humour as Roy did?

CHAPTER 9

PRISONS, MATRIMONY, AND OTHER INSTITUTIONS

The law is a ass—a idiot.
—Charles Dickens, *Oliver Twist*

"I've got a problem," the caller tells me. "In fact, my whole organization has a problem. I'm hoping you can help us."

"I'll do what I can," I say, wondering what my next surprise will be. It's 1983. I'm in my first year as the Speaker's executive assistant, and I'm still learning about the Speaker's job, the Legislative Assembly of Alberta, and the limits of my own authority. Every time I speak to somebody on the telephone, I imagine the Speaker listening. I'm afraid I'll say something I shouldn't and lose my job. Speaker Gerry Amerongen doesn't have a constituency office, and so I'm his constituency assistant too. Anybody who lives in his Edmonton-Meadowlark constituency might call to ask for help with any kind of problem or to share opinions on any subject: garbage pickup, vandalism, a proposal to allow stores to open on Sundays, back pain caused by a work injury, rising divorce rates, the lack of affordable daycare, the person's Member of Parliament not returning phone calls, et cetera.

Anybody who wants to ask these questions or something about how the Assembly works, what bills might be debated today, or how to get a seat in the gallery can phone 427-2464. One of the two secretaries picks up the phone, and if it's not a routine question, he or she passes it on to me.

I spin my chair around to look north at the barren stretch of mud and clay where backhoes and graders have been moving dirt for months on what, in a year, would become a series of reflecting pools, fountains, and walkways surrounded by trees, grass, and flowers. "What is the problem?" I say. "How can I help?"

"I am on the board of the Alberta SPCA, the Society for the Prevention of Cruelty to Animals." The man pauses to frame his preamble. It goes more or less like this: "Many of us have been lifelong members of the society because we care about suffering animals. But now we're being taken over by people who don't even care about animals. They're involved in a program to learn about proper procedure, how to run meetings. They want to get experience in running meetings, rules of order, that kind of thing. They were advised to join a non-profit group, to get involved in the meetings and participate. Now we've had our annual general meeting, and there were so many of these people present they have taken over the board. I'm afraid the SPCA will become a sham. I don't know what will happen to the animals we shelter and find homes for. These people only want to run meetings. What can we do?"

The bylaws of every organization outline who can become a member, but for most non-profits, those restrictions are usually minimal. To be a member of a political party, for example, a person has to live in a geographical area but doesn't even have to be a citizen. There is no ideological compatibility test. I could be Karl Marx's blood brother and still join the Conservative Party. I have been a member of the Edmonton Bicycle and Touring Club for many years, but a paraplegic or an infant could join for thirty dollars. Members don't have to like bikes.

Some societies have stricter regulations. The Northern Alberta Pioneers and Descendants, for example, admits as founding members only people whose family lived in Alberta prior to September 1, 1905; but even they welcome other members too, with the proviso that they "are interested in preserving the history of Northern

Alberta." To belong to the Legislative Assembly of Alberta or the House of Commons of Canada, a person has to be elected.

So I tell the caller that, as far as I know, the only way an organization like the SPCA can fight against people who want to take over the society is to organize the people who care about the society's purposes, harness their passion for the society's mission, and take control back. But it depends on the wording of the bylaws. If the bylaws don't cover certain contingencies, well, the law can be an ass. And non-profit societies are governed not only by their own bylaws but by the law of the land and are legally sanctioned institutions.

To join the "Federal Prisoners of Canada Club" a person has to be convicted of a criminal offence and get a sentence of two years or more. By my last count, the Criminal Code is 1,129 pages of federal legislation, and it constitutes the foundation of Canada's justice and corrections system. Corrections Canada has its own set of rules. The Bible of the prison system is the collected Commissioner's Directives. They spell out in some detail the rights of prisoners and the responsibilities of staff and management, and they include procedures for grievances.

Each prison has its own rules, and they are always changing, depending on circumstances. The prisons I am most familiar with have head counts several times a day. The daytime counts happen at 11:00 a.m. and 4:00 p.m. At those times, everything in the prison stops until every prisoner is accounted for. Meals come at set times every day. Staff on the units and in most positions in the prison have shift changes at 3:00 p.m., 11:00 p.m., and 7:00 a.m. Prison staff have their own places in a hierarchy, from warden to deputy warden to correctional supervisor to correctional officer and everything in between.

Every prison runs with military precision. Some military people would say that's an oxymoron, like a dry rain, a good illness, or an honest politician. Joseph Heller wrote a whole novel, *Catch-22*, about military inefficiencies and contradictions. Anything outside the prison routine has to be authorized in writing. The routines, of course, are also spelled out in writing, and any changes to them are duly written and posted for all to see. And everything is sub-ject to every guard's interpretation and to the circumstances of the moment. Rules are often stretched and broken as guards and other staff match their creativity against the prisoners', as happens in every war zone.

One of the unwritten rules is that people are not paroled directly to the street from a maximum-security prison. There are many rea-sons for that. One is that the entire system is organized on the prin-ciple that the security of society and the chances of the prisoner succeeding in the outside world depend on the prisoner's ability to live in a less structured environment. A Max has the most tightly controlled environment in the system, and to go from the Max to total freedom would require an extreme adjustment that not many could make.

Since I started at the Max in 2001, it has evolved from one integrated population into eight separate populations. None of these groups is allowed to mix with another. In effect, the Max is eight separate prisons, not counting segregation or solitary con-finement. Rarely did each of these populations have more than twenty-six in it until 2010, when CSC started double bunking. The one-person-per-cell practice guaranteed prisoners alone time, and they cherished that time. One of the most common stresses in the Max, in the whole system, in fact, results from constant vigilance. Every prisoner knows that an attack, verbal or physical, can come from anywhere at any time. Prisoners are not locked up because they're high-functioning social beings, and a big problem is pris-oners manipulating other prisoners. On the inside, the men who succeed are generally those who "do their own time" instead of trying to manipulate others or letting others manipulate them.

Sometimes the Max has no choice but to let prisoners out directly to the street. The odds of their success are small, but if a prisoner has served every last day of his sentence (warrant expiry) the sys-tem has to release him. The best-known example of this in Canada in recent years is Karla Homolka, who spent twelve years in prison in Ontario. She testified against her co-accused, Paul Bernardo, in a case that got national headlines for months. It involved the rape, torture, and brutal murder of teenage girls, which Homolka and Bernardo videotaped for their later viewing pleasure. The public was outraged when Homolka was released after her sentence, but there was no legal way to keep her in the system. She made a deal with the prosecutors and got a lighter sentence because she pleaded guilty and helped secure Bernardo's conviction. She was free to do whatever she wanted.

I've seen a few prisoners at the Max get released and return in a few days or weeks. One prisoner explained to me how he felt being sent from the Max to a halfway house in Edmonton. He had to check in and out of the halfway house, where they had a strict curfew. He resented that he had to account for every minute he was out. But as much as he craved freedom, he didn't know what to do with it. He had a car, and so he could go wherever he wanted. But he had to tell his case officer where he was going and for how long. He even had to tell the case officer where he planned to stop for gas. He wasn't allowed to make an extra stop for a Slurpee or a pop or he would be breaking his parole conditions and could be sent back to the Max.

That wasn't the worst of it, though. He had to buy his own groceries and cook his own food. He was in his late thirties and had lived on his own for a few years. He didn't have a problem cooking for himself. He did have a problem going into a grocery store and deciding what to buy. He told me when he first went into a supermarket, he just stood in the aisle staring at the shelves, overwhelmed by the choices. Dozens of different soup flavours, several different brands, different serving sizes, canned and dried. Meat coolers stacked high with beef, pork, chicken packages of various sizes and cuts. Fresh vegetables and fruit laid out in colourful displays, mouth-watering and attractive. He'd spent four years in prison, where somebody else made these decisions. He simply could not choose for himself any more. In Stephen King's novella *Rita Hayworth and Shawshank Redemption*, Red is released after thirty years in prison, and his bowels continue to move every day at precisely the time the guards used to let him use the communal toilet in prison.

The rigid prison regimen is extreme compared to the outside world, but the community has regulations, too, and institutions we as a society set up to give our lives structure. Just as we all have habits and routines that structure our daily lives, our community has laws, rules, and cultural practices to facilitate our living and working together. The challenge is to maintain our individuality while collaborating with each other.

For several years I was active in a men's organization called the Mankind Project. For four years I went to small-group meetings. The meetings were highly structured. Each meeting had four distinct parts reflecting the four quadrants of masculinity identified and described by Robert Bly and many others: the lover, the warrior, the magician, and the king. Each meeting started out with a smudging ceremony, adopted and modified from the Lakota tribes of the northern plains. Then we circled around a burning sweetgrass braid. As we proceeded through the four quadrants in order, we used structured processes to help each other work through personal struggles and to celebrate successes. Those processes are all well researched and spelled out in a manual and on the organization's website. I have a friend who has been a social worker and counsellor for over thirty years, and he is one of many who are in awe of the excellence of these processes. But the processes — protocols as they are called — are never enough on their own. Personal creativity, emotional awareness, and integrity are essential and can't be legislated. But without the protocols, individual men would not have the freedom to be themselves at Mankind Project meetings.

But in many respects, every institution, like a prison, is essentially dehumanizing. Making, supporting, and perpetuating institutions is also essentially human and necessary. Nothing is more human than the desire to take something good and make it into an institution and perpetuate it. That goes for religions, churches, schools, hospitals, societies, and corporations, as well as for rules to govern behaviour and prisons to enforce those rules. Laws are institutions. They are statements made by people in authority—monarch, legislature, city council, town meeting, referendum—to make certain practices the norm for the society that approves them. But institutions are two-edged, even multi-edged. They can kill us if we let them.

For fifteen years I was the editor of *Hansard* at the Alberta Legislature. That job became central to my identity because I'd done it for so long. I supported my wife and three children with the income I earned. The time and energy I put into my work was the better part of myself. I went to work every day energized and focused and came home exhausted. I spent the evenings with my family and sometimes doing something in the community, but I knew that my work had already taken the best of my day, that I was operating at eighty, sixty, forty percent or less. Weekends and summer vacations were highlights of my life, and I enjoyed them thoroughly. Looking back now I can't decide whether I worked all week for the weekend break and all year for the summer break or whether those breaks were simply rest periods so I could work better.

On Friday, June 22, 2000, at about 3:00 p.m., I suddenly was tired to the core. I'd been back two weeks from a three-week vacation, a long road trip from Edmonton to Kansas City to Des Moines, Iowa, to St. Louis, Missouri, and back again. I had my twenty-year-old daughter, Jennifer, with me and my seventeen-year-old son, Sam. It was a delightful adventure. We'd spent two nights in Fargo, North Dakota, a place Jennifer had wanted to go ever since seeing the movie *Fargo*. We ate barbecued ribs at a restaurant built to look like a flying saucer. We visited my parents and sister and brother-in-law in Overland Park, Kansas. In Iowa, we celebrated my wife's parents' sixtieth wedding anniversary with all the brothers, sisters, uncles, aunts, cousins, and grandchildren.

I should have been refreshed, renewed, reinvigorated by the break, but I was running on empty. I had been dissatisfied with my job for years, but my job search got me only a couple of interviews.

After a weekend to rest, I thought of going back to work but couldn't. Within a week I was so exhausted I couldn't even read. I slogged my way through *The Poisonwood Bible*, but I struggled with every sentence. I had so little energy that by the middle of every sentence I couldn't remember the beginning. I lay around all day every day because I could do nothing else.

At the end of my first month off work, I didn't know what had happened to the time. I went out to the backyard garden in late July to pick raspberries, but after ten minutes, I was so light-headed I couldn't stand up. In August I was determined to walk around the neighbourhood for fresh air and exercise, but I was constantly drowsy. I couldn't wake up. If I had been awake, maybe Dangerous G could've gone on an imaginary crime spree like Thelma and Louise, but even he didn't have the energy or the will for that. When I did take walks, I was somehow disconnected from my own legs and feet. I had to watch them carefully and will them over curbs and around obstacles. It took all the energy I had simply to walk around the block. I was a back-seat driver in my own body.

I went to my family doctor, to a gastroenterologist, to a psychiatrist, a psychologist. I had a colonoscopy. I had blood and urine tests, sonograms, psychological tests, a naturopathic examination. I took vitamin B12. I got a prescription for Zoloft, a common antidepressant. None of that did anything to cure me or to help diagnose me. The default diagnosis, therefore, was stress. It might as well have been institutionalization.

My identity was so tied up in my job that I was disoriented without it. I rested every day. Every day I pushed myself to do something: cook, sweep the house, do yard work, clean, do laundry, wash dishes—anything small and easily manageable. The summer days got shorter and cooler. The leaves on the trees turned red, yellow, brown, and fell onto frost-covered grass. Snow accumulated flake by flake. Six months felt like one day. My wife and kids would say things to me and we would do things, but I had a hard time remembering any of it. If I hadn't kept a journal during that period, those months would be forever lost to me.

When my energy came back a little, after about six months, I decided to volunteer at the Marian Centre soup kitchen downtown. I would hop on the Number 67 bus at about 8:30, and from 9:30 until 10:15, I cut up onions, potatoes, cauliflower, broccoli, carrots, and whatever other donated vegetables they had. Sometimes I made sandwiches out of tuna salad, egg salad, cold cuts, peanut butter and jelly. Sometimes I was on cleanup duty and mopped the floors or straightened out cupboards or moved things around in their basement cold room or their walk-in freezer. Sometimes I helped sort donated socks, pants, tuques, gloves, shoes. At 10:15 we had a tea break for about half an hour, and then we worked for another forty-five minutes and had lunch. Then we served lunch to whoever was lined up at 1:00 p.m. By 1:30 we were cleaning up the lunchroom. By 2:30 we were done.

The first few times I did this, I was sure I had pushed myself too far. I still felt light-headed but managed to work through it. Even after a year of this, I figured that I did well to make it through the short day. I had no energy to spare and had to take a nap when I got home. When I looked back at how much actual work I did—mindless, repetitive, simple manual labour—it came to three and a half hours of total work time, fewer than half of what I had worked on my slow days at the Legislature for eighteen years.

Every time I returned home from the Marian Centre, I felt like Jacob Marley in *A Christmas Carol*, dragging a heavy weight. But the weight wasn't behind me. It was in my bones, in my blood, in my muscles and skin. It was in my brain. For the next two days afterwards, I was too exhausted to get up and do more than cook supper or read a book. What was that weight I carried? For the twenty-two years I worked at the Legislature, I supported my family and I shared the work of raising three children, but who had I become? I was my job, the editor of *Alberta Hansard*. That work and the income from it were the foundation of my life. I had my own spirituality, my own values, my love for my wife and children, but if that work and income were taken away, the rest would collapse like a house of cards.

My family so depended on my level of income that it was unthinkable we could be better off with less. I had achieved much at the Legislature. I earned more as I got more responsibility, and by June 2000 the chance of my finding another job with comparable pay and benefits was virtually nil. The golden handcuffs. I gave all I had to my work and my family. I had nothing left.

After a year of being on long-term disability, I couldn't work more than three and a half hours a day a couple of days a week. I could read again, but I had no stamina, physical or mental. My psychologist and my doctor both started to wonder if maybe there could be problems at home, something that might be continuing to keep me from bouncing back, from healing from some deep wound that nobody could identify.

I'll forego the details. The end result was that on August 5, 2002, I separated from my wife of thirty-two years. I had worked with her for a year to get at what was wrong between us, and I know she worked hard too. But I reached a point where I knew I had to get space between us, at least for a while, so I could sort out who I was and where to go from there. It was a holiday Monday. I phoned up Pat at the Marian Centre to see if they had a place I could spend the night. He told me I could stay two nights, but after that, I would have to find somewhere else. I packed up some clothes in a small suitcase and left the house.

Because of the feelings that had built up in me over the previous months and because of the difficulties between me and Kathy, I was full of rage and grief. I struggled to sleep that first night. Every night after that I went to bed only because it was late, not because I felt sleepy. My mind kept going over and over what happened between us during the breakup period, as if the memories were a battering ram trying to shatter the door back into the relationship I thought we used to have. My mind wouldn't slow down or shut off. I was locked in a cycle I didn't know how to escape.

I had just taken on two new part-time jobs, and it was all I could do to go through the motions with them every day. Without sleep, that became impossible in a matter of days. I got prescriptions from my doctor for sleeping pills. It took a while to figure out what kind would work, and even then I struggled with sleep for over two years. I had bizarre and disturbing dreams night after night. I started recording my dreams to see if I could learn something from them. I talked to a dream expert. I told her I sometimes woke up seven times in the night. I recorded the dreams on audiotape. She told me analyzing so many dreams would be pointless. She told me I should simply honour those dreams in some way, that it might be enough to transcribe my recorded accounts of the dreams and file them away.

Aside from the insomnia and the dreams, when I was first out on my own, some of the smallest things made me mad. When I saw my fingernails needed trimming, I remembered Kathy had the fingernail clippers in the house where I used to live. I knew exactly where they were, in which drawer of the bathroom vanity cabinet. I was mad that she had them and I didn't. It was so unfair. I was mad that the shampoo we'd bought together and both used was there too. I had none. I was mad that I had to make an appointment to see my nineteen-year-old son. He still lived at home, but I had to phone him whenever I wanted to talk to him, arrange to toss a Frisbee, a football, or baseball around with him, something we'd done for years. I couldn't simply look across the dining-room table or walk down the hall to his room to talk to him. I resented that his mother had him with her all the time, and that I had him only when I approached him with times and dates and got him to agree to spend time with me. I had only a bicycle to get around on, while she had the family car.

Starting on August 5, 2002, I reconstructed my new identity separate from the institutions in which I had spent the last thirty-two years: my marriage, the civil service job I had at the Legislature, the family residence, and even my personal hygiene habits. I had followed all the rules, met all my responsibilities to my wife and family; I ended up depleted, empty, exhausted, and confused.

When I talk to prisoners about their plans for getting out, the ones who are the most committed to success and change tell me they want to go to a new city where they won't know anybody, where they won't have to deal with the circle of friends and the drug/violence/crime subculture that played such a big part in their pasts. I compare their chances with mine when I restarted my life after shedding the institutional influences that had so exhausted me.

I have a postgraduate degree. I have superior communication skills. I have developed healthy social habits and know where and how to make new friends. I have some savings, family connections, a good work ethic, strong moral principles, and I have never been addicted to alcohol, drugs, or even tobacco. I had enough connections and presence of mind to find friends I could stay with, and I associated myself with people I knew I could trust.

Until March 1, 2003, I boarded with a family I got so close to that they are among my best friends now, and I am an adopted uncle to their children. When I moved into a co-op house on that date, I realized I had never lived alone before. I woke up in the morning with only myself and my employers to please. If I didn't have to be presentable, I would simply relax unshaven and unwashed for the day.

I would look into the mirror and realize that the man looking back at me is the only person I have to live with. If I don't love that man, my chances of having positive relationships or a wholesome life are pretty slim. I learned to take delight in my own company. I was free of many of the institutions that had me manacled, mind, body, and spirit. I still struggle to avoid the dehumanizing power of institutions—government, church, employer, prisons, clubs, et cetera—even as I participate in them, try to influence them, and connect with others in them to do good. Every one, even a prison, has good in it.

In November 2002, I gave a sermon on restorative justice at the First Mennonite Church in south Edmonton. I called it "Fleas in a Jar." Training fleas to perform in a flea circus is a relatively simple task, from what I hear. The trainer puts fleas in a jar and closes the lid. The fleas jump and knock their heads on the lid over and over and over again. Finally they realize it's pointless to keep knocking against the lid. They start to jump a little lower, just low enough to miss the lid. They seem to understand the lid's not going away. They're not as crazy as some people. Maybe they simply get tired of the pain. I assume fleas can sense pain. Maybe they don't think about it — who knows if fleas can think or not? Maybe their bodies decide on their own to stop jumping so high, some kind of reverse Pavlovian response.

The trainer then takes the lid off the jar. The fleas keep jumping just short of where the lid was. After a while, the trainer takes the fleas out of the jar into the open air. The fleas keep on jumping to the same height. Audiences applaud the amazing spectacle. The trainer bows and pockets the proceeds of the ticket sales.

But if we knew about the training the fleas got, would we applaud? If we knew how a magician could always cut the card that only the person opposite him knows, would we be impressed? If we understood the way a child was raised, the kind of people the parents were, the values the child inhaled, swallowed, and absorbed through the skin, as it were, in church, school, peer groups, the community, we'd have a pretty good idea how a child might choose to become a policewoman, a loving father, a burglar, a doctor, or a murderer. Humans have more capacity to choose than fleas, but our lives, too, are shaped by the jars we live in and the training we get early in life.

I got into prison visitation a year after I went on disability from my Legislature job and a year before my marriage breakup. My energy was still low, but every day I pushed myself a little farther than I had gone the day before. I kept knocking my head against that lid to see if it might have moved in the night. I had volunteered when I was nineteen to teach high school math to a prisoner in the St. Louis city jail, but for thirty-five years, like most people in the community, I pretended prisons didn't exist. I was locked into the routine of my regular job at the Legislature. I got up every workday, ate breakfast, kissed my wife and kids goodbye; drove, bused, or bicycled sixteen kilometres from my suburban bi-level home; sat at my desk all day long, came home, kissed my wife and kids, ate supper, and did whatever I had energy for and went to bed. On weekends and some evenings I went to church services, community events, socials, movies, shopping centres, and farmers' markets. I took my family out to eat McDonald's cheeseburgers and Filet-O-Fish sandwiches. I bought Cabbage Patch dolls for my daughters and a Nintendo game system for my son. As a family we watched *The Wonderful World of Disney* on Sunday nights, just as I had as a boy. I hung out with people just like me, people who also bought Cabbage Patch dolls and Nintendo games, and watched Disney.

After a year of recovery from my burnout, I was bored and didn't know why. I wondered if I was simply tired of feeling rundown. But I was delighted to be bored, since that told me I had the energy to do more. At my church I heard a few people speak of visiting prisoners and how great a need there was for more volunteers. The turning point for me was a talk by Richard Rohr, a Franciscan priest. He said he sees people all around who buy more and more trinkets and toys and the latest and fastest cars and computers and how they get a rush of happiness when those things are new. He said those people feel down when the novelty wears off, so they look for the next new thing and the next rush — we've all done it! It's the dynamic of our consumer society.[9] Rohr said we are conditioned to think more is better. We get more, and it feels good until we get tired of it, and we want even more. He could have said we put ourselves into jars and keep buying bigger jars, but the problem is the jar itself. We need to get out of the jar altogether and do something besides jump. What I took from Rohr was that I could break free by deliberately associating with people who are different from me.

So I did. I volunteered for M2W2 at the Max. The first prisoner I visited was serving a life sentence for murder. He was an alcoholic

---

9 After the terrorist attacks of September 11, 2001, the U.S. economy stalled. People were afraid to spend money. President George W. Bush went on national television and encouraged the public to stand together against the terrorists who were jealous of the American way of life. He didn't tell them to pray or to volunteer to help the disadvantaged in their communities or to become politically active or to reach out to people who were different from them. He told them to go out and buy more stuff!

and a drug addict with a history of violence. My second prisoner was a serial rapist. We had nothing in common except our humanity. If I hadn't gotten outside the jar, I would have continued living as if being human could only mean being like me. Every time I go into a prison, I am on edge, wondering what's going to be different and how I'm going to respond to different situations and different people. I am never sure I'm going to get past the front gate, whether there will be a lockdown or a confrontation with a prisoner or a guard or the drug scanner machine.

When I imagine myself as a prisoner trying to make a new life for himself, I remember how hard it was for me to start over after my burnout and marriage breakup. I know that even after fourteen years, I'm still a work in progress. But I have a good education, lots of good work experience, and quite a few good friends. Most prisoners who get out have to stay away from family and friends because those associations are what made it so easy to do crime in the first place.

While working on this book, I got a letter from a prisoner I've talked to and worked with for at least six years. He's been in and out of the Max three times since I met him. He pleaded with me and another M2W2 visitor and friend of mine for help when he gets out the next time. He knows that if he doesn't get help outside his normal circle, he'll keep going back to prison.

My friend and I talked about the prisoner's request over lunch. We talked about the support he could get from the John Howard Society, Alcoholics Anonymous, Narcotics Anonymous, his Aboriginal community, and maybe a church community. But we both know him personally. He's connected with us in many conversations and in an AVP workshop. We know the man could be playing us for suckers. We don't know much about the crimes he's committed or how dangerous he is. We do know that if we don't step up, he has almost no chance of making it.

So we agree to support him, even though we don't know what that support might look like. We agree that together, the three of us can make this work if we can move past the CSC and parole board rules and create boundaries and rules for ourselves that fit this new relationship. We agree the relationship has to be personal, flexible, open, and dynamic. We know our help might not be enough and that we risk being taken advantage of or physically hurt. We know, too, that no human being can be fully alive inside a cage or a jar, even though some places, like prisons, have to have electrified, barbed-wire fences to keep people in, and high-tech equipment to keep people out.

CHAPTER 10

DRUGS AND SCANNERS AND KANGAROO COURTS

Kangaroo Court: A self-appointed tribunal that disregards or parodies existing principles of law or human rights ... one so controlled as to render a fair trial impossible.
—Webster's College Dictionary

On September 13, 2002, I have thirteen prisoners committed to our monthly M2W2 visit. I have exactly thirteen visitors lined up to come too. I tell my supervisor, Ken From, who's planning to come as well, "Isn't this interesting? All these thirteens coming together? I wonder what could possibly go wrong?" Ken rolls his eyes and we both laugh. Ken supervised four prison visitation programs in Alberta, and he'd been in prison work long enough to know the value of a good laugh.

We arrive at the usual time. The front desk officer goes through the routine with the new ion scanner. It was installed recently to help the prison detect traces of drugs on people who want to enter the prison. He gives us each a white paper disc and asks us to wipe it on some part of our clothing, our glasses, or our wallets. Out of thirteen, six—including me—test positive for heroin, LSD, or some other drug. The officer gives the six a second disc to wipe on a different part of clothing, and for me and another man, the second test is negative. He says nine of us can go in but not the other four. We all confer and agree to leave the prison and cancel our visit. We are reluctant to disappoint the prisoners, but we refuse to cooperate with this kangaroo court where we have no recourse and no opportunity for self-defence. We ask the guard to please send word in to the prisoners that we will not be coming in.

We reconvene at the nearest Tim Hortons for coffee and donuts. Every one of us sees something positive in what we just went through: we got to experience something the prisoners live with every minute of every day. Prisoners have told us many times about guards, administrators, parole officers, even the warden, how they make up reasons to deny visits, cut gym time short, refuse shower time, or simply decide not to announce on the unit's PA system that it's time for the prisoners involved to move to Visiting and Correspondence for the M2W2 program. Or to announce it and give the prisoners no time to change their clothes so they will be allowed into the visiting area.

The next week, Ken and I schedule a meeting with the then warden, Chris Price, to talk about the ion scanner and the volunteers it fingered. We question the scanner's reliability. We express concern that the record of these hits on the scanner might end up with the RCMP or Canadian or U.S. border guards. We speculate that these volunteers could be investigated by police or refused entry to the United States or re-entry to Canada on the basis of ion scanner hits. We ask that the records be destroyed. The warden says he cannot and will not destroy the records. He says he and his security staff might need that information. He says the information by itself might mean nothing, but if it's combined with other data, it could help identify a future risk to the institution. He values our program, he says, and acknowledges that nobody associated with it has ever been caught trying to bring drugs into a prison. He assures us these records are for internal use only. He explains that the information is internal to this prison and that it cannot and will not find its way into any external databases. Ken and I shake his hand and leave the office. In the car on the way back into the city, I say, "I'm sure the warden means well, but who does he think he's kidding?" Ken chuckles and says, "Well, we did what we could."

Six months later, Mike Sadava of the *Edmonton Journal* calls me. My name showed up on a leaked document, he says. He wants to ask me about the ion scanner and the night I hit positive on it. I take a deep breath. For the twenty years I worked at the Legislature, I had a tourniquet around my larynx. I could not say anything to the media. As editor of *Hansard* and director of public information, I could only refer calls to the Speaker's office. During the two years I was the Speaker's executive assistant, I was the person other staff referred journalists to so I could officially say, "No comment." Speaker Gerry Amerongen saw himself as a judge in Alberta's highest court, and he said it was inappropriate to talk to reporters about his decisions. His immediate successors were only slightly more open.

This is my first chance to talk to a reporter since my voice won its freedom. I tell him the scanner has a record of unreliability, that some cleaning fluids and hand lotions can cause false positives. I'm aware that if the warden thinks I'm saying too much, I could be locked out of the prison altogether and would lose my part-time job. But I've talked to Ken about this, and I know he wants to make a public issue out of how Corrections Canada's mission statement says it values community involvement and how some of its practices do the opposite. Ken and I both know that it's risky business, though, that the prison system could shut us out entirely if we're not careful.

After the *Journal* publishes the article on March 6, 2003, I go into the Max with Ken for another talk with the warden. He keeps saying he's sorry. And he's angry. He's not angry with us, though. He's fuming when he tells us the leak came from a staff member at the Max. He grits his teeth and jabs the desktop with his finger as if it were a gavel. The person who sent this stuff to the *Journal* and the *Edmonton Sun*, he says, has compromised the security of this institution. He grits his teeth and assures us he is doing everything in his power to find out who it was and punish that person to the full extent of the law. He says leaking information about the guard towers not being staffed some of the time and leaking our names to the news media are criminal offences. Ken and I have no doubt that the warden's anger and resolve are genuine. We both know, too, that given the culture of prison guard solidarity, it would be a miracle if the leaker's identity ever makes it back to the warden. It would take a second miracle for evidence to surface that could lead to a criminal conviction and prison time, or even to termination of employment.

For prisoners and volunteers, though, no evidence is required to put them down or to keep us out. Later in the spring of '03, another incident underscores this, with gusto. Early in 2003, I recruit a new volunteer, a salesman I'd known for quite a few years. He's a personable guy who's based his entire career on his communication skills and politeness. He'd been making a good income in sales all his adult life.

On April 15, I go into the prison for my regular weekly rounds. I am immediately directed to an assistant warden's office. A normally jovial official I've talked with many times before is frowning. He asks me to sit down. In a grim monotone voice he tells me a female guard complained about the behaviour of one of the volunteers during our last visit.

"What did he say? What did he do?" I ask. He shows me an incident report. The guard claims a visitor looked at her the wrong way and spoke sarcastically. The official says, "This is a serious accusation. We can't have volunteers coming here and treating staff this way. You'll have to tell your volunteer he can't come to the institution anymore."

I am momentarily stunned. I ask, "Shouldn't we ask the volunteer to tell us his side of the story? Maybe there was a misunderstanding, a joke or gesture that he thought was harmless, that he didn't mean anything by," I argue.

"I can't stop you from asking him," the official says, "but I've dealt with cases like this before. She's made the complaint, so she's serious enough to put it in writing. She's got a good work history here. She's not a troublemaker. I've got no reason to doubt her word or her judgment."

I can't be certain the volunteer wouldn't tell a female guard an off-colour joke, but I'm not ready to guillotine him without even the semblance of a hearing. So I say, "You mean there's no process for something like this? No way to give a volunteer a chance to defend himself? This man gave freely of his time to come all the way out here to help CSC achieve its own mission of engaging offenders with the community. That's what the M2W2 program is about."

The official takes a deep breath and leans forward in his chair. He looks me in the eye and lowers his voice to a near whisper. "Look. This guard could've filed a criminal complaint. I think she's being pretty reasonable, given the circumstances. I'd advise you simply to drop it. Drop this volunteer. This complaint is already damaging your program's reputation in here. It's only been a few days. If you drop him right now, it'll be clear that you won't tolerate this kind of behaviour. If you fight it, word gets around. Who are the staff gonna back, one of their own or a volunteer group that comes in here once a month?"

I'm reeling when I leave his office. It takes a few hours for reality to sink in. I always knew the prison could shut us out on a whim. But here is a clear example of an injustice that is intensely personal and not based on some machine's reliability. This is a clear case of one person's word summarily convicting another person. I'd read about *lettres de cachet*, documents signed by French kings before the revolution. These letters could come out of nowhere and with no basis in fact sentence a person to exile, imprisonment, or death, no questions asked. In the late eighteenth century, all of France finally rebelled against this hateful, evil practice.

I phone the volunteer to hear his side of the story. He's shocked when he hears of the complaint against him. He denies he said anything inappropriate to the guard. He says they spoke very briefly, that she was one of the guards who escorted him to the program room where we met with the prisoners. He says he joked with her, but that's how he talks to people all the time. He says he'd been through security screenings and customs a hundred times at airports and he knows those people have absolute authority to turn him away, just as prison guards do. He's not a pervert and he knows how to talk to people in authority. I can hear from the pitch and tempo of his words that he is spitting mad. Who wouldn't be? I'm being wrongly accused, he says; I want to know how to clear my name. I ask him if other volunteers were within earshot when he talked with the guard, and he gives me their names. When I call them, neither one of them is able to remember anything that was said. They both are sure the talk they heard was nothing out of the ordinary, but they admit they might not have heard everything.

The more I get into this, the more wrong it feels. I phone Ken From to ask what he thinks. He consults a lawyer. The lawyer says, if we had deep enough pockets we could sue CSC for damaging the volunteer's reputation. But, the lawyer adds, our case is weak, since their decision didn't cost the volunteer any money and they never went public with it. The lawyer says, this volunteer could go into just about any lawyer's office, and the lawyer would probably tell him, "Life is unfair." Ken offers to set up a mediation process where the guard and the volunteer could talk about what happened in the presence of a trained mediator, informally. I relay this proposal to the assistant warden, the assistant warden asks the guard, and the guard refuses.

I phone the volunteer again to tell him what we've found out. I hear his voice breaking on the other end of the line. What a helpless feeling! I wonder how I'd feel if somebody accused me of sexual harassment and I had no way to clear my name. This man had volunteered because he was a friend of mine, because he'd finally gotten to a time in his life when his kids were grown up and he had freedom to give something back to the community. He got accused, tried, convicted, and locked out after his third visit.

A few days after this, Ken and I have a volunteer gathering, one of the rare opportunities to get all the M2W2 volunteers into one room to share their experiences and get to know each other better. When we share the sexual harassment story, everybody feels bad about what happened, but nobody is surprised. It comes with the territory. Here are some other examples of summary prison "justice" and its impacts:

- Countless times volunteers make the drive out to Edmonton Institution for the visit only to be told at the gate that the place is locked down and we can't go in. Sometimes a staff person phones me ahead of time so I can tell the volunteers not to come, but often I get no call. Sometimes an incident occurs just before we get to the prison, and there is no way anybody could have warned us.

- A volunteer is married to a school principal, and he drops out of the program after the leak to the *Edmonton Journal* of names of people who hit positive on the ion scanner. He fears that if his name gets connected with drugs in any way, his wife could lose her job.

- Guards take the mattress away from a prisoner in solitary confinement (D&S), apparently to punish him for filing grievances against the prison staff and administration. An M2W2 volunteer, whose training as a nurse gives him a fair bit of credibility, reports to me the cuts and bruises he sees on the prisoner he visits. He says they probably resulted from physical abuse, which is what the prisoner told him. He says to me, this is the kind of thing that most people think happens only in tinpot dictatorships. At my next opportunity, I talk to a staff person I trust. The person talks to the prisoner and the guards, and then a courageous supervisor forces the guards to give the man back his mattress. There is no follow-up that I know of on the claim of physical abuse.

- A volunteer is turned away at the front gate because his security clearance had expired, but when I check into it the next week, I discover his clearance had not expired. I point this out to the warden. He admits the guard made a mistake, but there is no apology.

- An eighty-year-old volunteer who has been coming to visit prisoners for twenty-five years hits positive on the ion scanner and is refused entrance before I arrive at the prison. I find out afterwards that, contrary to prison policy, the guard at the front gate did only one scanner test on the visitor. As well, the volunteer never got to talk to a correctional supervisor, which has been standard procedure for years. I talk to the warden about this afterwards, and he apologizes that procedure wasn't followed. He promises a letter of apology to the volunteer but never sends one.

The ion scanner is an ongoing issue the whole time I am M2W2 coordinator. We go through long periods when one or more volunteers, often including me, hit positive on the ion scanner. In most cases, prison staff follow the proper procedure and do a second scanner test, and then call out the supervisor to interview the volunteers. Usually the interview consists of one question, which is, essentially, "Do you know how you might have come into contact with _____ (name of illicit drug the scanner claimed to have found traces of)?"[10] Typically, volunteers are flabbergasted that the

---

10 Once a supervisor asked a volunteer, "Are you bringing any illegal drugs into the institution today?" When the volunteer told me, we both had a good laugh. A few weeks later, I asked an ion scanner operator I knew well what he thought of these supervisor interviews. I said, "I can't imagine someone who has illegal drugs on him simply saying yes to a question like that." He told me a story of a visitor who broke down when he got that exact question. He said the prisoner he was visiting threatened the visitor's wife, said he would have someone assault her if the man didn't bring drugs into the prison. When the man got caught, he suddenly realized he had no choice but to turn the matter over to the authorities.

machine finds something on them, and they simply say no. Every time someone hits positive, he or she naturally feels accused of drug possession. How else should someone feel? Here we have an agency of the Government of Canada responsible for public safety, staffed by people in uniform and backed by an impressive array of razor wire, twelve-foot-high chain-link fences, guard towers, and a nearby firing range to emphasize that the guards are well-trained in the use of firearms. Every volunteer knows all too well that 240 men are confined in cages and under heavy guard just behind that fence. We've all heard tales of wrongful convictions, trumped-up charges, and physical abuse of prisoners by prisoners and guards, and although it's dangerous to believe what prisoners tell us, it's also naive to think that none of it is true.

On Monday, January 30, 2012, a number of the new Catholic chaplain's friends come to the Max to participate in his official installation into his new position. This is to be an official liturgical celebration to bless Paul Vanderham's ministry at the Max. Four of us test positive on the ion scanner, and we are held back to be interviewed by the correctional manager. When he comes out, he tells us we have been deemed a threat to the security of the institution and will not be admitted. I point out that I have come into the prison hundreds of times over the last eleven years, and two of the others have come in many times too. We have never been involved in anything inappropriate. I ask if that doesn't count for something. He simply says that the ion scanner's decision is final. I write the next day to the warden. I quote Commissioner's Directive 566-8-1, which says the scanner is only a tool, that the supervisor's judgment must take precedence. I ask if this directive is still in effect or not. The warden, Kelly Hartle, writes an apology back to me. As far as I know, none of the other three gets an apology. I am certain, however, that sincere though the apology is, the same thing will happen again to somebody else.

I've talked to many people about the ion scanner's reliability. Staff have insisted the scanner never makes a mistake, that if it says you have a trace of a drug on your clothing, there is a trace of that drug on your clothing, period. But some of them have admitted that the machine can sometimes be fooled into thinking that hand lotion or cleaning fluid is marijuana or heroin.[11] We've also been told over and over that virtually every twenty-dollar bill has traces of some illicit drug on it and that simply touching the inside of a city bus will leave traces on clothing and skin.

I taught English at a small university in Edmonton for three years, and when I hit positive on the scanner during that time, guards and chaplains would say, "Well, it's no wonder! The odds are that maybe half of those students are drug users." I facilitated an AVP workshop at the Max one weekend, and I wore the same pants on Sunday that I wore Saturday. I had a scanner hit on Sunday, and the supervisor scolded me. She said, "It's no wonder you hit positive. Inmates must've brushed against your pants yesterday. Drugs are all around in here. You have to wash the clothes you wear before you come in here if you want to avoid problems like this."

But I've worn clothes that came right out of the washer that morning and still had positive hits. One time I had a new pair of pants on, pants that had never been worn, and the machine still dinged me. I couldn't believe it! When the supervisor asked me the standard question, I was even more puzzled than usual about where the drug could have come from. I had just come through a period when I hit positive on that thing about half the time I came in. My name kept coming up during the morning staff meetings after these things happened, and I would run into people in the hallway who would joke with me about my encounters with the machine.

So I was particularly cautious about what I wore and what I touched. I even made a practice of using only my right hand to

---

11   During the eight years I was coordinating M2W2, the technology was always evolving, and the operators' training grew more sophisticated. In the early years, including the September 2002 incident, operators apparently didn't know that the device had to be recalibrated to account for changes in barometric pressure.

open the doors to the main entrance to the prison and using my left hand to wipe the white paper disc on my clothing. The day I wore those new pants, I asked some staff I knew well where the drug traces could've come from since I'd never worn the pants before. The fourth person I talked to thought about it and figured that the pants were probably made in China or some other place in Asia and that there was a good chance drugs were part of the scene on the shop floor. I hadn't thought of this before, but his comments made me realize that any number of people could've tried the pants on in the store before I bought them, and the staff there certainly handled them too.

During one of the last visits I coordinated at the Max, the staff showed all of us a brief video before they allowed the prisoners to come into the visiting area. It was a new correctional services video that they required all visitors to see. It was a dramatization of one prisoner threatening another with violence to him and his family if he didn't persuade one of his visiting relatives to bring in some drugs. The video spelled out the dynamics of prison drug blackmail and showed visitors how their prisoners faced pressure from other prisoners all the time. It made clear that turning the matter over to the authorities was the only way to keep drugs out of the prison, to keep the prisoners safe, and to keep visitors from being dragged into the mess and even getting charged with drug smuggling and ending up in prison themselves.

I had indirect experience of the danger drugs bring into prison. One prisoner I had in M2W2 got caught with a woman visitor who had smuggled in a stick of lip gloss saturated with LSD. They almost got away with it. A staff person who told me about the incident said that that amount of LSD would have promoted the prisoner overnight into the de facto head of the prison. The prisoner would have been able to command any price or favour from anybody in the prison who wanted anything. I heard of another prisoner who made big money on the outside running a drug distribution net- work and who then operated the drug business on the inside, at a prison down east. I heard of guards moonlighting by bringing drugs into work with them, making five thousand dollars a month or more on the side. I've heard prison authorities justify the practice of not subjecting staff to ion scanner testing. Some say that their clothing would always test positive because they're always around inmates, that they inevitably pick up traces of drugs from inmates' clothing whenever they do a pat-down. Some deny that staff ever get involved with drugs, that it's always the visitors. But I know of an incident, at the women's prison, where a prisoner overdosed on drugs when in solitary confinement, after a significant time of no contact with anybody but staff.

I had several brief chats with an ion scanner operator I know well, a man whose judgment I trusted because he treated me and every volunteer I brought in with care, respect, and even a sense of humour. When I told him I thought that I might have hit positive on the scanner because I touched the same door handle that everybody did on the way in and used that same hand to touch the paper disc, he scoffed at the idea. But a few times after that, he acknowledged that I might have been right. Not too long afterwards, the system was changed. The last time I went into the Max, they used a wand to hold a piece of cloth for me to wipe against my clothing; my hand never contacted the material they tested.

The same scanner operator once told me about the worries he has every day about his own teenage daughter going into her high school and having to deal with the drug culture there and how grave the risks are for students. He said he wished there were ion scanners in schools to keep drugs out so she wouldn't have to deal with the drug culture. He told me he was proud to be one of the gatekeepers at the Max and that even though drugs still got in, he played a key role in minimizing their impact. And this good man is one of many good men and women who do great work on our behalf in our prisons.

I have a lot of respect for correctional services staff. They live and work in a war zone. They are charged with the responsibility for keeping the prisoners safe from each other even though the hazards are legion, from a prisoner flinging his feces at a guard to staff being sexually assaulted or killed. They are charged with keeping visitors like us safe in a dangerous environment. They live under a great deal of stress. Many prison staff feel they are pariahs in the community because they work in a place that is so separate from the community and so profoundly misunderstood. They have the constant temptation of moonlighting for drug money and of brutalizing prisoners, displaying the contempt most in our society have for criminals.

Staff are also charged with deciding when to recommend that prisoners get parole. When even one parolee reoffends, their judgments are immediately suspect. Consider the case of Daniel Gingras. He was convicted of murder in 1978. After serving nine years in prison, he was out on a day pass and murdered two women. He got out because a parole officer, backed up by the parole board and no doubt some other people, decided he had demonstrated he was rehabilitated enough to be out on a day pass with an unarmed escort. Because of cases like these and the public outcry that inevitably results, the staff responsible have to err on the side of caution, even when it puts extra stress on a system that can only hold so many prisoners inside.

Some non-security prison staff explained to me how security guard culture is incredibly similar to prisoner culture. One strict rule both groups observe is about ratting. Guards who see other guards breaking the rules—assaulting a prisoner, bringing in drugs, leaking confidential information to the media—cannot report the violation without great risk to themselves. Because prison staff have to work as a team in dangerous conditions, they have to be able to trust each other, and staff who break that trust by ratting out someone may find that other staff will withhold important information from them or simply not be as engaged in watching their backs when there's a need.

Another aspect of prison guard culture, which seems to include other prison staff too, is their perception of time. Prisoners do time; so do prison staff. Every prisoner who has a hope of getting out keeps track of how much time he or she has left in his sentence, how much time before his next parole hearing, how much time before his next security review. Pensions are a big issue with staff, and with few exceptions, the staff I've gotten to know are all aware of how many more days, months, and years they need to serve to get released and get a full pension. They know, too, how much time they need to serve to get a reduced pension and exactly how much it will be reduced for every year they are short of the magic eighty-five number (age plus years of service).

These cultures don't exist in vacuums, as much as our Western society demands that prisons be separate universes. Professional organizations of doctors, nurses, lawyers, teachers, and just about any other organization of peers I can think of all have a taboo against turning in or criticizing one of their own. And I've met plenty of baby boomers like me who are in jobs they no longer find satisfying who decide it's better financially to count the days until the pension clicks in than to start a new career or look for a new job with less pay and less seniority.

When I watched the movie *The Sixth Sense*, I was blown away by the effectiveness of its surprise ending. But the most memorable part of that movie is what the gifted boy says about his ability to see dead people. He tells the Bruce Willis character, "A lot of people who are walking around are dead and don't even know it." I was virtually dead myself after my burnout at the Legislature. I've met a lot of other people who are just putting in time. Not just prisoners or prison staff, but everybody who clings to job security and waits for the calendar pages to turn over and over and over.

Six months after I left M2W2, I was in the Max again to substitute for the program's coordinator, Janet Anderson, who was taking a month's leave. On Tuesday, March 8, 2011, I rented a car and drove to the Max to organize the next Friday's visit. That went reasonably well, despite the work being done to remove asbestos flooring in the main hall. I had to go the long way around to get to the program area. I talked to the acting program director and made sure she knew who I was. I checked to see what special arrangements we'd need to make to get the visit to happen. Janet told me that in

February, M2W2 had to meet with prisoners in a program room at the back of the prison because of the construction, and she wasn't even sure they could physically accommodate us in March. But the acting program director assured me the visit would happen.

Before I left home, I phoned ahead and made an appointment to see the unit representative on D unit. I also phoned H unit because I needed to get a list of prisoners to have as a backup in case there was a problem with D unit. The H unit guard said he wasn't sure about seeing the H unit representative in the morning but that I should phone when I got into the prison and he'd know more then. I got eleven names from the D unit representative, and we had a brief chat. I'd talked with him a few times before, and he was curious how I was enjoying my new life.

I tried phoning the H unit guard, but the line was busy. When I went back to the program director, she phoned, and the guard on H said to come after 1:00 p.m. When I got there, the guard was miffed that I didn't call ahead, and so I explained that I had phoned ahead and that the program director had too. The guard reluctantly agreed to let me talk to the representative, and I managed to get the list from him. The unit was temporarily locked down, and so I got to walk down the range and past a row of closed cell doors. In most of the cells I passed, prisoners immediately noticed a stranger in the hall, and as soon as they found out who I was, most of them wanted to get on the list. Before long I had another ten or twelve names I could fall back on if I needed them.

Two days before I went into the Max, I had phoned the volunteers, most of them people I'd worked with for years but a few new ones too. Janet told me that all their security clearances were up to date and I didn't have anything to worry about there. As I had done once a month for over eight years, I made up a list: ten volunteers were available to come. I gave the list to the acting program director on Tuesday when I gave her the prisoners' names, and she assured me the memo authorizing the visit would be looked after. I had everything under control. Or at least as much as anything at the Max can ever be under control.

When I left the Max that Tuesday afternoon, I felt good that I'd slipped right back into the groove and gotten things done with only a little hassle. On Wednesday I got a call from another staff person at the prison. She told me four of the ten volunteers on my list had expired security clearances. I asked her when the clearances had expired, and she said she didn't know. She told me she'd just talked to the person who does the clearances, so I knew there'd be no point asking that person to check again. So I made a note for Janet, and I phoned the four volunteers and told them not to come, since they wouldn't be let in anyway. There was clearly no chance of getting them a new form to fill out and having it processed before Friday night. They were disappointed, of course, but there was nothing more any of us could do.

By Friday afternoon, I'd received two calls from other volunteers saying they'd just come down with the flu and couldn't come after all. So instead of ten volunteers, I was down to four, including me. I wondered how the visit might go, with us being outnumbered eleven to four, but I reminded myself that it's not about numbers. Showing up is the important thing.

I arrived at the front gate, showed the guard my driver's license, and got in the outer door. Soon after, the other three volunteers were there too. The guard inside the main entry then started running us through the screening process: checking each name off the memo, getting our IDs in exchange for a bright yellow visitor's tag to clip onto our clothing, having us sign the register, issuing us each a locker key so we could secure our wallets and keys while we were inside, and, most importantly, testing us for drugs using the ion scanner.

When the guard handed me the wand with the little white cloth on the end, he asked me to rub it on the inside of one of my pockets. I asked him which one, and he said for me to pick. I chose my left pocket and gave him back the wand. He carefully removed the cloth from the wand with his fresh latex gloves and inserted it into the ion scanner. Almost immediately the scanner went beep beep beep like a video lottery terminal or a pinball machine does when somebody scores big. I joked, "Hey! What did I win?" But the guard wasn't laughing. He told me I had a positive hit. He gave me the wand again and asked me to put the cloth into the other pocket. This time the machine was quiet. The guard phoned the supervisor's office, reported my positive hit, and asked me to sit down and wait for the supervisor to come out.

When the supervisor came out, I saw that he was someone I'd worked with a few times before, somebody who at least knew our program. He wasn't smiling either. He said to me, "Do you have any idea how you could've gotten heroin on your clothing?" I said, "I haven't got a clue. I avoid drugs like the plague. Those things are evil."

He told me I had one positive hit and one negative hit. He said anything over one hundred is enough to raise a red flag. My positive hit was over four hundred, which he said indicated more than casual contact. I simply repeated that I had no idea how I could've gotten any heroin on me. He said, reluctantly, "I'll let you in, but I have to tell you, one more positive hit on the scanner, and you won't get into the institution again." I thanked him, but I still wondered what the fuss was about, what possible reason there could've been for the hit, a higher hit than I'd ever had in the over nine years I'd been going out to the Max.

When the visit was over and I was sitting on the loveseat at home relaxing, I wondered how much would be missing from my life if I couldn't go into the Max any more. I was glad I didn't have to worry about passing the ion scanner test every week, as I had for eight years. But there was an uneasiness in my gut akin to what I'd often felt as a child and numerous times since, a feeling I recognized as guilt accompanied by a twinge of shame. I had been accused of something I didn't do. I had no recourse, no possibility of appeal, no evidence I could bring up other than my history of integrity and responsibility. And that was a history that was already littered with dozens of positive hits on the same ion scanner.

I remembered, too, what a staff person at the Max told me a few years before. She also worked with volunteers, and she had a volunteer who tested positive several times. That volunteer eventually admitted that she had a teenage son who used drugs, and that she was so ashamed of it that she was in denial about it. This staff person said she'd talked to one of the experts in internal security at the prison, and he emphasized to her that the machine cannot lie, that when it detects drugs, there are drugs. She then told me, "I think you need to take another look at your life and see where you find drugs. There has to be some presence of drugs in your life, and you're having a problem seeing it."

I had thought this staff person and I had a good relationship, but I saw then that she was also a part of the institution, much as she insisted she was an independent contractor, a person with good judgment. I did agree with one aspect of what she said, though. People do lie. People lie to protect themselves from uncomfortable truths. And there's no way any person can say for sure what any other person is capable of — violence, drug trafficking, fraud, sexual assault — and denials aren't worth much.

A couple of days later I got an email from Janet. She was sad to hear that four volunteers couldn't go in because of security clearances, and she said she didn't understand how that could be. A week after, when she returned home and went into the prison again herself, she checked into the clearances further and found out that somebody had simply made a mistake. Those four people did have good clearances after all, despite the institution's claims to the contrary.

CHAPTER 11

DOIN' TIME

Time is the coin of your life. It is the only coin you have, and only you can determine how it will be spent. Be careful lest you let other people spend it for you.
—Carl Sandburg, at his 85th birthday party

A lifer at the Max—I'll call him Q—is eager to have a volunteer visit him. Q is a man of average height, with well-developed arm and shoulder muscles. He's lifted a lot of barbells. He's in the early years of a life-twenty-five sentence for murder. He's a unit representative, which means he's earned respect from staff as well as prisoners. He already has a reputation as an organizer for his work on prison socials, for developing consensus among the prisoners on their issues, and for speaking up at warden's meetings and getting results.

Q talks to me about the need for men on his unit to mix with people from the outside, even though most of them are not willing to commit to M2W2's one-on-one visitation. They'd rather watch television in their cells than risk opening up to a stranger. It's safer. But Q knows how unhealthy that is. The passion in his voice, the intensity in his eyes, convince me to create a monthly social program for M2W2 to complement our music and visiting programs. Q is always clean-shaven and neatly dressed whenever

I see him. He has clean, short, neatly combed hair and clear, bright eyes. He's smart too. He's convinced that this is a great program, so he's signed up, and he's persuaded a few other prisoners to sign up too. So I pair him up with a volunteer. Three months in a row the volunteer comes to the Max to meet him. Three times Q doesn't show up.

No-shows at the Max are as common as frost in Edmonton. Not only for our program. For any program. When I ask the no-show prisoners why, they recite from a checklist of reasons. "I had to watch the hockey (football/basketball/baseball) game." "There was a great movie on TV." "We were never called. The guards never told us you were here." "I was on the phone with my mother (wife/ son/daughter/lawyer)." "I was depressed/mad and didn't want to lay that on anybody." "I had to go to the gym." The first two times I asked Q, he quoted from the list. The third time he gave me a reason I had never heard before or have heard since, but I'd bet money that a lot of guys besides Q have thought it and never said it.

It's November 2006, and I'm especially disappointed in Q, because now I have to enforce my longstanding rule: when a prisoner fails to come three times in a row, he comes off my list and I put somebody else on. I almost always have a waiting list. I ask the unit's guard to call for Q so I can talk to him. I'm hoping his reason will be so good I can give him one more chance. When he comes into the servery, he smiles and shakes my hand, as always. I get right to the point. I say to him, "We missed you last Friday. What happened?" He stares down at the little black flecks in the poured plastic flooring. He looks over at the wall where the stainless steel milk dispenser and industrial-strength microwave oven sit on a long steel table. I can see him blushing through his olive-brown skin. He stammers and makes a fist, his right arm straight and rigid at his side. He lifts his head and looks me in the eye.

"I'm doing life-twenty-five," he says. "They're never gonna let me out. The guy I killed. A Chinese guy. A drug lord. Even if they did let me out, I'd be killed in a minute out there." He pauses to catch his breath. "I don't keep track of what day it is. I don't want to know the time of day. I don't have a clock. I don't have a calendar. I don't want a calendar. You come in here on Tuesday. You tell me the visit is Friday. But Tuesday, Friday, Sunday. They're all the same. I don't care what day it is. I don't keep track."

He raises his head and looks me in the eye. "You know, I just found out last week that this is 2006." I don't know what to say, and he must sense my surprise. He says, "I thought I could do it. I wanted to do it. But this just isn't gonna work for me. You oughta give that volunteer to somebody else."

////////

Everything at the Max is about time. I've often thought that would make a good slogan to put on prison signs across Canada, just below the name of the institution: "It's all about time." Not that everything's on schedule. These places don't run like clockwork. I've seen days when lunch is still being served after 2:00 even though it's scheduled for 12:00. But the afternoon shift change always happens at 3:00 p.m. Some staff do double shifts, and shifts get stretched with overtime, but the union contract guarantees that there is at least a schedule to vary from. Head counts always happen at 11:00 a.m. and 4:00 p.m. But I've been in programs where we're promised we can keep the prisoners until 8:30 p.m., and guards sometimes come for them at 8:00 and sometimes at 9:00 or even later.

No. I'm talking about passing time. The years of a sentence, the months until a security review, the days with nothing to do, the decades spent until the engraved gold watch and retirement farewell party. My first few years doing M2W2, I spent plenty of time waiting for the guard at the front gate to get around to letting me in. Prisoners talk a lot about "doin' time." The ones whose time goes the slowest and who have the most trouble with other prisoners, with guards, with administration, are the ones who are "doin' somebody else's time." They're the ones who can look in another guy's eyes and see something they don't like and start beakin' off, and somebody ends up with a broken nose or missing teeth or worse. They're the ones who start rumours about something somebody else said just to stir up trouble. They're the ones who take somebody else's mail and read embarrassing private bits out loud to other prisoners. Prisoners refer to this kind of troublemaking as "drama."

Time goes faster if it's spent on vicarious drama. Every prison cell has a television, which makes spectator sports a very popular time sink. The most common excuse prisoners had for skipping one of our visit nights was a game on TV. When the Oilers used to make the playoffs, I knew the turnout would be low on game nights.

Federal prison authorities long ago recognized television as a highly effective means of prisoner control. Or I should say prisoner sedation, since television induces a state of mind that's very much like sleep. The TV gives a prisoner a choice: be a criminal in a cell or a hockey player free to skate end to end, to slap pucks at a hundred miles an hour or snatch them out of the air like a cat catching flies, and to bodycheck and slug it out with another player. And everything on television is in colour, instead of in dull grays and monotones.[12] I've spent a fair bit of time around little kids, and I know from personal experience that when a kid thinks his or her life is boring, the easiest solution — for parents and caregivers — is to turn on the tube. And prison life is inherently boring.

I used to watch a lot of sports myself, not because of boredom but because I needed a diversion and was too tired to think of something better. Back in the glory days of the 1980s, I was a passionate

---

12 In the mid-1990s the Alberta government instituted a new type of punishment for prisoners in provincial jails. Steve (a.k.a. Attila) West was Solicitor General, and he decided that giving prisoners access to colour television looked too much like pampering. So he took all the colour TVs out of provincial jails and installed black-and-white ones instead. He also insisted that prisoners who wanted to watch television should have to do it in groups. This was partly to save money, but it fit neatly into the Klein government's philosophy that life should be as hard as possible for criminals.

Edmonton Oilers fan. I had a well-paying but demanding job at the Alberta Legislature. I came home every night—or early morning, as the case sometimes was when I had a late shift—and I wanted to unwind, to relax. I spent time with my wife and kids, but what we did together most often was watch television and movies at home. We spent a lot of time engaged in fictitious people's lives. And we watched plenty of hockey games. Those were the days when Wayne Gretzky, Mark Messier, Jari Kurri, Paul Coffey, Grant Fuhr, Glenn Anderson, and their supporting cast were breaking records, and winning five Stanley Cups. I admired their speed and energy because I didn't have any myself.

I remember one Stanley Cup season when our television died during the middle of an early round. I got home from work, ate supper, and rushed to the nearest electronic appliance discount warehouse to buy a new TV so I wouldn't miss a single game. I was in the showroom at game time, and I heard more of what the commentators said than I did of the salesman's pitch. I was more interested in the numbers on the screen—the score, the period, the time remaining—than I was in the numbers on the price tag or the total on the MasterCard chit I signed my name to.

In Kansas City, I grew up fanatical about baseball. (How many people realize that the word "fanatical," of which "fan" is the first syllable, means a person obsessed by, uncritically devoted to, crazy about something as if it were a god?) I listened to every 1950s and 1960s Kansas City Athletics game on the radio. Most of which they lost. Almost none of them made it to television. The networks always showed the big-market teams, the pennant contenders, the New York Yankees and the Los Angeles Dodgers, where big stars like Sandy Koufax, Don Drysdale, Mickey Mantle, and Whitey Ford always ended up. I cherished my favourite baseball. It featured the autographs I'd collected, in person, of local heroes Frank Tuttle and Harry Chiti.

When the baseball season was over, I shifted to football and the Kansas City Chiefs. When my wife and I moved to Canada, we both got into hockey, but I'm still not sure if she really cared or just went along. I lost interest in all spectator sports after my burnout in June 2000 and my marriage breakup in 2002. I was more interested in making a new life for myself. I saw all the media hype around professional sports as a way to distract the masses from economic injustice, political manipulation, environmental crises, from fundamental questions of life and death, war and peace in Afghanistan, Iraq, Chechnya, Uganda, China—and the list goes on.[13] In the early 2000s I went on all the protest marches I could find. I even travelled to Quebec City in 2001 for the big anti-globalization protest.

From 2003 to 2005 I settled into a new life of teaching freshman English at the King's University College and doing prison visitation. My social life consisted of protests, poetry, and pedalling my bike all over the countryside with newfound friends. I lost track of the sports seasons. I saw front-page newspaper stories about big games and ignored them as I did advertisements for Lexus, Coors, Caribbean cruises, and other things I wasn't going to buy. I was more into the seasons of nature. Watching the leaves turn yellow and brown and shimmer in the cold October rains. Waiting for the snow to fall so I could get out on my cross-country skis. Cleaning the rust and grit off my bike chain to be ready when the ice melted off the roads and bike paths in the spring. Revelling in the glorious eighteen-hour summer days when I would crank and crank and crank and relish all the smells of clover blossoms, new-mown hay, cow manure, truck exhaust, and freshly oiled asphalt as I cruised by at thirty kilometres an hour.

By the spring of 2006 I had zero interest in hockey. That was the year the Oilers made the playoffs the last week of the season,

---

13 At a social justice event a speaker criticized the mainstream media by saying their power isn't so much in telling us what to think as it is in telling us what to think about. He said that if they keep their reading public focused on sports or sex scandals, most people give their attention to those things instead of to the more boring but more important issues of the day, like shipping jobs offshore, where subcontractors don't need to worry about environmental regulations or working conditions.

came in as the eighth seed in the west, and went all the way to game seven of the final. For three years I'd seen precious little of my son, Sam, who'd moved to Toronto with his mother in 2003. He's never been a keener about writing letters or emails or talking on the telephone, so when I say "seen" I mean to include all the senses and all the means of communication. I only knew he was taking a year off his studies to work because his older sister gave me regular reports.

I did manage to reach him to wish him a happy birthday that April, when the first round of the playoffs was happening. He told me he was still an Oilers fan, that he listened to or watched every game. Just as I did the Kansas City Athletics fifty years before. The passion in his voice about the Oilers reminded me of me, and it made me miss him that much more. He was in Toronto. I was in Edmonton. It was hard even to get him on the telephone, since he has a practice of rarely being home and not answering messages. Then I realized: he's going to be watching all the Oilers' playoff games! If I get into the playoff spirit, I'll be sharing it with him. If I watched the games, followed the Oilers news, not only would we have something more to talk about when we got together, but I could recapture some of that father-son camaraderie in the meantime. So I watched some of those games and thoroughly enjoyed them. I was a kid again. Sam and I were kids together. He and I were two thousand miles apart, but during those games we were sitting on the same sofa, sipping the same lemonade, grabbing handfuls of buttered popcorn out of the same clear glass bowl.

I went to a prison ministry meeting at Lendrum Mennonite Church the same night the Oilers and the Anaheim Ducks played game one of the semifinal. When the meeting was over, somebody reported that the Oilers had won. I got on my bike and pedalled north on 109th Street toward the north side of the city, where I lived. Car drivers were honking their horns, waving their hands and flags, and yelling out their windows. Pedestrians were dancing on the sidewalks. People were high-fiving me as I went by. It was party time for the whole city. The next time I talked to Sam,

I let him know what was going on back here, how the whole city was caught up in the Oilers frenzy.

After the Oilers made it to the finals, Sam told me he and a few friends bought tickets to game seven and planned to drive to Charlotte, North Carolina, to cheer the Oilers on in person, if the series went that far. At the time, the Oilers were down three games to one, and it looked like a short series. But they won games five and six. I'd planned to visit my daughter Liz for a week that June, and game seven was on the first full day I was in Toronto. Liz and I watched the game on television, and whenever the camera showed the stands, we looked for Sam. We never found him, but we didn't need to. We knew we were with him in the same event, remotely linked by video cameras and cable television. It was wonderful to share that experience with two of my kids, but it made me wonder: where do I draw the line between healthy and unhealthy spectating? Where is the line between spectating and real living? As spectators, we can learn from others' experience, but how much is too much?

My present partner's late mother's favourite maxim was: Moderation in all things. It's a proverb that paraphrases something out of Aristotle's *Nicomachean Ethics*. It sounds like a good, simple rule to live by. The first problem with it, though, is that I find it impossible to be moderate about some things, like murder, pedophilia, and lying. The second problem is I might think watching an hour of television a night is moderate, but a prisoner might decide it's moderate to watch television all the time instead of injecting drugs, beating up another prisoner, or trying to hang himself. It's hard to argue with that. Moderation means different things to different people. It means different things to me at different times in my own life.

When I had my burnout in June 2000, I spent most of my days lying down or sitting down, trying to read but mostly resting, simply because I didn't have the energy to do more. I had to take time out to recreate myself. Looking back now, it feels like I was in a time of deep meditation as my body and mind healed cell by cell, synapse by synapse. When I was two months into the burnout, I got a call from my boss about something I'd been working on, and it seemed to me like I'd only been off work for a few days. Every day I tried to push myself a little, to see how much I could do that day. I refused to accept a life of lying around resting. I hoped each day that I could do more than the day before. I had no idea what moderation was any more, whether I was being lazy or whether I was really disabled. After all, I was on long-term disability.

One of the oddest feelings I had was that I was a back-seat driver in my own body. My body was in charge, not me. Or maybe somebody or something besides me was in charge of my body. I went through a period when I literally relearned how to walk. Not quite in the way a person with a broken leg or a knee replacement does it, of course; more like how stroke victims relearn basic motor skills. I had all day, day after day, to work on my recovery, and one of the basic things I pushed myself to do was to take walks. After my crash and burn, I started slowly. I used to be able to walk for hours without getting tired, but that first time back on my feet I decided I would only go around the block. It was a walk that, before my burnout, I could easily do in ten minutes.

When I stepped out onto the front porch, I watched my feet carefully, making sure I lifted them clear of the cast aluminum threshold and all the ridged lines where the door's rubber weatherstripping fits in between to keep the cold air out. I knew I couldn't trust my muscles to hold me up on their own, so I added what willpower I could to the effort. Every hair root on my scalp tingled and ached, as if they'd just been vigorously massaged and pulled to the breaking point. Or maybe those were nerve endings inside my skull sparking in new directions, trying to rebuild after a trauma. I was terrified I would fall and my bones shatter like glass on the concrete porch. As I looked down I was shocked to see my feet moving on their own, way down below. I was a crane operator inside my skull pulling levers and pushing pedals to get the heels and toes moving up and down, to lift the right thigh, bend the right knee, place the ball of the right foot on the next stretch of sidewalk. It had been days, maybe weeks — who knows? — since I'd seen the neighbourhood, but I couldn't look up unless I stopped. Which I did often, because I had to rest. After I'd gone maybe twenty metres, I had to cross the street. We had curved curbing that's common in suburban communities, a mere six-inch, gradual slope down to the asphalt, but I'd scrambled over Arizona mountains made of jagged, knife-edged granite that were less frightening than those six inches of concrete. As I lowered my left foot millimetre by millimetre onto the curve, I bent my knees like a skier, kept my centre of gravity balanced between both feet, leaned into the descent, pushed back with the ball of the foot, and edged forward. I have no idea how long that first hike around the block took, but it wore me out. I had to have a nap when I got back home and didn't get off the chesterfield the rest of the day.

On other days, I'd try other things. A trip into the backyard garden to pick raspberries. Sitting on the ground between raspberry clusters because I was too light-headed to bend over for them as I always had before. In the fall, a visit to the backyard apple tree to gather apples. Each of those efforts took a whole day. And then another whole day to cut up apples, assemble the topping, and bake apple crisp. I pushed myself to read again. I didn't have to relearn reading, but I did have to put up with a mind that had to go over and over and over the text before it would sink in. Yet reading, editing, and writing had been my life's work. For those months, that was my life. But one thing I'm sure of now: it was my own life and nobody else's. I watched my wife and kids coming and going around me. I talked to them and was as present to them as I could be, but my job was to care for myself. It was the best I could do.

Bo Lozoff published *We're All Doing Time* in 1985. His primary audience was prisoners, but he says the challenge for everybody is to live his or her own life. He says the best way to do that is to find a spiritual path that suits each of us so that we can be more fully connected with the divine spirit and in that way be truer to who we really are. In *The Power of Now*, Eckhart Tolle says that life is only possible in the present time. He talks about his own struggle with despair, living a life that was miserable and hopeless until he decided he couldn't live with himself any more. Then he realized that simply stating the decision that way begged the question: Who is this self I can't live with? And who is the I who can't live with this self?

I never did dislike myself, during all those months of burnout. I was frustrated with my body because I couldn't do things I wanted to do. My body did feel as if it were somebody else's. But I had always been an inherently spiritual person. I prayed every day. In fact, I constantly put myself in the hands of the divine, trusting that somehow things were going to work out for me. I went to doctors and a psychologist to make sure that if I had some physical or mental illness, I could get a diagnosis and treatment. But the main thing for me was to let go of the outcome and hope for the best. I did my best to be fully present in the moment even as every moment melted into the next without any apparent change in my condition, even as twelve, sixteen, eighteen, twenty months passed with only limited recovery. At the time those many months felt like hours.

In the spring of 2002 I faced the possibility that there were problems in my marriage that had to be dealt with before I could move on with my life. I had imagined ever since Kathy and I were married in 1970 that we would grow old together, that our kids would grow up and leave home and come back for Christmas, Thanksgiving, and other special occasions. That we'd celebrate their careers, their personal accomplishments, their marriages, the births of their children, and that we'd support each other during illnesses, hardships, and problems. I saw before me the image of Kathy and me turning gray and getting crotchety, using canes and walkers, our eyesight growing dim, holding each other's hands during hospital stays, and for me happiness meant facing all of that together.

I looked into the future and that's what waited for me. Then I looked at the present, and I realized that I couldn't get there from here. Our kids were just about grown up. Sam, our youngest, was nineteen, the only one of the three still living at home. Jennifer was twenty-one and engaged to be married in June. Liz was twenty-five, and she'd been living on her own on and off for seven years. Pretty soon, the family home would only have me and Kathy in it, alone together. Conversations with Kathy about who we were and where we'd been together, about how each of us saw the other, about our hopes for the future invariably stirred up anger and frustration for both of us. I realized that I had no problem living with myself, even though I had no idea what was possible for me after the Legislature job. But I realized that Kathy's reality was so different from mine that I couldn't live in it. I could live with me, but I couldn't be me and continue to live with her.

Separating from her—which I hoped at the time might be temporary and give us each space and time to work things out between us—was the most difficult and the most important decision I ever made. I could only have made it by being fully present and by focusing on the present. I sometimes wonder if our marriage could have lasted longer if, during those first thirty years, we'd focused on our relationship more, if we'd taken more time to be with each other and with ourselves instead of spending all our time and energy on our kids and our work—her work being full-time motherhood for most of those years.

I know it's impossible to change the past. As impossible as it is for a murder victim to come back to life, for a rape victim to get unraped, or for a prisoner to erase his or her life of drug dealing, addiction, and violence. In real life, there are no second takes, no erase and reshoot options, no chances to cut and paste. Except in our own memories, where we edit and revise the past to suit ourselves.

I've never seen a bicycle with a reverse gear. Nobody makes them that way. Bikes are designed to go forward. My road bike has twenty-seven gears, twenty-seven different ways to convert my legs' pumping up and down into rubber tires rolling forward. I've got gears for steep mountain grades and for equally steep descents on the other side. I've got gears for headwinds and tailwinds. I sometimes need to look behind me for traffic, the cars, trucks, buses, and RVs that roar by a few feet from my left elbow as I ride the paved shoulders of highways. I've tried using a rear-view mirror, but the most reliable kind, the ones that fasten to a helmet's visor and have a reflecting surface the size of a loonie, are more trouble than they're worth. I've found it's better to use my ears, to listen for the sound of those trucks, and to turn my head around for a quick glance. At least that way I see the whole picture. I used to worry about getting run over from behind, and I know a lot of people who shy away from cycling on roads for that very reason. After a while I realized that the only good way to protect myself from those drivers behind me is to keep going straight ahead, to stay on my part of the pavement, and if I need to change direction, to signal and take a quick backward glance.

Since my burnout, I've experienced time in lots of different ways. I spent so long living in low gear, crawling through life as if I were going uphill against a headwind that I thought of time as the enemy. I thought time was a burden to bear, a mountain to climb, a storm to battle. I gradually taught myself that time is really the road in front of me. It's the only road there is, but I can use it to go wherever I want to. It's Alberta Highway 93, the Icefields Parkway, past the Athabasca Glacier in all its frigid, windblown glory. It's the bike path through the parks in Edmonton's North Saskatchewan River valley. It's the way to the Grand Canyon, to Uluru, to my mother's condo in Phoenix, to my daughter's wedding in Toronto, to my new home in Edmonton's McCauley neighbourhood with my new partner and her two grandchildren. It's my way to whatever I'll accomplish in the years ahead of me, however many I've got left.

Which brings me to one last thing I want to say about time and how to do it. Elite athletes like Wayne Gretzky, Sidney Crosby, Dominik Hašek, Kobe Bryant, Venus Williams, George Brett, and Sandy Koufax played different sports but have one talent in common: timing. Only an elite athlete can watch a little ball rocket towards him at a hundred miles an hour and smack it four hundred feet in the opposite direction with a stick of wood. Or stand in front of a goal and dart, stretch, and snatch a small rubber disk out of the air after it's passed through a rapidly moving menagerie of skates, legs, arms, torsos, and helmets. Or stand fifty feet away from a metal hoop that's ten feet off the ground, leap into the air, launch a ball over a defender's outstretched fingers as the final buzzer sounds, and watch the net flex as if a mere breath of air is blowing through it.

Elite athletes and commentators often talk of being "in the zone." What they really mean is that when they're performing at the highest level they're capable of, time slows down. It takes a lot of raw talent, which few people have, and it takes a lot of training and practice to get to that point, the point where time and time-lessness intersect. In my experience, this happens in every aspect of life, not just sports. I've never been much of an athlete myself. I've been a volunteer writer for the Artist on the Wards program at the University of Alberta Hospital for over eight years. I go into patients' rooms, usually patients who don't even know about the program, and I ask them if they'd like me to write a poem for them. The most successful meetings of this sort end with my reading the patient the poem I've written using words, ideas, images, memories I coaxed out of them during a conversation. While we're talking and I'm jotting down words and putting them together, I am so focused on being present in the moment that I don't notice how many minutes have gone by, even though there's always a clock right up there on the wall. When I finally look at it, maybe twenty, thirty, sixty, ninety minutes have passed. My internal clock, my conscious sense of time tells me that's just a number and it has nothing to do with what really happened here.

I've experienced that sweet spot in time that I'm talking about in plenty of ways. A passionate kiss with my partner. A bewitching performance of *Peter Pan* at Edmonton's Citadel Theatre. A frigid December afternoon at the local rink with my grandson on ice skates for the first time. A bicycle trip along the Going-to-the-Sun Road in Montana's Glacier National Park in crisp mountain air, the snow-capped Rocky Mountains towering over me, my heart and legs pumping vigorously, endorphins surging through me.

I've had similar timeless experiences that were anything but sweet. When a 1990s midnight-blue Pontiac turned left into me as I rode my bike across an intersection and I watched the hood, bumper, and pavement attack me in slow motion. On a tour bus at a checkpoint outside Jerusalem when a teenage girl in army fatigues walked down the aisle checking passports, a machine gun slung over her shoulder. At a strip mall in Nelspruit, South Africa, when four teenage boys forced me at knifepoint into a deserted, enclosed stairway as they casually asked, "Do you want to die?"

I wasn't keen on dying then, and after my burnout and marriage breakup, I have found myself more determined than ever to live every day. Part of that has been reawakening my creative side. Eight years ago I started taking guitar lessons. I was fifty-six years old. The last time I'd taken music lessons was in grade eight, when I was thirteen. I remember I was a pretty decent flute player, but I gave that up and lost interest in playing anything for almost forty years. After I'd worked on learning the guitar for three years, I asked my guitar teacher and a friend of mine who taught piano what it might be like if I took up the flute again. Would I have to start over from scratch? Would I remember anything I knew about the flute when I was a kid? Would I be better off devoting myself to the guitar or some other instrument instead of reconnecting with my past? Both of them told me that everything I learned about the flute was stored somewhere in my body, that I merely had to reawaken it. One of them even claimed that after two weeks' practice, I should be just as good at playing the flute as I was when I quit forty years ago!

But first I had to get a flute. I have a friend, Jan, whose life's work is crafting notebooks out of discarded paper and old LP album covers, jewelry out of used bicycle spokes and chain links, furniture out of used corrugated cardboard boxes. Jan plays a piccolo-like instrument he made out of a section of half-inch copper water pipe. I didn't want to spend much money on a real flute, and I thought I could commission Jan to make one of those piccolos for me. When I asked him about it, he said he didn't do that kind of thing anymore. He asked me why I was interested. When I told him, he reached down to the bottom shelf of a bookcase in his living room, pulled out a black plastic case, and handed it to me. "A friend of mine gave this to me," he said, "and I've got no use for it. I was hoping I'd find it a good home. It's yours. Enjoy." It was a Gemeinhardt silver-plated flute virtually identical to the one I played in grade eight.

It took me four years to dredge up those childhood memories of playing the flute and build on them. If I hadn't been on such a tight budget, I could've taken lessons and developed more quickly. Two weeks? Not a chance. But now I can sight-read music and play many songs and classical pieces right off the page. My fingers know the notes well enough to get simple melodies right the first time. And when I play songs I know by heart, songs like "El Condor Pasa," "Danny Boy," and "The Swan," they take me into that place where I'm totally unaware of time passing. Into the zone. I'm thirteen years old and I'm sixty-six and everything before, after, and in between.

For a year, Jan and I got together about once a week to play duets; me on my flute, he on his recorder. Playing with another person is an even more magical experience of time—when we do it right. When we played a piece in swing time, "Jumpin' Around" by Brian Bonsor, I realized how much I had to learn about timing. Jan became the drill sergeant; I the raw recruit. He had me play one measure at a time over and over and over until I got it right. When he ran out of patience with me, we'd either go back to a song we played well before or try a new piece that looked simple. When we played through something that worked, especially if it worked the very first time we tried it, we'd escape through the bars on the page into a new place, a place outside of time yet totally in time. If we got the melody and the tempo right, the bars couldn't contain us. But if we didn't have the bars to start with, to hem us in and give us some kind of form and direction, we couldn't get to that new place, that place some would call a taste of heaven or nirvana.

It seems to me that time is primarily social. It's only important to me that it's 5:00 p.m. Monday afternoon if I know I have to meet somebody at 5:30 and it takes half an hour to get there. Or if I have to get two kids from daycare and take them to a soccer game at 6:00, but I have to feed them and drive them half an hour across town during rush hour. If I lived by myself and had no deadlines to meet and I didn't want to go to any concerts and I didn't need any groceries before the local store closed at 9:00 p.m., it wouldn't matter what the time of day was. And as long as my health is good and I'm fit enough to do what I want to do, my age doesn't matter either, until I look around at the teachers at my grandkids' school and realize they're younger than my own kids.

I started this chapter with a story about Q, the lifer who didn't know what year it was. I know I'm sixty-six years old and this is 2015, but when I write about my job in the Speaker's office, I'm in my early thirties. When my mother reminisces about me climbing up to the top of our kitchen cupboards in Pueblo, Colorado, I'm two. I look back at pictures I took in the late 1970s when my oldest daughter, Liz, was a baby, and I'm a young father again with the prime of his life ahead of him. I don't know where Q is now. He got transferred out of the Max years ago, and I never heard any more about him. I do know that when I met with him, we respected each other and we were present with each other during those moments in time. I also know that he and I will both die some day. The trouble is, we don't know how many days we have left. I could just put in time and act as if I'm in some kind of prison waiting to be let out, but I won't get out alive.

CHAPTER 12

THE PEOPLE IN THE TORY BLUE UNIFORMS

People like myself say fix the problem. Put [Clifford Olson] in the general population. The moral prisoners will deal with him in a way we don't have the nerve to do.
—Stockwell Day, October 1997

One responsibility of prison chaplains is to help prisoners handle grief when a close friend or relative dies or is in danger of dying. I spent many lunch hours with chaplains at the Max. Many times they had a prisoner's relative's death or life-threatening illness to deal with that very day.

One day I'm on my weekly rounds. I'm in the A unit office waiting for the guard to get off the phone so I can ask to see a few prisoners. The chaplain comes in. I've been around the prison a few years by this time; neither the guard on duty nor the chaplain ask me to leave so they can talk in private. They both know the prisoner involved is someone I know well. The prisoner's brother just committed suicide in the remote northern community where they grew up. Their father was on the phone with the prisoner the day before to tell him the news, and this guard was on duty and witnessed the call. Prisoners' phone calls have to happen in a hallway, where someone is guaranteed to overhear half the conversation and see the prisoners' body language and facial expressions.

The chaplain asks the guard about the phone call, and the guard starts to weep. After a few minutes, he wipes his eyes, turns to me, and says, "Most people don't think we care about these guys. But we have feelings too." This was the most emotion I ever saw a prison staff person express on a prisoner's behalf. The uniform normally doesn't allow it. Prison is a place for tear gas, not tears. Prison staff and prisoners both have to keep their guard up and act tough all the time. That's what the hard, cold walls demand. But every guard, every staff member at the prison is an individual with feelings, passions, family connections, flaws, and values.

As an outsider, I've caught glimpses of prison staff in many moods and situations. I've left the program room to go to the toilet and had a guard glare at me in the hall and gruffly tell me "NO!" before I could say a word. I discovered later that a group of prisoners was staging a sit-down in the gym just a few feet away; this would be front-page news tomorrow. I've had a guard accuse me of being belligerent to his partner even though I was surrounded by witnesses who said otherwise. I've relied on staff to write and circulate memos authorizing my volunteers' visits; usually the memos get written and circulated, sometimes the memos are full of errors, sometimes they don't get written, and sometimes they get written and aren't circulated. I've heard staff complain that their own memos get misplaced and that the only way to make sure memos get delivered is to do it themselves.

I've had open and friendly conversations with plumbers, parole officers, kitchen workers, teachers, guards, Elders, supervisors, managers, and wardens. Many times I've been told to go away. I've had guards make up a new rule every time I see them and talk down to me as if I were stupid for not knowing the rules. I've had a guard at the front gate look at every playing card in the six decks I brought in, apparently to make sure I don't have some kind of contraband in between them. I've had guards bend the rules to help me, letting prisoners come to visits even when their names aren't on the memo. I've had staff phone me up to beg for a volunteer to meet with a prisoner who's desperate and alone. I had a staff person who'd been at the Max twenty years thank me for doing M2W2 because "Of all the programs that happen here, this is the only one that has a real, positive impact on these guys."

Since I started going to the Max in September 2001, I've seen security get tighter and tighter. I've walked through the prison yard with staff who remember the early days when prisoners roamed free here, in the shade of trees and bushes, when there was one general population and every prisoner could exercise, or go to school, the chapel or the Aboriginal cultural centre with every other prisoner. The trees and bushes are long gone. The yard is a bare expanse of grass, weeds, concrete sidewalks, and, of course, snow in the winter. The eight units are eight or nine or ten populations who have to be isolated from each other. (Units are sometimes divided in half and the prisoners in each half are kept apart from prisoners in the other half.) Each unit has its own tiny exercise cage where prisoners can go two at a time. That's how the higher-ups responded to the gang rivalry and violence that have caused so many problems in recent years. As I write this in the spring of 2013, there's talk of reintegrating the populations, even as the number of prisoners grows to double what it was just three years ago, a direct result of the Harper government's tough-on-crime policies. Not everybody agrees that this fragmentation has worked, even though the number of violent incidents declined and only part of the prison has to be locked down when there's a fight or a weapon is discovered.

But there's no public debate about policies like this. A culture of secrecy pervades the place, and it goes all the way up to the Prime Minister's Office in Ottawa. Communications officers can't even issue a press release for something as innocuous as Restorative Justice Day without approval from Ottawa. Staff don't talk publicly about what happens at the prison because they could lose their jobs if they did. But the staff who talked to me agree on one thing about the culture of the Max: it's a very stressful environment where many people burn out, have to take stress leave, quit, or simply run on autopilot day to day.

One staff person I had many conversations with over lunch and coffee at the Max agreed to speak with me on the record, as long as her name was kept out of it. I'll call her Jane. She's a prison program officer and we meet at her home. When I ask her if she thinks turning the Max into eight or ten little prisons—in addition to segregation—is the answer to the waves of violence that kept the place in the news these last few years, she answers with a question: "Do you think there are too many accidents on Highway 2? If we could control accidents on that highway, do you think that would be a good thing?"

"Yeah," I answer. A no-brainer, it seems to me. But what does this have to do with prisons? I've known Jane a few years, and I can tell by the wry smile on her face that she's eager to reel me in now that I've taken the bait.

"Okay. We will put police at every exit and on every ramp. We'll control it so that only one car can be going in one direction at any one time. I guarantee there will be almost no accidents on Highway 2."

I've travelled that highway hundreds of times. It's the aorta of Alberta's transportation system, the four- to six-lane blacktop that links Edmonton to Calgary and handles over 130,000 trips a day on some stretches. I shake my head and say, "But the highway would be useless!"

"Exactly!" Jane says. She agrees that violence at the Max is down in the last couple of years since management divided up the prison, but the trade-off is, "They've crippled non-security. At health care, they've just thrown their hands in the air. Inmates can't get in to see the doctor. They can't get in to see the dentist. Guys on methadone—they're supposed to see the doctor every week in the beginning." Some new prisoners on methadone, she says, "haven't seen the doctor for months."

"How much of that is a reflection of the federal political climate?" I ask.

"It's all the federal political climate!" she says. "It's all the propaganda: get tough on crime. In my view, this is completely stupid.... These guys are getting out, and they've had no programming."

The voting public's fear gets stirred up whenever there's a serious crime or a perceived miscarriage of justice, and the public buys into the propaganda. But inside the prisons, the get-tough-on-crime ideology plays out in lots of little things that make life more difficult, not only for prisoners but for staff and, eventually, for the community these prisoners will almost all be released back into.

I've talked to chaplains, teachers, parole officers, psychologists, and I've seen it myself. Ever since there was a stabbing on a gang unit that caught the staff totally off guard, prisoner movements have become more and more complicated. To get prisoners to the chapel or to the gym or to health care or to visits or to work in the kitchen or to the metal shop has become a logistical nightmare. Staff get called off their units to do pat-downs. Whenever there's a movement, the public address system announces, "Clear the yard," and everybody has to wait for prisoners out there to move to their units or to a secure area. Once, a gang member told me he went out to the yard to go to health care, and prisoners from the Transfer and Release Unit were already there. He was so shocked, he forgot how much he hated those guys and wanted to kill them. He froze just long enough for staff to step in between. And all those movements, pat-downs, and yard clearings take time and shorten an already short period between mandatory head counts, the only time available for programs.

"When I was on core training in April 1988," Jane says, "we were taught that dynamic security was far more reliable than static security." Dynamic security, she explains, is a person's "Spidey-sense," intuition, the gut feeling that something's safe or not. It's what customs officers have always used to decide whether a traveller's shifty eyes are simple nervousness or a sign he or she is smuggling drugs across the border. Static security is steel doors, concrete walls, security cameras, and guns.

On the units she worked as a guard, Jane says, the guards knew their guys, and they could sense whether something wasn't right with a guy. "Now," she says, "they're all behind barriers. They don't know them. There's a strong push toward 'I don't want to know you. It's enough that I have to know your name.'"

In fact, some guards secretly wish they could be judge, jury, and executioner for some of the prisoners in their charge, and some of those guards are not so good at keeping that secret. Many members of the public, too, are so afraid of people in prison and so angry about what they've done that they wish they could simply do away with them, as President Obama and his commandos did with Osama bin Laden. In my time at the Legislature, I heard Stockwell Day—who would later become the federal minister responsible for corrections under Stephen Harper—comment that although capital punishment has been abolished, maybe we should release killers like Clifford Olson into the general population of his prison and let the other prisoners have their way with them.

Jane argues that prisoners need to have relationships with non-prisoners if they are to have any hope of changing their lives. Prison programs have to be more than a staff person talking and a prisoner attending and regurgitating the right answers so he or she can get a piece of paper in his or her file. Yet with the Max being, in effect, twelve small, separate prisons, even having minimum classroom time is logistically difficult.

Despite all the obstacles, Jane says, "We run some programs. But you do a program for two months, and then you're done. Programs should be a day-to-day thing, intermingling with staff. And give them some job skills. Now, with the separated units, there's nothing for jobs. Not that it wasn't difficult before, but it's impossible now. There was something. But this is dead time for these guys now. They'll have a two-month program, and then it's cell time.... These inmates muscle each other because there's nothing for them to strive for. It's almost like being in suspended animation."

When Stephen Harper's Conservative minority government came out with its Transformation Agenda, things got worse, she says. When the majority Conservative government passed its omnibus crime bill, they got worse yet. The emphasis is more on punishment, isolation, building more prisons, and locking more people up; there's even less support across the country for programming, education, compassion, and prisoners bettering themselves.

The frustration in Jane's voice is palpable. She's at the end of her rope. She's in her early fifties and a long way from when she can get a full pension, but she's told me over and over how she's just putting in time at her job and wants to get out. She tells me she can get a reduced pension if she can just hold on for another four years. Every time I talked to Jane over the last few years, she was eager to unload, to chat about her children, her dog, her plans to go to Europe, her latest run-in with security staff. She tells me how hard it is to drag herself in to work every day. She looks to me like a person who's lost her spirit, a bird in a cage with a dim memory of what it's like to fly.

I think back to the letter my own psychologist wrote for me after I burned out at my Legislature job in 2000, the part that says "emotional exhaustion with flat affect." Jane is me ten years ago: burnt out, dispirited, with zero energy, zero capacity to use mind or body for much beyond mere survival. Virtually a zombie. I remind myself that she would not have agreed to this interview with me, on the record, if she felt she had anything more to lose. I hope that giving her a chance to talk about her frustrations will help her find a way out of the trap she's in, or at least to move forward a little bit. She's in suspended animation herself, "putting in time." "I've gotten burnt so many times," she says, "that I just don't have the strength to battle it."

I assume she hasn't always been like this. That there's a lively Jane underneath the "flat affect" I see whenever we meet, a younger woman who might come back to life if she were given a chance. So I ask her why she got into prison work in the first place. She shrugs and says, "I had a degree in psychology. I was working with juvenile offenders. I was on UI. I thought I'd work here a year and decide what I want to do. Well, one year went by, and another, and you know ... I was thirty-one then. I'm fifty-four now."

She tells me her first job was playground supervisor. Then she worked with autistic children, with high-functioning, mentally

handicapped children. She did a year at a juvenile offenders centre where she had to work long hours and sleep on-site, where
"juveniles were maniacs," staff were assaulted, and she burned
out after a year before going on unemployment insurance. When
she got the job at the Max in the late eighties, she had to take three
months of core training, "the weapons and the gas," she calls it.
She started as a security guard, a CO-1, became a CO-2,[14] a parole
officer, and a program officer.

"I would say almost from the moment I walked in there, I didn't
fit....Generally speaking," she says, "I want to be a helper. I want
to go in there and make a difference in a positive way." But trying
to help prisoners at the Max looks to other staff like being a "con
lover." Despite the fact that one of the key objectives of Corrections
Canada is "actively encouraging and assisting offenders to become
law-abiding citizens."[15]

About two years ago, she says, before the Max was as tight as
it is in October 2010 when we do this interview, she remembers
talking to a suicidal prisoner on his unit, when a guard rushed into
the room to cut off the interview. The guard says he has to go do
pat-downs and the prisoner has to be locked up. Jane talks to the
guard privately and begs for just two more minutes. She tells the
prisoner not to do anything, that she'll get back to him as soon as
she can. She asks the guard to phone her as soon as it's possible
for her to come back to the unit.

"The guy doesn't get back, and so I phone several times and
said, look, I have to get back there and see that guy." The guard
won't let her back, so she phones the supervisor. No action. She
phones psychology, and the psychologist she speaks to says it's
probably faked, that he's "just grandstanding." She gets more and
more frustrated and worried, and she finally gets the guard to let
her talk to the prisoner through his locked door, out on the range

14 Two levels of correctional officers with two different levels of responsibility
    and salary.
15 From Corrections Canada's mission statement.

where everybody can hear them. Eventually, she's able to get the prisoner moved. Afterwards, she writes a letter of complaint to the internal preventive security office, and she hears later that they found a noose in his cell. She went to the staff briefing the next day, and "there was no mention of it." She tells me that if the prisoner had actually committed suicide, management would have hidden everything under the carpet.

In my nine years of going into the Max, I've heard plenty of prisoners complain about being beaten up and mistreated by the guards and by other prisoners. I've heard stories of escapes and murders, of prisoners managing drug operations from their cells on smuggled "cell" phones, of prisoners wrongfully convicted, of parole officers who place obstacles in the way of their clients to ensure they suffer long and hard, of guards making up a story of a gun thrown over the fence so they could justify locking down the place for weeks. At least some of these stories must be true, but I've learned to be skeptical. It's human nature to see our own actions, especially shameful ones, in a better light than, say, the victims or the courts might. It's human nature to make up or embellish stories to make our enemies look bad.

All the M2W2 volunteers I've worked with know how important it is not to judge a prisoner's stories and complaints. The prisoner may be working a con on us, trying to make us feel sorry for him. He may simply be in denial. A woman in the women's prison in Edmonton has served more than fifteen years of a life sentence for killing her own daughter and still won't own up to the fact that she did it, simply because the shame she carries is too great. A prisoner may actually be innocent, but if a volunteer acts on his belief in the prisoner's innocence, the institution would almost certainly deny the volunteer the chance to continue as a volunteer. One volunteer I know wrote a letter to CSC headquarters in Ottawa to complain about the unfair treatment of a prisoner, and the volunteer got banned from the institution.

When I talk to Jane, I know she's telling the truth as she knows it, as she's experienced it, first-hand. I can tell by the way her voice comes alive and her words follow each other more quickly as she tells her stories, a stark contrast with how I've often seen her act in the privacy of her own small office. Every time I've gone in there I think the only thing this place needs is a toilet and a bed and it would be a cell. Jane gets to go home every night and every weekend, but psychologically she's still locked up.

Every time I see Jane, I remember my own golden handcuffs at the Legislature. What I never had to deal with there was the physical danger. Even in my nine years at the Max, I was never threatened or even yelled at. I never felt I was in danger, even though I knew what the prisoners had done to get themselves in there and what they were capable of doing on the inside. Jane, however, knows all too well that her job involves risking her life. The Max is a dangerous place. Guards have been killed on the job, and many have been seriously wounded, physically and emotionally. In 1994, Jane was taken hostage at knifepoint and held for ten hours while other staff scrambled to get her free. But she doesn't make a big deal about it.

Instead, she talks about what she calls a typical workday. She goes to a unit to interview a prisoner. Both guards are sitting there with their feet on their desks. She asks to see the prisoner, and they say they're too busy. She sees two empty interview rooms and asks if she could use one of them. After a bit of persuasion, a guard relents and says okay, it won't be long. While she's waiting, a prisoner comes to the steel barrier that separates the unit from the stairs up to the office. The prisoner says, "Hey, Boss, can I have some toilet paper?" The prisoner makes a few good-natured jokes about how badly he needs the toilet paper. Jane says the office door is open all the time, but both guards ignore the prisoner. He keeps begging for toilet paper for ten minutes. Zero response. Finally, she says, the prisoner calls the guard a name, and the guard turns to her and says, "See what I have to put up with?" The guards keep her waiting so long that she finally has to leave without doing the interview.

When I say, "How much of this is because the guards themselves are dehumanized by the system too?" Jane rattles off a litany: her previous jobs, her daughter's jobs, immigration and customs jobs, et cetera. Then she says, "How are guards more dehumanized than anybody else in any job?" It's part of the union's negotiating tactics, she says, to spread "a lot of propaganda about how terrible their job is." Why? "Because they want a raise." Ever since 1994, she has defied the union's pressure to come forward as a case in point to illustrate how dangerous the guards' work is. "In all the years I've been here, only one staff person has been hurt badly.... We've had a few slapped." In twenty-three years, she says, she only knows of one correctional officer in the country who was killed on the job. Instead of talking about the hostage taking, she tells more anecdotes about guards manipulating other guards, stealing games and other property from prisoners, guards getting away with unethical and even criminal behaviour because the subculture protects them. She's clearly got a lot of anger about that, and so I let the anger run its course.

When her energy flags a little, I ask if she'd like to tell me something about the incident. She says okay, but it takes some coaxing to get her started. Pretty soon her voice and her face are animated again, and she's a guard back on a unit in 1994. It's 10:00 p.m., and she and her partner wait for the prisoners to come back from the gym.

"I noticed they were kind of acting funny," she says. Then in an instant, everything changes. "He held the knife to my throat and said 'This is a hostage taking.'" And this isn't a homemade knife. I've seen a few of those in a display case in the internal security office. The most common ones prisoners cobble together by melting half a dozen pieces of flimsy plastic cutlery into one and then sharpening it to a point. "It was a metal knife, eight or ten inches long," she says. Since the prison didn't use metal detectors in those days, she says a prisoner could easily tuck even a weapon that size down the front of his pants and get through the pat-down without raising suspicion.

She and her partner both press the buttons on their panic alarms. "A bunch of guards piled into the vestibule," she says, that enclosed, secure area just outside the unit's main door. The prisoner holding her takes her out to the door's window and tells the guards out there, "Don't open the door or she'll be dead."

"There was such a feeling of unreality," she says. "It was just like you're watching a movie," an out-of-body experience. "I didn't resist. He had his arm around my neck. I knew what was happening." She says people have often said to her, "You must've been terrified." She says she wasn't. "It was just sort of like Whoa!!! I had a bit of post-traumatic stress at the end, but it took a long time. Because it was so unexpected. It takes a second. It comes out of the blue. I remember early on that I was thinking of a film about the Santa Fe riot. Guards were tortured and murdered, their eyes gouged out. It was terrible."

But Jane keeps telling her story without a tear, amazed herself to remember that she'd been part of this dramatic episode in the Max's history, that she could've been killed. "They started papering up the windows to the vestibule, and the guards were going crazy." After a short time, the prisoners tell her partner to get out, and they send him away. Then she is totally alone on one side of the metal door with a group of prisoners, some of whom she had developed a respectful working relationship with. An army of security staff is standing helpless on the other side of the door.

"I didn't have any problems with the inmates," Jane says, with a couple of exceptions. "That gave me some confidence, maybe falsely. I didn't feel they would hurt me." Jane was worried for one of the prisoners who was in the office but seemed a passive observer. He had a deer-in-the-headlights look on his face. She didn't want to see him get charged with being a party to the incident, and so she tried to use body language and eye movement to persuade him to get out of the office. "But he knew he couldn't leave." She adds, "There was another guy. In a trance. He started doing things like moving cabinets. He picked up...an extremely heavy filing cabinet and moved it against the door. He was writing on the wall and things like that. But he never hurt me."

After the leader of the uprising gathers all the prisoners together in the office, he says to them, "What are our demands?" Jane is flabbergasted. The prisoners did all this without a plan! Then they decide on one demand: to trade Jane for another hostage. Jane explains to the prisoners that the staff aren't allowed to trade hostages and it would be foolish even to try. So that's the end of that. She tells me the prisoners ask for sandwiches after a while. The leader asks for some painkillers, and at one point he asks to be sent to the special handling unit (SHU),[16] which is where they'd have to send him anyway after an incident like this, the place he actually did end up.

At one point in the night, she hears guards banging on a back door into the servery, looking for another way into the unit. She learned later that staff couldn't find the key, "So they were trying to break down this door. The inmates were going crazy. At that point I thought, 'My God! This is gonna go south. I'm gonna get shot.' Not by the inmates but by these guards. Everything was going wild. But then they stopped."

Jane remembers that from her side of the glass, the staff appeared completely disorganized. On the inside, the prisoners were disorganized too. In the briefing afterwards, she says, staff admitted they handled the whole episode poorly. First they couldn't find the key to that back door. Then they couldn't get hold of anybody in the kitchen so they could get some food onto the unit. She says they finally did get a few sandwiches in. After it's all over, they give her the name of a psychologist to help her recover from the trauma, but she sees him only once. "I didn't feel I needed a lot of treatment," she says. The irony is that she has to pay for the treatment up front, and when she realizes the receipt is in the wrong name, she can't even claim for reimbursement! "I kept phoning and phoning and asking this guy if I could get a receipt with the correct name. He never did send it."

16 It's one level of security higher than a Max, and the Edmonton Max doesn't have one. It's where the system sends prisoners deemed to be of extreme danger or in need of extreme punishment. See chapter 13 for an account of life at the SHU.

"What finally ended the hostage taking?" I ask. Jane doesn't remember. She says even at the trial, "I wasn't a very good witness. I was supposed to write everything down, my notes and everything, but I didn't." As the incident wound down, Jane remembers prisoners one by one agreeing to go back to their cells, so that by the end of the night the hostage-taker was alone, and he simply surrendered. It was winter, she says. The heat was turned off. They were cold and hungry. "Somehow they negotiated with virtually nothing." Apparently, somebody did something right to rescue Jane from a deadly situation.

Jane says that her relationship-building with the prisoners minimized the risk of being under the power of the hostage-takers. "I didn't feel they would hurt me if they could help it. I mean, sometimes they don't know their own minds. But if you have a rapport with them, you don't need to feel that danger from them. And I tried." I gather that it's a matter of setting clear boundaries and sticking to them, just like supervising staff, raising a child, or training a dog. And I've done all three of those. Jane says, "I'd try to give them a phone call when I could, without getting myself into trouble." But she says she could be a "hard-ass" at times, and she often wrote up charges against prisoners who refused to stand for the standing count or who cussed at the guards.

I ask her how much time she took off to recover from the hostage experience, and I'm shocked that she had only a couple of weeks. Her partner took several months off, and he was only involved for a few minutes. She says the reason was that she was involved in a competition for a new job, and she couldn't afford to take the time off and miss the promotion and the change of scenery. A few months after I interview her, I hear she's off on long-term leave. I wonder how much of that could be delayed reaction to the hostage taking. Or is it an accumulation of the stresses she's been dealing with for twenty-two years: a person determined to help prisoners caught in a system and a culture that frustrates the effort at every turn.

Jane is far from alone in this dilemma. I know people in the prisons I've worked in who are able to play the game and still do good for prisoners, people who manage their own personal boundaries at work and recreate their real selves in their downtime. The system needs people like that. It also needs to let people cry when they have to before the pressure of suppressed tears rips them apart.

At the Alberta Legislature, I was Jane. The politics and jockeying for power among the politicians and the staff eventually broke me. I tried my best to maintain my integrity, but after nearly twenty years of being a human in a meat grinder, I had to leave. I left Jane's home that day praying she could find a way to escape from *her* prison without having a nervous breakdown. I hope her stress leave has given her the chance to heal.

Since the 2011 election, Canada has moved into a new political reality. Stephen Harper's majority Conservative government has acted on its promises to build more prisons, lock up more people, and make it harder for them to get back out into the community. Before the election, with a minority in Parliament, they instituted a prison transformation policy that was supposed to put more emphasis on programming, to ensure that prisoners improve themselves and earn their paroles. But the government has shut down prison farm programs, and the prison system struggles to find instructors who want to work in such a punitive, dangerous environment. I've talked to prisoners who have waited years for a program their correctional plan requires them to take. The government calls the system "corrections," but most of the people in prisons I've talked to agree it's more about punishment and warehousing than it is about correcting people who have broken the law.

In the aftermath of Harper's tough-on-crime legislation, even conservative prison guards have marched outside his constituency office in Calgary to protest increasingly dangerous working conditions. Is this another ploy to justify demands for higher pay, or is it the overcrowded system itself starting to break under the extreme pressure the government is putting on it? Several U.S. states have already tried similar tough-on-crime approaches. In Texas and Kansas, two of the most conservative jurisdictions in the country, the governments realized a few years ago they could not afford their high incarceration rates and instituted more open parole policies, a more community-oriented approach. In 2011, California's Supreme Court ordered the state to release thirty thousand prisoners from the state's overcrowded system. Years before, the prison guards' union had decided that even though the guards favoured tough-on-crime policies, the prisons where they worked were unsafe to work in. Maybe these systems have gotten so stressful that the systems themselves, as well as the staff who work in them, are burning out. Maybe Canada has a few things to learn from the U.S. experience about the value of community involvement in public safety policies.

CHAPTER 13

FROM CRACKHEAD-MURDERER TO CHEF

All human wisdom is summed up in these two words, —
'Wait and hope.'
—Alexandre Dumas, *The Count of Monte Cristo*

Four friends, men in their fifties and sixties, shoot the breeze over lunch at Chachi's Sandwich Bar in the Chinook Centre Mall in Calgary. It's a sunny, warm October day outside. They sit at a table near the window where they can see the clear blue sky off in the distance. The other three have sandwiches, but I eat a salad because wheat products give me indigestion. The place serves beer and wine, but we're all into soft drinks. I'm the heaviest drinker at this table: I order ginger beer.

There's the occasional serious comment, but mostly we talk about the food, the weather, federal politics. We crack jokes and laugh. Typical gray-haired, balding baby boomers killing time together. One of us was in prison for thirty years, and he credits the friendships with strangers who visited him for his release and his successes on the outside. One of the others is the M2W2 volunteer who continues to support him. The other two are current and former coordinators of the program.

I've known Gord Hutchinson for over eight years. He's coordinated the M2W2 program at Drumheller ("Drum") prison for over ten years. The volunteer sitting next to him I'll call Jack. He's been in the program for over four years. The fourth man, B, has been out on parole for a year, living at a halfway house. The three of them know each other well, and they talk about the most recent M2W2 visit at Drum. B asks about some of his old friends on the inside. I talk about my eight years as coordinator at the Max. I say I just finished my time there, my warrant expired September 30, 2010, and "I'm never goin' back." B laughs. He has clear memories of the Max, where he started his prison career in 1980. It was "home" for ten years.

B says, before he got arrested, he was a crackhead. He says he killed his best friend because he was out of his mind on cocaine. If it hadn't been for cocaine, he says, he never would've killed him. He tells me he found out later there's an officially recognized mental illness called cocaine psychosis, that cocaine really does make people crazy. I recall that I've met at least three other prisoners with cocaine addictions who killed their best friends. I ask him if he considers himself responsible for the murder: Was it your choice or was it the cocaine's fault? "I'm guilty as hell," he says. But we're both more interested in his last thirty years than in going over the details of the murder or his long-gone cocaine addiction.

I ask him what he remembers about the day he got his life sentence at the age of twenty-seven and how it felt to go into the Max knowing he couldn't get out for at least twenty-five years. B doesn't hesitate. He answers a totally different question. For him, the last thirty years were about fighting for justice, fair treatment, and human dignity. He says for him the dehumanization process started in the Edmonton Remand Centre, where he spent eighteen months before he was even convicted. Remand, he says, is where "they rob your soul out of you before you get a chance to go anywhere. They don't feed you enough. You don't get proper health care or anything in remand centres because you're not a ward of any government until you've been sentenced." What a lot of people call remand centres, he says, are "plead guilty facilities," "because most people, after they've been there a couple of months, they'll plead guilty to anything just to get out, so they can go to a federal pen, get three hots[17] and a cot and some fresh air." I ask him how they take away your soul, and he says, "They don't feed you. You don't get no fresh air. You're totally desensitized. You lose all contact with the outside except on the phone."

I walk by the Edmonton Remand Centre nearly every day on my way downtown. I've often seen men up there looking out narrow slits in the gray concrete walls.[18] In the federal system, there's a legal requirement that every prisoner has to have access to fresh air at least one hour out of every twenty-four. That's a right federal prisoners defend more energetically than just about any other. "You couldn't even get fresh air?" I ask, "Not on the rooftop or anything?"

"There is no rooftop," he says. "There's a little thing that goes out there. It's caged in and you're out there—maybe, if you're lucky—forty-five minutes a day. If they feel like letting you out. Do that for eighteen months, spring, winter, summer. I never seen a tree. I never seen leaves turn or nothing. All you could see was the sky, daytime, nighttime."

"After the first six months you say, I'm gonna try to make a special sandwich out of this and save it for later or to buy a little bit of canteen every week." B explains that in remand, none of the prisoners has a job, nothing to occupy his time, and no way to earn any money. All the money you have to spend on canteen is "what you had in your wallet when you got busted." To supplement that, he says, his mom, dad, and cousins would sometimes stop by and put money in his account.

After six months of that he was just plain tired. After eighteen months, he says, "I was looking forward to going to prison. I knew I would get real food. Even though everybody complains about it after they've been there a few months, it's still good food. And

---

17 Hot meals.

18 For thirty-three years, the Edmonton Remand Centre was downtown on 97th Street, between 104th and 105th Avenue. A new, much larger remand centre opened on the northern limits of the city in April 2013.

fresh air. You get interaction with people. Visitation. You get family. They have an opportunity to come there and you can sit across the table from 'em and talk to 'em."

He says some people stay in remand and fight their charges, knowing that if they're convicted, they'll get two days' credit toward their sentence for every day in remand. That was the system's way of recognizing that remand time was harder than prison time. But in 2009, the Harper government stopped the two-for-one practice. That's part of the Transformation Agenda that at the time had its principles pasted on walls and doors in prisons across the country. The Transformation Agenda was the first step in the Tories' plan to build more prisons. One principle is that prisoners have to earn parole, and they do that by good behaviour and by taking programs, programs about things like anger management, substance abuse, cognitive skills, family violence, and the like. The theory is that prisoners have to prove they are responsible enough to be released back into the community without endangering others. But back in the 1980s when B was new to the system, lifers didn't get programs at all.

I reframe my first question and ask it again: "How did you adjust to your new reality once you came into the Max? There you were facing a twenty-five-year sentence before you could apply for parole. How did you cope?" B says he met prisoners he knew from remand who had been in prison for a few years, and "They said the first thing you should do is get yourself a job. So I always had lots of work in there. Get yourself a job. Get a routine. Get a job in the kitchen because you'll never go hungry if you work in the kitchen." B smiles. "Here I'd been starving every day for eighteen months. I think I'll go work in the kitchen. Sure enough. That was great. So you get into the routine, and after a while you don't even think you're in prison anymore because it's you go to work, you go to exercise, and you go to sleep. The next day, the same thing. Most of the kitchen jobs are seven days a week."

So B started looking after himself, doing what he could to forget where he was, and the time passed quickly. At the Max, he says, and throughout the system, prisoners are encouraged to work. I know from my time there that the incentives to work are strong at the Max, even though jobs got very scarce once each unit became a virtually separate prison. If a prisoner doesn't want to work, he doesn't have to, but that means he has no money to buy himself pop or noodle soup packages or protein supplements. Six dollars a day is way less than minimum wage anywhere in North America, but it's way better than nothing. And in B's case, his work in the kitchen at the Max was the start of his career as a chef thirty years later.

But B could only forget he was in prison until the next weekend, when his family would come to see him. "That was the hardest thing," he says. "It was very, very hard because you can't say, I'm getting out in a year, or I'm getting out....I don't know when I'm ever getting out and going somewhere better."

In the early years of his sentence, when B wanted to get into a program and couldn't, he wrote letters of protest to the warden, to the correctional investigator, to the head of Corrections Canada, "to everybody," he says. He got responses basically saying, "You're in here for life. You've got lots of time to take programs." He agitated for lifers' programs, and the more he agitated, the more blowback he got.

"In 1986," he says, "the warden of Edmonton Max and the head of security thought they'd send me to a place called the Special Handling Unit, the SHU as we called it, in Prince Albert. They thought I needed an attitude adjustment. I found out eleven years later that all the stuff they used to get me to the SHU—because it was very serious stuff—was fabricated."

"The head of security swore," B says, "under oath at my judicial review, that everything they used was fabricated by the administration because they wanted me out of there." He says the man realized what he did then was wrong and he wanted to tell the judge and clear the record. The man knew the Crown was claiming that B's time in special handling and what he did to get sent there proved he was too big a risk to let him out onto the street.

B says, "They sent me to the SHU because they said I'd planned an escape, that I had someone throw a handgun over the fence at Edmonton Institution, which I would use in a violent escape attempt." Testimony at the judicial review, he says, confirmed the handgun was not operational and was thrown over by a staff member. I ask him how they connected the gun to him: if it got planted in his cell, if they got his fingerprints on it, or what. He says it was never connected to him, but they showed the gun on television and got the news to connect his name to it.

B said to them at the time, "Let's take it to court." They said, "No, no. We don't have to take it to court. We'll put you in jail [the SHU] for two years, and you'll never, ever get out." B says they figured he'd be there at least two to five years.

· "The only reason I got out of the SHU," he says, "I took the head of security and the warden to court. I got a young lawyer out of Prince Albert, Saskatchewan. He got me in front of a judge. Within twenty-four hours the judge had me back in the Max with a court order stating that I am to be treated no different than anybody else and everything I had when I left would be returned to me. Which in those days wasn't much. It meant I could get my $6.90 a day pay and have my job back in the kitchen and I'd have a single cell."

"Could I just say something at this point?" Jack interrupts. "I've been with [B]—it's over four years. Almost from day one, I noticed [B] had a heightened sense of justice. I mean, the things we talked about had a lot to do with other prisoners' rights, his own rights, what's fair in the system." Jack says he considers B a friend, and so when his parole hearing came up, Jack volunteered to write him a letter of reference. "The thing about a heightened sense of justice when you're a lifer," he says, "is that you can really screw yourself. You go in with no rights, and you basically are non-humanized. You've lost everything you had. So if you don't have a voice and you try to get a voice, it's not gonna work. But you know what? I really credit [B's] sense of integrity here. He could've knuckled under. He could've just gone really quiescent, the yes-sir no-sir kind of thing, and I think he probably would've gotten out before he did."

"Ten years earlier," B insists. "At least."

In my time as M2W2 coordinator, I've heard a lot of prisoners complain about guards, parole officers, wardens, and the system. All prisoners have their own styles, their own way of surviving on the inside. Some never talk back or fight back; some do nothing but. The unit representatives are the guys I have the most sympathy for; they're the ones who have to take flak from both sides while they negotiate for and against policy changes.

One guy at the Max spent four years in solitary, and every time I talked to him, he brought a two-inch-thick folder of handwritten notes into the interview room. This prisoner grieved everything. He fought for access to his computer—back when they allowed computers in cells at the Max. He filed a grievance whenever a guard touched him or refused to give him something. He phoned the correctional investigator repeatedly. The guards and other staff I talked to about him considered him a major pain in the ass. He created more work for them than a dozen other prisoners. He got taken to segregation in the first place because somebody in the general population tried to kill him, but he refused to move out of segregation to a protective custody unit in the prison because he was sure he'd be marked as a rat from then on, or even mistaken for a sex offender. I met with him repeatedly, and he went over and over the timeline of his crime, claiming it was not physically possible for him to drive to the scene of the crime from where he was in the time the prosecutor claimed.

I admired his focus and meticulous record keeping. He was intelligent, articulate, and stubborn. He fought the courts and the prison system at every turn, and the guards and other staff pushed back with equal vigour. His life was a wrestling match in which he and his adversaries got more and more energy and focus the more they pushed against the other. Despite setback after setback, he was always upbeat when I talked to him, even though his dogged determination was digging him into a deeper and deeper hole. It looked like a lose-lose proposition to me: refuse to buckle to the system so you can maintain your humanity and you get squeezed into a smaller, tighter, ever more isolated corner and lose your humanity that way instead. Yet if I were in prison for a murder I didn't commit and guards treated me badly, would I respond any differently? How long could I fight alone against a system without going crazy? It's hard enough for me to focus on writing this book day after day, and I don't have a series of uniformed guards working round the clock to keep me isolated and off balance.

Six years later I still hear the odd report that this prisoner is fighting the system and being shuffled from place to place. I don't know how his appeal is going or what's been happening with his grievances. But B is out on parole, has a full-time job as a chef, and is relaxed and self-confident enough even to have talked to two hundred people at a restorative justice conference the previous year about his life in prison. He stood up to the system and fought for his rights. It cost him ten years or more, but he finally made it back onto the street.

The Special Handling Unit was supposed to be the place where the hardest criminals in Canada had to do the hardest time. What was B up against? How did he manage to survive, to maintain his humanity? There was twenty-four-hour lock-up, he tells me, which meant that between 7:00 and 8:00 a.m. he got to clean his cell, have a shower, and try to get some fresh air in a "yard" that was really a cage ten feet by twenty feet. Before going into the yard, he says, "you have to stick your arms through the slot and they cuff you up." When he first arrived, he had to go into the yard alone. Once he demonstrated he was "sociable" and wasn't likely to hurt anybody, he was put in with two other prisoners. After a while, if there weren't any problems, he'd be able to exercise with more prisoners at a time.

His cell had no furniture, only a toilet and a bed. B says he got two pairs of socks, two pairs of pants, two T-shirts, and a jacket he could wear into the yard. "You don't get any regular shirts because you're not going anywhere," he grins. They gave him ninety days to prove he could be trusted not to destroy his clothing, and then they gave him a radio and a set of headphones. He could pick up three radio stations. "That was like Christmas time when I was six years old," he says. "That's how I felt when I got that." Before that, it was dead silence all the time except for whatever song kept playing over and over in his head.

"I did take up meditation and yoga while I was there," B says, and "it said in the fine print in the little pamphlet they give you at the SHU that you're allowed to go to the library one hour every week. So I put in that request every week." B says he read all the time, whatever he could get during his time in the library. He read anything on any subject. "I wanted to be a better person. I wanted to learn stuff. All the stuff I didn't have time for before, I had now; it had taken me a lifetime to get it." One of the most important finds was a book on yoga he read early in his time in the unit. After that, he did yoga three hours a day, one hour in the morning, one at lunch, one at night. He says the yoga, more than anything else, kept him focused and positive.

I want to see if there's a connection between that time and M2W2, so I ask, "Did you have any visitors in the SHU?" He says his family used to come from Calgary every weekend to visit him at the Max, but not in Prince Albert, "because it's six hundred miles away from nowhere." One visitor did come to see him there, however, on Christmas Eve: Claire Culhane, a leader in the prison reform movement in Canada until her death in 1996. B smiles at the memory that "the warden wouldn't let her stay past visiting hours. So the warden got a call from a judge in town. He said, 'Mrs. Culhane can stay there as long as she wants.' That's how much clout she had."

Gord has been sitting silently through our conversation. Suddenly, he turns the conversation in another direction. "What about medical attention in the SHU?" he says. "Did you get timely medical attention?" I expect B to speak of complaints about long delays getting wisdom teeth extracted, getting a root canal, about having requests for antibiotics ignored over and over again to deal with strep throat, bronchial infections, or pneumonia. I've heard these things so often I assume prisoners simply take them for granted. Instead, B talks about the way the prison system — not just the Special Handling Unit — used drugs to mellow prisoners out.

Back in the eighties, he says, "Corrections Canada had a new scheme on controlling prisoners with a pill. It was pharmaceutical intervention. That's what I call it. They had probably seventy-five percent to eighty percent of the maximum prison population and probably ninety-five percent of the Seg[regated] population on some sort of sedative." B says he'd see a psychologist, who'd ask him if he had trouble sleeping, and when he said no, the psychologist would give him dalmane, but he wouldn't take it after he did a little research in the prison library and found out it was a sleeping pill. He told us how he'd save up the pills for the Saturday or Sunday, when he'd get an extra hour of exercise, and he and his exercise buddy would get hammered on the things and sleep for two days afterwards.

In '86 when he got back to the Max in Edmonton, he says, there was a lineup from the medical wicket right out to the centre of the courtyard at nine o'clock at night because they'd pass out mood-altering drugs, and everybody wanted them. Almost everybody in the place wanted them, he says, and the prison authorities liked the drugs because they kept prisoners from staying up all night to make knives, brew liquor, or plan trouble. "Halcion was the big thing out there because it knocks you out and that's it. It's very quick acting."

He says that all stopped in the nineties, largely because Halcion and some of the other drugs of its kind were taken off the market. One of the big problems with giving prisoners these drugs, as management found out, was that once a prisoner got out, he'd go through withdrawal and depression, and become suicidal. "I couldn't figure out why these guys in the SHU were slashing up all the time. Sure enough, because they were arguing with the guards about something, they got cut off their meds as punishment."

In 1997, he says, he got his judicial review under the "faint hope" clause of the Criminal Code. That provision enabled a prisoner serving a life-twenty-five sentence to apply for parole after fifteen years in prison instead of twenty-five. He says the judge and jury recommended that he get day parole and unescorted temporary absences "the minute I walk out of the courtroom door. And you know what? I didn't even get out of a minimum facility for three years after that. When I got back there, the parole officer said, 'We don't have to pay any attention to what they said. That's just a scam.' I said, 'I've got a court order here.' They said, 'That means nothing in here. You should know that by now.'" His parole officer, he claims, cost him another three years. He protested over and over, but the warden backed her up. When she got transferred to British Columbia, his new parole officer saw the court order, was thoroughly disgusted with how it got ignored, and had him out in a week.

B was in Drumheller from 1992 until 2007, with a few years out in the middle. In our conversation, it's as if those years never happened, they went by so fast. "I got sent back," he says, "because a guy from Bowden sent a letter that I've never seen. My lawyer's never seen it. The judge has never seen it. Even the warden that kept me in Drum has never seen it." The letter was enough to cause his parole officer to revoke his day parole. "The letter was asking me to bring drugs into Bowden Institution," B says. "I says, can I see the letter? No. Can my lawyer see the letter? No. Can the judge see the letter? No."

The story takes me back to the scene in *The Count of Monte Cristo* where Edmond Dantès is escorted from the Crown prosecutor's office with a promise of freedom and taken instead to a boat and ferried to the infamous Château d'If prison, where he remains in a cave-like, dark cell for fourteen years. He's the innocent courier of a letter from Napoleon in his exile on the island of Elba to the prosecutor's father in Paris. He doesn't know what's in the letter. Instead of marrying Mercédès, the beautiful woman he loves, he's condemned to a life of misery and despair for something he didn't do.

So I ask B, "Do you read much fiction? Have you ever read *The Count of Monte Cristo*?" He roars into a belly laugh that turns the heads of all the people in the restaurant toward us, momentarily.

"Yeah. In fact, that was one of the first books I read when I was in the remand centre."

"Are you serious?" I'm shocked. Why would a prisoner want to read a nineteenth-century French classic instead of fiction about contemporary life, in contemporary English? Then I remember: this novel is escapist literature in at least two senses. The main storyline is Edmond Dantès' life: his daring, miraculous escape from the French version of Alcatraz; his cold-blooded, intricate plan for revenge against the enemies who put him away; and his emotional struggle to come to terms with his former fiancée, who married and had a son with one of those enemies. But B has no interest in revenge against the wardens and parole officers who kept him locked up for so long. He has certainly acted on the novel's concluding advice for people in despair: "Wait and hope."

But now he's interested in celebrating his freedom. "I've been riding the bus now for almost 364 days. The bus and the train every day except when I'm going out to Gord's place or somewhere." B tells me the seniors in the facility where he works are planning a "Happy Birthday" party for him tomorrow. It will be his first anniversary of getting out for good. At least we all hope it's for good. We all know it wouldn't take much to get his parole revoked again. It's pretty clear to me that fear of being sent back is one reason B will not give any thought to revenge. It's one thing to imagine becoming rich and powerful enough to have his way with the people who treated him badly, but B knows Edmond Dantès is a fictional character he can never be. And B knows he doesn't have any more years to spare.

He tells us about the time he asks Howard Sapers, the correctional investigator, if he can see the file Corrections Canada has on him. Sapers says to him, "B, we have a whole room full of your stuff!" Jack, his M2W2 sponsor, assures B that all his letters and grievances have helped prisoners who've come after him, but I can see in B's face and hear in his voice that he's tired of all that. He loves his new life more than a cave full of treasure chests loaded with gold coins and cut diamonds.

Just a few months before our lunch, the *Edmonton Journal* ran a series on the value of arts programming in prisons. Richard Moosewah, a lifer I've known for some time at the Max and in Bowden, had his picture in the paper. He talked about how important making beadwork was to him, how grateful he is that he's been able to turn his life around with the help of the programs he's taken in prison. I mention this to B to show him how his struggle to get lifers access to programs has paid off. I have another reason too. The series sparked some strong reactions from redneck Alberta readers. A few letters said things like, "This guy's a lifer. Why are we wasting money on him? We should've just put him out of his misery. Why don't we have capital punishment? These guys should've been toasted a long time ago."

So I ask B if he's met people like that, people who say he should've been hanged thirty years ago. He says Ron Forget, a LifeLine worker, once took him to the University of Calgary to speak to criminology students. Some were lawyers, and some were going to be prosecutors. "I was getting prosecutor questions left and right," B says. "You've gotta realize, this is society, and there are going to be people madder than wasps."

"How did you handle it?" I ask.

B says, "I tell them if I was in your position and had your background, I'd probably be thinking the same way, but I've seen a lot more now, so maybe in time you will see the same thing that I do." His voice softens and he says, "I've noticed with a lot of prosecutors they only stay in it for about five years, and they go to the other side, defence lawyers. For one thing, there's more money in it. For another thing, you can probably sleep a lot better at night." He pauses to reflect. "I don't know. It's a hard call. I can't get mad at people who say that, because they've lost someone and it's ripped their heart out. They just want some sort of revenge. They want to make it better. It won't make it better, but what do you do?"

As we get up from our table, say our goodbyes, and walk in different directions to our cars, I wonder, who is more human, me or the security chief who lied and recanted, or the wardens who run our prisons, or the volunteer M2W2 visitor, or the letter writer who wants capital punishment, or the best friend who died because of B's cocaine addiction, or the fifty-seven-year-old lifer I just met who's celebrating a year of freedom. There's the old saying, "To err is human; to forgive divine." But it's just as human to kill as it is to laugh, as human to love as it is to make mistakes.

CHAPTER 14

BUT, JUDGE, I DIDN'T DO IT

Better that ten guilty persons escape than that one innocent suffer.
— William Blackstone, 18th-century English jurist

A bright, beautiful, sunny day in February, and I'm cruising east on Highway 1 into the morning sun. I've just spent a productive five days at the Banff Centre working on this manuscript, and now it's time to get back into my daily routine. I look in the rear-view mirror at the receding peaks of the front range of the Canadian Rockies, their brilliant snow cover a stark contrast to the deep blue sky.

The pavement is rolling by at 112 kilometres an hour, the road is clear and dry, and I'm listening to a CD I made of some songs I want to memorize and play on my guitar. The Creedence Clearwater Revival are using their gravelly southern drawl to tell about life in prison, life under the thumb of "the man." "If you're ever in Houston, well, you better do the right; / You better not gamble, there, you better not fight, at all / Or the sheriff will grab ya and the boys'll take you down. / The next thing you know, boy, Oh! You're prison bound."

I'm driving an economy car, a Nissan Sentra that doesn't have cruise control, and so I frequently check the speedometer. Up ahead, a sheriff's patrol car has its blue and red lights flashing. It's parked on the shoulder, and an officer is standing beside the car he pulled off, getting documents from the driver. I glance in the rear-view mirror again, turn my head to the left for a quick shoulder check, signal, and move into the left lane, my foot off the accelerator until my speed drops to sixty as I pass by the two parked cars — as required by Alberta law.

I gently accelerate once I see them in the mirror, and I get back up to speed. A few kilometres down the road, I see another sheriff's car on the shoulder. I look down at the speedometer. 110. I pass by it and look back in the mirror. The flashing lights come on, and he comes closer. There's no other car in front of him but mine. I brake gradually, signal, pull off onto the shoulder, and turn off the ignition. I wonder what the problem is. Maybe I've got a broken tail light or my licence plate is obscured somehow.

I know I haven't done anything wrong, but my hand is shaking as I feel around the passenger seat for my sunglasses case. My regular glasses are in that case, but the case isn't there. It's so dark inside the car with my sunglasses on that I can't see my black fanny pack or my black sunglasses case or much of anything. I think about taking the sunglasses off, but I'd simply be trading blackness for blurriness. I look at the outside mirror. The officer walks past my rear fender. I reach for the window crank. There isn't one. I try the switch, but the ignition is off. It doesn't do anything. I crack the door open.

"Open your window, sir," says a cold, hard voice.

"A rental," I say. "Electric windows. Not used to it." I shut the door. I turn the key partway and feel for the window switches. I can't read the lettering or symbols on the door. I push the one I think is in the upper left. The window comes down about three inches.

"Your registration and driver's licence please."

I just ran my hand over my fanny pack in the passenger seat, so I know it's there. I pick it up, undo the zipper to the main compartment, and pull out my wallet. My pale-blue Alberta operator's licence is the first thing I see. I hand it to the officer. I lean over and unlatch the glove box. I grab the slip of paper on top and pass it out the window too.

"This is the insurance," says the mechanical monotone. "I need the registration."

I lean over again. This time I pull everything out: owner's manuals, service records, how to operate the stereo. Underneath it all is a small white piece of paper the same shape as the insurance document. I pick it up and hand it over. Without a word, the officer walks back to his car. In the rear-view mirror I see him writing something. He's a thumbnail snapshot in the glass, a uniform beside a standard-issue sheriff's car. He could be the captain in *Cool Hand Luke*, the man in uniform who wears two mirrors for sunglasses.

I was stopped another time for no reason. It's 1974. I'm still facing charges in the United States for failing to report for duty in the U.S. Army; I got my draft notice in 1971. My wife and I are driving our red Volkswagen Beetle across southern British Columbia to spend a week at Long Beach when an RCMP patrol car pulls us over. We are in our mid-twenties and still naive enough to think that in Canada people who look like hippies — as we did — won't be harassed by police as they are in the U.S. Midwest, where we grew up. We heard stories of draft dodgers and deserters who'd been captured and spirited across the border, though, and we wonder if they could be more than legend. As we wait for the policeman to check us out, we try to convince ourselves that the RCMP could not get away with kidnapping somebody on a busy highway. I get out the map to confirm exactly where we are. She jokes about the policeman's bowlegged walk, says he belongs at a rodeo somewhere. We laugh, but our bowels are clenched, and our breathing is quick and shallow. We steal glimpses in the mirror. The policeman holds the two-way radio in his hand, speaks into it, holds it away from his face to listen. I imagine somebody at headquarters flipping through paper files and photos, checking arrest warrants and unpaid traffic fines, relaying information in formal, clipped phrases. We banter. We sweat. After what seems like at least an hour, he saunters back to the driver's side of our Bug. He hands me my registration and driver's licence, thanks us, and tells us to have a nice day.

On that February day east of Canmore sitting in my rented Sentra, I don't have a worry in the world. I know I've done nothing wrong. A yellow slip of paper slides through the Nissan's open window, wrapped around my licence and registration. "This is a citation for 140 in a 110 zone," says the uniform. "You can plead guilty and pay the $177 fine. Read the back of the form."

I wonder, "Could I have blanked out for a moment and floored it?" No. Not possible. I say, "Where was I going 140?"

"On the highway." Not a flicker of a smile or laugh.

I'd like to say, "Thanks for the clarification. I thought you meant I was driving 140 on that rough pasture of prairie grass." Instead, I ask, "What stretch of the highway?"

"Where I was parked. Morley Road."

"But I never go that fast," I say. I recall how closely I was monitoring my speed. "Could the speedometer be broken?"

"Watch your speed, sir," he says and walks away.

All the way to Calgary and then on Stoney Trail to Highway 2, for the next three and a half hours to Edmonton, I test my theory. Could the speedometer be broken? I go ninety in a ninety zone, and people pass me. I go eighty in an eighty zone. People pass me. I go 105 on Edmonton Trail where the speed limit is 110, and I'm the slowest car on the road by a long shot. I go 110 and people still pass me. Nothing wrong with this speedometer.

I could plead guilty, write out the $177 cheque, and be done with it. I'd get three demerit points on my license that I don't deserve. But why should I admit to doing something I didn't do? If I plead not guilty, what evidence can I present? There's no DNA evidence, no witness, no skid mark on the road, no blood, no fingerprints. I could get a letter from Enterprise Car Rentals saying that I've rented from them for years and never had a ticket. I could get a copy of my driver's abstract showing I've never had a moving violation in my thirty-nine years in Canada. I could swear to the judge that the only mark against my driving record since I started driving forty-four years ago was a yellow light I stretched in Kansas City, Missouri, when I was seventeen.

Why should a judge believe me, though? A person's past says something about his character, but it's no proof that he didn't, this one time, do something out of character. The peace officer who wrote the ticket has the support of the Alberta government or he wouldn't be out on the road writing tickets. He's got the latest photo radar equipment and cold, hard evidence to back up his claim. He's got the code of conduct of his profession behind him. He's got thousands of men and women in uniform who would stand in solidarity with him. Besides that, the citation says I have to appear in Cochrane, a town of fifteen thousand, where the judge and the officers probably see each other at local rodeos and dances, where their wives chat at the IGA produce counter, and where their children perform at the same school Christmas pageant.

The ticket says I can plead guilty and pay the fine, or I can plead not guilty by mailing the ticket in before March 19. I talk to several friends about it, and I'm surprised to find that virtually all of them have had speeding tickets. Some admit to a history of several speeding tickets a year and note that photo radar costs them a lot of money in fines.

So I plead not guilty and don't even think about the ticket; after all, the court date is a long way off, November 5. On July 27, during one of my regular Tuesdays at the Max, I drop into the chaplains' office for lunch. In Pastor Oliver's office is a man I've never met before even though I've seen him in the hallways from time to time. He's dressed in a dark suit and tie, white shirt, shiny black shoes. As I stand in the doorway, I hear Oliver and the man talk about a legal issue. They know I'm there, and I assume that's why they don't mention anybody's name. I gather that the man's a lawyer. Apparently he's going to segregation to talk to a client. Oliver introduces me to him, and I engage in some small talk with the lawyer, Oliver, and Chaplain Teresa. The conversation turns to traffic tickets, and I mention mine. I tell the story, and they all nod skeptically when I say I was only going 110. "That's what they all say," Teresa laughs. But when I tell them I've had only one moving violation in my life, forty-four years ago, they're all hushed into a reverential silence.

I tell the lawyer I've pleaded not guilty, but I have no idea what to expect at the trial. He says that the first thing I should do is request disclosure. The Crown prosecutor's office is required to provide me with all the evidence they have against me, including the officer's notes. He says that I can represent myself, but I should know that all I need to do is establish some reasonable doubt about the Crown's case. He suggests I ask the officer, directly, questions like: Do you specifically recall this particular case? Has there ever been a time when you didn't reset your radar after giving out a speeding ticket? Is it possible that you made a mistake in this case? When I tell him the trial date is November 5, he's surprised they would delay it so long. He said he thought that would be another point in my favour: How can the policeman remember much of anything nine months after the fact? He said I had a good chance of winning the case and wished me luck.

But I have a busy couple of months ahead of me, and so I simply note the advice and file it away. I spend a week in September at a family reunion, the first time we've gotten together since 1977 except for funerals. It's my mother's ninetieth birthday. I decide to quit my M2W2 job and spend more time writing, including working on this book. I help my partner raise her two grandchildren, whom she got temporary custody of in June.

On September 28 I am visiting my friend Gord Hutchinson in Redwood Meadows. He needs to go into the medical clinic in Cochrane to get blood taken, which he does twice a week. It's part of the monitoring he's been getting during recovery from his recent heart attack. We go to the provincial building that's just a couple of doors west of the clinic, find the location of the courtroom, but the court section of the building is locked. I pick up copies of some brochures on the rack. One of them gives some advice about what to do in court. It says it's my right to seek disclosure of whatever evidence the Crown has against me.

Now that I've only got six weeks before my court date, I realize I'd better follow up on that disclosure stuff. But I can't find anything about disclosure on the Department of Justice website. I phone several places and get the runaround. I remember my time as the Speaker's executive assistant back in the eighties, and I phone the minister's office. The person who answers first tries to refer me to one of the places I've already tried. Then she finally is able to connect me with someone in Calgary who actually deals with disclosure requests. She promises she'll get the officer's notes to me well before the trial date, but the last week of October, I have to phone again to see where they are.

On November 3, I finally get an email from Justice with one sheet of the police officer's notes. It has a diagram of the highway, an exit ramp, and three Xs, two in the driving lane and one in the passing lane on Highway 1 at Morley Road. None of it makes any sense to me. I show it to a friend, and he can't figure it out either.

Two days later I'm in the Cochrane courthouse with my friend, Tom Walker, from Bragg Creek. I am confident that since I'm innocent, I'll be exonerated. All but one of the cases before mine are either deferred or there's a guilty plea. They save my case for the end. Nobody's left in the courtroom except the judge, the prosecutor, a few staff, and a couple of policemen. When it's over, the judge says I'm guilty and I have to pay a $177 fine. It still doesn't seem possible, even after I pay the fine so I can still legally drive. In the eyes of the law, it's now on record: I am officially guilty, regardless of what really happened on that highway back in February.

When I get home to Sara and we put the kids to bed, I have a lot of emails to catch up on and a video project to work on. Then we cuddle up to watch *Groundhog Day*, the Bill Murray classic from 1993. We laugh every time he wakes up under the same homemade quilt in the queen-sized bed at his bed and breakfast in Punxsutawney, Pennsylvania, where he's gone to film a special television feature for WPBH, Channel 9, in Pittsburgh. We watch him wake up to Cher singing "I Got You Babe" over and over again as the numbers in his mechanical bedside clock click over from 5:59 to 6:00. He has enough redos that he's able to learn the piano, get to know all the people in Punxsutawney, save a kid falling out of a tree at precisely the same time every morning, and finally woo his producer, Rita, and, as in *Beauty and the Beast*, learn to let go of his intolerably irritating ego and love her.

Sara and I go to bed talking about what day we'd like to have a do-over of. I say I'd be delighted to take one of those days we were in Paris and experience it again, even better the next time. After she identifies a day or two herself, I say, "I sure don't want to do today over again. It was a real bummer getting convicted of something I know I didn't do."

When we turn out the lights, my subconscious takes over. My brain takes me back to the Cochrane provincial building, courtroom one — the only courtroom there — back to me standing at the defendant's table facing the judge without any weapons except my integrity, my intelligence, and my innocence, where that simply was not enough.

My mind replays the episode. The prosecutor and Officer S are a tag team. The prosecutor asks him how much training he's had on the radar gun he used on February 9. She asks him the make and model of the machine. She asks him how many years he's been on the force and how much traffic patrol he's done. She asks him to describe the scene that morning on Highway 1 eastbound at Morley Road.

Officer S says there were two cars in lane number two, the driving lane, and one car in lane one, the passing lane. He says the car in lane 1 was my blue Nissan Sentra. He says my car was going over 130, that from personal experience he knows this just by eyeballing the car. He says he then took out his radar gun and aimed it at the three cars. The prosecutor asks about the operation of the radar gun. Officer S says it's designed to give two readings, a strong reading and a fast reading. He says that the fast reading was on my blue Nissan Sentra. The prosecutor asks him if he ever lost eye contact with the blue Nissan between then and when he pulled me over. He says no.

When I cross-examine him, I ask him how many tickets he's written over the year, just to get some idea of how many incidents he's witnessed, but he says, "I'd just be guessing." All I want to know is if it was in the hundreds or in the thousands, but he won't go there. I ask him if he has a specific recollection of resetting the device between the reading he says he got off my car and the previous ticket he issued that morning. He says the device automatically resets itself.

I get up on the stand. I swear on the Bible I'm going to tell the truth. I have some notes in my hand, notes that my friend Tom and I had worked on earlier. I've written out my statement in four crisp sentences because Tom said the process would be chop, chop, chop, that there'd be little time for explanations or tangents, that I had to keep it very short and to the point. When I start to look at the notes, the judge asks me what I'm reading from. The prosecutor chimes in too. The judge says to me, if you were cross-examined by your own attorney, he'd have the ability to use notes, but you can't use notes on the stand. So I give my statement without the notes: "I have never had a speeding ticket in forty-seven years of driving. I received one moving violation in my entire driving career, and that was for stretching a yellow light in 1966, when I was seventeen. I have a habit of not exceeding the speed limit. I never go 140. On the day in question, on that entire stretch of Highway 1, I never exceeded 115. On the stretch of the highway where the officer's car was, I saw him well off in the distance, and I never exceeded 110. I kept close watch on the speedometer and am certain that I was within the speed limit at all times."

In cross-examination, the prosecutor asks me if I ever took my eye off the speedometer, and I say, of course I did, because I needed to watch the road and the traffic. She asks why I was in the passing lane. I say I don't remember passing anyone at that time, but if I did, they were going under 110.

In his judgment, the judge says I didn't give him anything that would cast doubt on Officer S's testimony. If my aim was to cast doubt on the reliability of the radar gun, I had to do more than claim my innocence. He even makes the outrageous claim that in cross-examination I cast doubt on my own testimony when I admitted that I wasn't watching the speedometer constantly. I struggled not to gape at him over that. The judge didn't wonder how the officer could constantly keep his eyes on my car while he was watching the radar screen and merging into high-speed traffic. I wanted to get up and debate with him, but I'd seen too many television programs where judges get royally pissed off when people disagree with them once they've made up their minds. Our system gives the judge the final word. That's that.

What evidence could I have provided? If I had a do-over, what would I do differently? But the same video kept playing in my head. I am innocent. I know I was watching the speedometer closely. I know I didn't go over 110. So what could I have done to convince the judge that I hadn't broken the speed limit? Was I missing something in my memory of that morning on Highway 1 eastbound at Morley Road? It's a very flat stretch of road, the first significant flat stretch east of Banff. I'm driving along, aware of the road being empty in front of me, of the police car on the shoulder and the officer who just turned his flashing red and blue lights off after stopping somebody else.

The road is empty! How can the officer get two other cars out of this? What about those other two cars? Where were they? Behind me! Of course!!! Officer S didn't make anything up. He had nothing against me. He was just doing his job, enforcing the speed limit to keep people like me safe from drivers who thought they could go any speed they liked simply because their muscle cars and suvs have too much horsepower. He saw something that I couldn't possibly have seen unless I had been watching my mirrors constantly instead of the road ahead. He said that a car in the passing lane closed rapidly with two cars ahead of it in the right lane, that he guessed it was doing over 130, and then his radar gun told him it was doing 140. He said he maintained constant eye contact with the speeding vehicle the whole time, and that it was me in my blue Nissan Sentra.

If I'd asked him what the colours of the other two cars were, could he have told me? He could've made something up, of course, but why would he have noted the colour of those cars in his report? He had me cold, he thought. And so did the prosecutor and the judge. But if he didn't know the colour of those two cars, I could've asked him if either one of them could've been blue. I could've asked him to demonstrate to us how he maintained constant eye contact with the blue Nissan Sentra and still pulled out safely into traffic. Didn't he have to look around to see there weren't other cars he might be pulling in front of? At 110 or 140, how many microseconds does it take for a car to shift lanes? And was the blue Nissan Sentra he saw still in the passing lane when he shifted his patrol car into gear and pursued it? If so, wouldn't the two other cars have blocked his view of that car as it passed by?

If I had had more time with that scanned copy of the officer's notes, if I'd wondered what those other two cars were doing in that diagram, if I'd asked someone who could read shorthand what all his squiggles meant on that note, the outcome of the trial could've been different.

How many times had I heard one of the prisoners tell me when I visited him at the Max that the testimony of the other witnesses didn't agree on what his role was the night when that murder happened? A few prisoners claimed to me they were innocent and complained about the incompetence of their legal-aid attorneys. Some prisoners told me they were framed, that the police had tampered with evidence, and begged me to help them. How many prisoners actually get to have do-overs in court?

One man I saw repeatedly said even the prosecution told him the evidence wasn't strong enough to convict him, much less sentence him to life for murder, that the case should've been thrown out. For two years he was always confident he'd get exonerated and released, but I saw him transfer from unit to unit in the Max and then to the medium at Bowden. He was so sure he'd get out that he told me he'd already decided he would become a volunteer and come back into the prison to support others. The last time I saw him, he was still hanging on, waiting and hoping.

At the beginning of my trial, the prosecutor notes that two of us plan to defend ourselves in court. So she summarizes the process for us, gives us an outline of what will happen. Less than a minute's instruction from my opponent in the courtroom, a person whose job is to convict me, a person who's spent at least four years studying at law school and who has decades of courtroom experience. I am clearly out of my element. I have no courtroom experience. When I sit down in the witness box after I'm sworn in, the prosecutor says, "We stand up in the witness box. It's only on American TV that people sit in the box." Those places that advertise that they can help people charged with traffic violations clearly have a role to play.

Innocence is no defence. More than that, if an innocent person is convicted and sentenced to prison for a serious crime, like murder, innocence is a burden and a nearly impenetrable obstacle. In *The Shawshank Redemption*, Morgan Freeman's character, Red, meets Tim Robbins' character, Andy, and says he's in for murder. Andy asks him if he's innocent, and Red replies, "Only guilty man in Shawshank." But of the hundreds of prisoners I've met in Bowden, the Max, Grande Cache, and Drumheller, many complained they should've been convicted of lesser charges, but only a handful ever claimed innocence.

To claim innocence after all your appeals are lost requires either a large dose of delusion or a mountain of courage. If you really are innocent, you don't feel remorse for what you didn't do. Without displaying remorse, chances of parole are virtually nil. It's a principle that makes sense: how can a person claim not to be a danger to society if he's not sorry for killing somebody? One prisoner, who had already served fifteen years of a life-ten sentence, told me he could've been out on parole for five years already if he'd demonstrated remorse. He said: How could I lie about that? How could I live with myself if I told them I was sorry for something I didn't do? His position even earned him sympathy from a few of the guards.

One ex-prisoner I spent some time with is David Milgaard. He was convicted of murdering Gail Miller in January 1970 and spent twenty-two years in prison for a murder he didn't commit. He maintained his innocence all that time, never showed remorse, and paid a heavy price. In her book *A Mother's Story*, Joyce Milgaard quotes from a parole report written in 1977. It notes that David's family is "concerned and supportive," but since that support is based on a presumption of his innocence, the report questions how constructive that support really is. "If subject is guilty, familial belief in his innocence provides a firm block to subject ever admitting to or working through the intrapsychic aspects of offence." Fifteen years later, David is released and then exonerated. The McCallum commission of inquiry concluded in 2006 — thirty-six years after the murder — that the police, the prosecutors, the defence attorney, the courts all did their best, that there was no wrongdoing involved, no incompetence, and no conspiracy to frame David Milgaard.

At our M2W2 volunteer appreciation event in May 2010, David Milgaard was the guest speaker. I circulated to the people there a summary timeline of David's case. When the floor was open for questions, someone expressed outrage that the inquiry found nobody to blame. David's response was that the justice system did this to him and it could do it to any of us. He even said there was nothing to stop the system from doing the same thing to him again. Privately, he told me how much support he's gotten all along the way from the Association in Defence of the Wrongly Convicted (AIDWYC). If not for the passion and commitment of the people at AIDWYC, he said, innocent people in prisons across the country would be in an almost hopeless position.

Without community support like AIDWYC's, all prisoners, guilty or innocent, would have a lot less hope, their chances of success on the outside would be much smaller, and the community itself would be less safe. That's especially true for released sex offenders.

CHAPTER 15

THE PARIAH FACTOR:
SEX OFFENDERS INSIDE AND OUT

Don't ask what the world needs. Ask what makes you come alive, and go do it. Because what the world needs is people who have come alive.
—Howard Thurman, American author and theologian

The Most Reverend Thomas Collins, Roman Catholic archbishop of Edmonton, comes to the Max for Teresa Kellendonk's official installation as Catholic chaplain. Along the west side of the chapel, several long tables are covered with an array of cakes, brownies, donuts, sandwiches, cold cuts, cheeses, veggie slices, soft drinks, and coffee. Guests are welcome to help themselves to the drinks before the official ceremony but must wait for that to end before they can have a go at the food. For me, for other community people, for prison staff, the food is simple fare, what I would expect at a working-class neighbourhood's community hall. But for prisoners, such food is a rare delicacy.

Before the formalities begin, I see a prisoner I talked with a number of times a few years before but haven't seen for about two years. I'm surprised he's still here. The turnover rate is high, and most of that is because the Max is doing what it's supposed to do: prepare prisoners for medium-security placements. Over a three-year period, I counted 150 prisoners who came in and out of M2W2, and the most

I ever had active at one time was twenty-five. He recognizes me right off and comes over to say hi. "I'm getting out in just ninety days," Dave (not his real name) says. "I'll be glad to be out of this hole."

I ask how he's been doing. Dave says he's been going to chapel services every week, and he's planning to find support through the community chaplain in Edmonton. Dave's met the chaplain a few times and is determined to become a regular member of a Christian community. He says he's found Jesus and he's been saved. I ask him what kind of work he plans to do on the outside. He's not really sure, but he'll be so happy to be free. "There's no way I want to come back in here," he says. Dave pauses and then grits his teeth and slams his right fist into his left palm. "But you know, if I run across one of them skinners [sex offenders] on the street, I'm gonna stab him up and maybe kill him. I don't care if I end up back in here or not. I owe it to the women and little children out there." Dave looks me in the eye and vows, "It's my duty to protect them. The cops and the courts won't do it."

In the con code, the prisoners' traditional code of ethics and conduct, there's a hierarchy of crimes. I should call it a 'lower-ar-chy'. The worst crimes are sex crimes, especially against children. Other crimes against women and children—kidnapping, unlawful confinement, assault, et cetera—are just above that, but not by much. Even a rat or a "goof"—a prisoner who betrays a fellow prisoner, who has broken ranks with his gang, or who is perceived to be too friendly with staff—is not as bad as a sex offender.

Before the summer of 2008, when each of the eight units essentially became a separate prison, the two main divisions were General Population (Pop) and TRU,[19] otherwise known as protective custody. The Pop guys saw the TRU guys as low-life and taunted them whenever they could, with shouts of "Skinner!" Many times

---

19 As stated in chapter 7, TRU is short for "transfer and release unit." There used to be such a unit at the Max, where prisoners moving in or out of the prison would be segregated and protected. For years, though, TRU has meant protective custody. Pop prisoners typically assume that TRU prisoners are sex offenders, even though there are many reasons a prisoner ends up in TRU.

I've been in the prison when the public address system barks out "Clear the yard!" The first time I heard that, I panicked, thinking I had to get out of the yard *now*! I learned that announcement was for prisoners, so that prisoners from the other group could pass through to the gym, to a program, or to work. Once, the fire door between two units was "accidentally" left unlocked, and Pop prisoners rushed into a brawl with TRU prisoners on the other side. That time, nobody was seriously hurt. But according to the con code, Pop guys are supposed to kill TRU guys.

In the community, sex offenders are pariahs too. Out of concern for victims and potential future victims, the media regularly publicize sex crimes and issue public warnings whenever a sex offender is being released. For Catholics, the scandal of pedophile priests has been an open wound that won't heal. It has cost the church hundreds of millions of dollars and countless parishioners, as well as its credibility in speaking out on moral issues. But pedophilia and other sex offences have been committed by non-Catholics, hockey coaches, Scout leaders, teachers, and many others. It's generally accepted now that sex offences cause profound damage to the victims and that victims cannot heal without help. It's generally accepted, too, that like alcoholics, sex offenders can never be cured of their addictions.

With the right kind of support, though, sex offenders can live productive lives in the community. In 1994, Rev. Harry Nigh was asked to help a sex offender who was about to be released into Hamilton, Ontario. The man had served every day of his prison sentence, and the justice system had no further claim against him. The local media stirred up fear in the community about the potential for future victims. Yet here was a man who needed to work to earn a living, find an apartment, buy groceries, and establish connections with other people if he had any hope of making a new life for himself. A program called Circles of Support and Accountability (COSA) grew out of Rev. Nigh's work with that man.

Moira Brownlee has been the program's Calgary coordinator since 2002, the year I started working with M2W2. Both are programs of Community Justice Ministries and Mennonite Central Committee Alberta. I met Moira at the Bower Ponds in Red Deer that summer. About eight of us got together for a staff meeting and recreation. The sun was burning hot through hazy cirrus clouds that streaked across the sky. Moira was giddy as a schoolgirl, as she and her husband, Tom, in his curly gray beard, launched their rental canoe to explore the riverside swamps and rushes teeming with ducks and geese. When we gathered around the picnic table to eat hamburgers, Moira giggled and joked in her lilting South African English accent. I wondered: Who is this flighty woman, is she putting on some act, or is she a little girl trapped in a middle-aged woman's body? I'd worked for several years with a woman like that at the Legislature in the 1990s; her syrupy-sweet greetings had "phony" written all over them, like an overdone sales pitch. But in the years since then, I've learned this is the real Moira: a girl dancing through life blowing bubbles full of laughter.

In August 2009, I agree to spend a whole weekend camping in the foothills south of Sundre, Alberta, because Moira invites me. "Oh, Gary! It would be so wonderful if you could come! We had such fun last year! And this year it'll be even better! We're renting a rubber raft so everybody can ride the rapids!" I hesitate. Moira pleads, "I'd love for you to meet some of my COSA people. And it would be so good for them to meet you!" She adds, "You wouldn't have to worry about food, either. I'll get gluten-free bread for you and make sure there's no wheat flour in the stew. Melanie and I will look after everything. It'll be a riot! We'd love for you to come!"

I have a quote from Howard Thurman over my desk. I frequently refer to it when I feel unfocused or doubt myself and what I do: "Don't ask what the world needs. Ask what makes you come alive, and go do it. Because what the world needs is people who have come alive." Moira Brownlee has certainly come alive, and she spends her life spreading the contagion.

On Thursday, August 13, I drive to my friend Gord's place near Bragg Creek in pelting, drenching, chilling rain, the type of just-above-freezing downpour more temperate climates get in mid-winter. The forecast for the next three days: more of the same. We plan to go to his cabin early on Friday, the fourteenth, and prepare the place for the twenty-plus campers who will arrive for supper after working all day and driving up from Calgary. Gord shakes his head and shivers as he stokes the fire roaring in his living room fireplace. "Gary! Gary! Gary!" He moans. "How can we do this? There's no place to cook out there in the rain. There's nothing to do in the rain. People will be miserable."

I say, "Gord, it's only weather! Alberta weather. You're not responsible for the weather. I'm sure things'll work out somehow."

He stares at the burning logs for an hour while I strum my guitar and sing Joni Mitchell's "Both Sides Now" and Leonard Cohen's "Hallelujah," and a few other folk songs. Gord is lost somewhere in the fire, focused on the warmth, like Sam McGee being cremated in the firebox of a Yukon River steamboat. He walks into the kitchen. I hear him talk on the phone. He comes back and announces, "My cousin Dan's an old cowboy. He's got a big wall tent he can bring. He has a stove to heat it with. He'll meet us in Cochrane in the morning. The three of us will work on it together." His forehead is clenched and his lips are a thin, straight line. "But I still don't like it. That dirt road will be slippery. Will people even come? We can't spend the whole weekend in a tent!"

The rain is still falling the next morning. It's six degrees Celsius. This could be snow at higher elevations just a few miles west of us. Gord frets and stews and grumbles as he thinks through what we'll need as we pack up his Honda. We meet Dan at the Tim Hortons in Cochrane and drive north on Highway 22 in three separate vehicles, and then off on a side road. The last ten kilometres are watery mud on slick clay with a few gravel chunks scattered about, rare as beef in prison stew. We skitter and glide down the steepest hill, the one that looks like a ski jump. We arrive at the site at 3:30 p.m. The tall grass is bent over by the weight of the rain, but only the occasional droplet falls on us as we erect Dan's tent, stretch tarps around the outdoor kitchen, and set up a three-person and a four-person tent for ourselves and some others who don't have their own.

Gord and I are shivering and wet when we finish the small tents. My hands are numb from handling the muddy pegs. I cannot imagine myself sleeping in this and not getting pneumonia. I already have three layers of fleece on, as well as long underwear and a poncho. Gord and I stride back to Dan's wall tent, hoping the fifty metres of strenuous walking will warm us up from the inside. We step through the tent flap, and suddenly it's summer again. Dan has his feet up on a log near the glowing stove. A thin plume of steam rises off his leather boots.

Two hours later, the dim gray sky is much dimmer. Sunset is less than an hour away, but we haven't had sunshine all day. At least the drizzle has stopped. Cars, pickups, and camper trailers pull through the gate onto the grass. They are spattered with mud halfway up the sides. When Moira arrives, she looks at the tarps, the tents, the soggy firepit. She bounces onto the grass and runs up to hug me. "Thank you so much! I love you forever!" I chuckle, "And everybody else here too!"

A month later I phone her up to do an interview for this book. She's agreed to talk about her work. As soon as I say hello, the floodgate opens. Her words rush over me before I can get a question in. She just returned from a weekend at a women's camp near Prince Albert National Park in northern Saskatchewan, she says. She says how little time she's had to sleep, how long the drive was, how she got up early in the morning and went right back to work. "So this was a vacation?" I ask. No, she says, it was work, sixteen-hour days, just like the last two weeks.

"But isn't this a part-time job?" I remember she had her hours cut back a couple of years ago when Mennonite Central Committee Alberta was in a budget squeeze. "How many hours a week do you work?" I ask.

"Oh my god!" She shrugs. "I don't even know. I have absolutely no clue. I don't count my hours. I cannot count my hours.

"I'll give you a little example. The other night, Monday. I'd been at my women's camp. I drove up on Friday, get up by Prince Albert National Park, spend Saturday and Sunday there. I'm supposed to do a little speaking part. The other speaker, the main speaker, didn't turn up. We don't know why. I turned into the major speaker about COSA for the weekend.

"I was asked an hour before, can I be the main speaker? Because they just couldn't find this woman. So I said okay. I'd done the speaking on Friday night. I could do more of that, but I think what I'll do is tell you what my program's all about. It was easy for me," she says, "but I had no notes, nothing. Ha! And it was for over an hour! It went really well because I'm a verbal person, and I can do that. That was my Saturday. Then Sunday afternoon and evening I visit my daughter. Monday morning, first thing, I have to track down—I'm bringing a man's ashes back."

It turns out that a man she'd been working with for five years had died in custody at the Regional Psychiatric Centre in Saskatoon. The man's son was a core member of a COSA circle. That means the circle was formed to support him when he got out of prison: he was the reason for the circle to exist. As she unfolds the tale, I feel I'm entering the deep circle of hell where a whole family has been living for a long time.

"We've been involved with the family since 2004. The son's brother committed suicide while incarcerated. The father finds the body. He'd hung himself. He was an addict. The other son is also an addict. The parents are raising another young man because their daughter, being an addict, produced a child with fetal alcohol syndrome. It's a hugely addicted family, really bad."

I suddenly feel a heavy millstone on my back: the huge responsibility these grandparents have taken on, the only healthy people in this web of addiction. I remember the chronic illnesses my own children battled when they were growing up and how I felt supporting them through those. My gut tightens, my stomach aches just thinking about that. I wonder how the grandparents' struggles compare with mine. How does substance abuse compare with physical disease? "So the grandparents aren't addicts?" I want to make sure I have it right about this one bright spot in the extended family.

"The grandmother, the wife of the man who died..." Moira pauses, the rush of her energy pooling into a still eddy. She seems suddenly aware of the tape recorder, and for an instant, treads as carefully as a witness in a courtroom. "She likes her marijuana." Moira chuckles. "I don't know what the man was like, if he was an alcoholic, because he started to get a little senile by the time we met him."

"You cannot imagine anybody being able to live like this!" She gathers force and speed and rushes on. "And they have twenty cats and five dogs! There's cat shit and dog shit everywhere!" The world she and her circle of volunteers enters to support the son of these grandparents literally stinks. My stomach churns even to think of the place, overrun as if by squirming maggots, the stench and disarray and teeming life mirroring the profound dysfunction of the people who live in it.

Moira organized a Circle of Support and Accountability to help the man at the centre. One of her volunteers, she says, is a retired family therapist. Another is a chaplain-like family friend who had connected with the daughter, the mother of the boy with fetal alcohol syndrome. A retired director of a treatment centre for alcohol and drugs becomes part of it, and a couple of other people as well. Moira and the volunteers have supported the man for five years, and they've been engaged with the whole family. In the middle of it, around the time the other son dies, other members of the family accuse the father of sexual abuse that happened thirty years before. The man is in the early stages of dementia, and he says he can't remember anything. While the son is on parole, the father/ grandfather gets a fourteen-year sentence. The son breaches the parole conditions by taking drugs, and both of them end up in Bowden together.

Before long, the son is out again and the father is at the Regional Psychiatric Centre in Saskatoon because his dementia is getting worse. The retired family therapist writes to him occasionally. The wife visits now and then. But it's a poor family, she lives in Calgary, and money is tight for gas and maintenance for the car. The man is diabetic and unable to care for himself because of the dementia. He spends all his canteen money in prison buying sweets and candies. His parole hearing date approaches, and they want to move him back to Bowden for it. So a doctor examines him. By this time he's put on nearly a hundred pounds and his skin is splitting open from water retention. The doctor says, "This guy'll never make it to Bowden. He's dying." They rush him to the university hospital in Saskatoon and find a mass behind his heart. They stabilize him, send him back to the hospital in the Regional Psychiatric Centre, send him back to the university hospital, and there's cancer through his whole body. Only the wife is cleared to go in to visit him, but the parole officer pulls a few strings and gets a telephone in his room at the last minute so at least the kids who still have a relationship with him can say goodbye.

Then Corrections Canada tells the family they have to pay for the man's funeral, Moira says. He leaves about a thousand dollars in his prison account, the family pays another thousand, and that covers the cremation. But the ashes are in Saskatoon and the family is in Calgary. Moira volunteers to pick the ashes up on her way back from Prince Albert. She makes the drive to Calgary the Monday before I talk to her.

"I just made it in time for Caring for Families on Monday night." Moira's adrenaline is pumping again as she relives the experience. Caring for Families is a program Moira helped start as a volunteer. She saw a need for someone to support the families of people charged with criminal offences, and she decided to meet that need herself. "During that I get phone calls. Melanie[20] tells me one of the COSA guys is in real crisis because a relative died on the weekend. Tom[21] is dealing with another guy on the weekend who has a terrible drug addiction. The probation officer and all the people are

---

20 Melanie Weaver, Moira's sidekick in the COSA work, the other part-time staff person in Calgary at the time.

21 Tom Brownlee, Moira's husband, who not only supports Moira's COSA work but was also, at the time, a full-time chaplain at the Calgary Remand Centre and the Calgary Correctional Centre.

like, 'Yeah, you've got to go out and get a job. You gotta do this and that.' The guy says, 'I need treatment.' When Tom finds him, he's bathed in sweat. So I have to go and see this other guy and make sure he's okay. Luckily both these guys live in the same complex." Moira, evidently, can speak and inhale at the same time, like an Aboriginal Australian didgeridoo player.

"Then I get a phone call from a third guy—ha!—and he's had a terrible weekend as well. The long and short of it is that he started school at Southern Alberta Institute of Technology (SAIT). He's a good-news story in a way, but he's had a number of horrible things happen. He gets to the school and realizes he has no money and no bus fare or anything to get home that night. It's a long way. He can't walk it. And he's just put in a full day of work, gone to the thing, and realized he can't get home. It's late at night. His class ends at 9:30. So I have this Caring for Families meeting where some women are in real crisis. I see the one guy and the other guy. Then I realize I'm not going to have the emotional energy to deal with the third guy. That's where I'm so lucky I've got Tom. Tom went and got him a book of bus tickets and got him down to the CTrain station so he could catch the bus home.

"Yesterday, after getting up early in the morning and going to Bowden—only to find it was locked down—and pulling the circle together yesterday afternoon, I'm supposed to be at a church meeting last night. I'd totally forgotten about it! I remember fifteen minutes into the meeting. I jump in the car and almost fall asleep at the meeting. I drive home, pull into my driveway, and what is it? The guy is back in SAIT now. It's 9:30 p.m. He's lost his book of bus tickets and he's stranded at school again. He wants to jump the CTrain and not pay. I say, 'No. You can't do that.' So I think, 'I'm too tired to drive. I'm exhausted.' I walk in the house and say, 'Tom, he's lost the bus tickets, and I'm so tired.' Tom says, 'Okay. We'll go down together.' By the time that's all over it's 11:00."

She tells me this is a typical day for her, that she's on call 24-7. Then she remembers that today, Tom and one of the prisoners he works with plan to pressure-wash the paint off their fence and that she's supposed to feed them supper! "Ha ha ha!" she laughs at the work she's piled onto herself. "It's not boring!" She smiles and I squeeze in a question about how long she's been doing COSA work, wondering how anybody could maintain such a frenetic pace for long. When will she burn out?

Moira says she was a volunteer for the program in Saskatchewan in 1999, and she moved to Alberta in 2002 to be part of the first COSA in Alberta paid for by Corrections Canada. I try to get an idea of how many prisoners and volunteers she works with, but Moira thinks in people, not numbers. She tells me they work with guys in prison who ask for help prior to their release. COSA has circles that are up and running, weekly meetings with about four volunteers in each. Then there's ongoing support, guys who've been out for a few years. And sometimes circles get resurrected when a guy's life goes off track again.

Eventually I gather that COSA works with eighteen guys right now and twenty-five to thirty-five volunteers, that some of the guys don't have circles yet, and that some volunteers are involved in up to five circles. "Where do you get the volunteers?" I ask. "What's in it for them? What's driving them?"

"I can honestly say it can only be God who does this, because I don't know." Moira assures me she's not a fundamentalist type. She tells me about the circle she's working up now for a guy who's getting out this month. One of the volunteers in the circle came to hear Tony Campolo speak at one of our special events in 2006. The man fills in a form and gets on the email list. His life changes, he has more time, and so he wants to get involved. Melanie goes to visit him. The man's wife walks in. She gets interested, and they both want to volunteer. There's another man at their church whom they talk to, and he wants to do it too. "I didn't do anything," she shrugs.

She tells me, once a volunteer has signed on, there's a one-day orientation and special training for working with addicts. Once the circle gets started, people have to get to know each other and develop trust. The volunteers tell the circle about their life experience, and the core member shares his too. That's tough for the core member because there's so much shame attached to it. When they're able to do that, Moira says, it's a "Sacred moment." Then they draw up a covenant. Everybody in the circle agrees to do certain things as part of the relationship, the volunteers and the core member. The covenant and the whole existence of a circle are voluntary, both for community members and for the guy getting out of prison.

But before they get to know each other, it's common for a circle to help guys avoid the inevitable media circus that happens when they get released from prison. COSA staff and volunteers help the man find a place to live and a job. They make sure he has food, clothing, and the basic necessities.

Imagine starting off a new life with the media on the lookout for you. Your face is in the newspapers and on television, along with a story about the horrible crime you committed six, eight, or more years ago, for which you were sentenced. You've been in prison every day of that sentence. You've developed coping strategies in prison and managed to survive. Now you come face to face with the fact that the public considers you a pariah, a sicko, a terror, a danger to all women and children. The Crown has convinced a judge that you're still a danger to the public, and so you have restrictions on your activities. You can't be within one hundred metres of pre-teen boys. You can't drink or drive. You have no money, no job, and no friends. You have to submit to searches of your apartment without notice—once you get an apartment. You have to report to a police officer once a week, as if you were on parole. You are under constant surveillance.

You know everybody out there is certain you will reoffend, even though studies have shown that, with appropriate programs, sex offender recidivism rates are comparable to the rates for other types of offenders.[22] The community's fear has built a wall between

22 John Howard fact sheet Sex Offender Recidivism, http://www.johnhoward. ab.ca/pub/C24.htm.

you and them, a wall every bit as real as the double twelve-foot-high chain-link fence topped with concertina wire around the prison you just got out of. You don't have money, so you have to get a job. You have to find a place to live. But people hate you because of your crime and fear you because you will do it again, and they don't want you to live in their building or work in their shop.

You are determined to avoid prison, to avoid hurting people any more, but you still have the same attractions, temptations, and addictions you had before. Then, the day before you're going to be released, you get shipped to the Calgary Remand Centre and have a hearing. You're put in with a bunch of other men who would attack you or even kill you if they knew what your crime was. You spend the night there and get shipped back to Bowden. You get released the next day, but you aren't sure ahead of time what day you'll be released because the prison wants to avoid publicity. You are driven to the Red Deer bus terminal, and from there you get the Greyhound to Calgary, where you're on your own—unless somebody from COSA is there to help you.

The members of the circle commit themselves to contacting the core member every day, and offer themselves as a sounding board, like a sponsor in Alcoholics Anonymous. The core member needs to know he can call somebody if he's feeling down or if he's struggling with temptations, despair, or other problems. And the volunteers do not simply nurture him; they challenge him to look honestly at himself, who he is, and what he's doing. That's where the "accountability" in the name comes from.

When I recruited volunteers for the M2W2 program, I looked for men to visit other men in prison. Sometimes men brought their wives with them. Contact with women is extremely valuable for prisoners, but inter-gender relations are a sensitive matter in prison, given the all-male prisoner environment and the social deprivations intrinsic to prison life. This applies to all prisoners, not only those convicted of sex offences. So when Moira tells me that COSA volunteers are mostly female, I'm shocked. I've heard too many stories of women getting drawn into destructive relationships with prisoners: a pen pal, a chapel volunteer, a contractor, a friend of a friend marrying a prisoner, writing, visiting, and waiting year after year for him to get out and struggling to have a life and a distance relationship in the meantime.

"Women volunteers," Moira explains, "a number of them have suffered abuse themselves. But they've moved on. They're not in the victim stage. They've come to understand that this work prevents more victims." Another reason the program has more women, she says, is "the men not coming. A lot of men have, if not done it, thought about it, maybe by going on the Internet or whatever. So it's too close to their own thinking," and they have shame about that. "Then there's the nurturing role of the woman too. For example, in my Caring for Families group, most of them are mothers of sons. The fathers disown the kids."

But would a female volunteer be safe alone with a core member, a guy who's been convicted of a serious sex crime? "It takes a long time before that happens." Moira clearly has answered this question before, but instead of giving a canned answer, she speaks from the heart. Typical Moira. "Once they've got a profile they usually don't switch. If they're going to offend against young boys, they're not going to switch to an adult female. So the volunteer is actually safer than going on a blind date with someone, for example.

"I go bike riding with this guy," Moira says. I visualize her on a mountain bike pedalling at a leisurely pace on a paved trail beside the Bow River, the water reflecting blue sky and sunshine, office towers sparkling from above, pedestrians strolling hand in hand beneath towering poplar trees, their leaves yellow as lemons, one or two fluttering to the ground. "He's a pedophile who's offended against little girls. He's got conditions that he can't go through parks, yet he loves to bike ride. And it's good exercise for me. He asked me once, 'Why do you do this with me? Aren't you scared of me?' I said, 'Heck, you're the safest person. You're not interested in me.' He said, 'Yeah, you're right.' I said, 'I'm even safer because I'm with you. Any guy lurking around while I'm riding on the pathways, he's not going to do anything. I'm not a woman alone.'"

He's allowed to ride through the park if he has somebody with him who knows his criminal past, even though there may be little girls in the park. Moira sees a parallel with the man who somehow got over the fences and out of Bowden just a week before we have this interview. "People will think that he murders and rapes and molests children, but actually, he robs banks. There's a chance of him switching, but they don't usually. They usually stick to their specialty." The man who just escaped, she says, is "a good bank robber and escape artist, as we discovered." That's why one of the guys is allowed to go into a volunteer's home so long as her grandchild isn't around. Another guy is attracted to young boys, and so a woman volunteer is safe with him, unless she has a young son. In that case she'd be put in a circle with somebody else.

The ride Moira takes me on to explore the world of sex offenders is way different from the ride I get on television and in the newspapers, and virtually the opposite of what I read in the householder newsletter my Conservative Member of Parliament sends out every month. The fact is that COSA works. That's why the federal government funds it in most major cities in Canada and why police departments support it. A study has been tracking sixty core COSA members and sixty other offenders with similar backgrounds for five years. Preliminary results show that sexual recidivism by the core members is seventy percent less than for similar offenders without circles.[23] The study also shows that sixty-eight percent of the people responding to community surveys would feel safer if a released sex offender in their community were part of a circle.

Nonetheless, the pariah factor looms large over COSA. I recall a conversation I had with Myron Krause, then the director of the Mustard Seed in Edmonton, about the COSA program he used to run. Serial sex offender Karl Toft's criminal history was well-known across the country. He served a thirteen-year sentence for thirty-four counts of sexual assault against eighteen boys at New Brunswick's Kingsclear Youth Training Centre, but he has

---

23 http://www.csc-scc.gc.ca/text/rsrch/reports/r168/r168-eng.shtml#49.

admitted assaulting as many as two hundred boys from the mid-1960s to the mid-1980s while he was at the reform school, and the number of victims could be even higher. A compensation report says there could be as many as 1,400 offences.[24] When Toft was getting out of prison and then living in a halfway house in downtown Edmonton, he got front-page coverage in local newspapers. Some Mustard Seed donors threatened to cut off their support for the church entirely when they found out COSA was one of its programs and that it supported sex offenders like Toft.

So I ask Moira how Calgary COSA manages to keep going. She says, "We keep it under the radar." When a sex offender gets out, "we keep it very quiet that we're supporting him." One way around the pariah factor, she says, is that they take on people with fetal alcohol spectrum disorder (FASD) and others who are high risks to reoffend and lack other community support. Moira tells me that COSA supports an FASD man she visited in a psychiatric ward. "Some of those guys you work with," the man says to her, "have they committed sex offences?" "Yeah," she says, "We take everyone." He says, "That's terrible! Why do you care about them?" She says, "Why do I care about you? *You* traumatized *your* victim." He'd robbed a liquor store. He says, "Yeah, but *those people* were victimized!" Moira says, "Yeah, and you went in with a gun and victimized somebody yourself."

Even though he had FASD, this man then realized he had much in common with sex offenders. It's not exactly the same, Moira admits, but the liquor store clerk, the bank teller, the knife attack survivor, and the rape victim all have had their lives changed by trauma and suffer lifelong repercussions from it.

But there is life after rape and sexual assault, both for the victim and for the perpetrator. Their lives may not be as action-packed as Moira's, but they do go on. Nobody can be fully human if he or she hides from life, whether out of fear, shame, or hatred. Sex offenders victimize vulnerable people, but sex offenders are human beings,

24 http://members.shaw.ca/pdg/karl_toft.html.

not monsters. They have families and feelings too. Of course, we have to protect ourselves and our children, but we do a better job of that if we use informed judgment case by case than if we lock 'em all up and never let 'em out.

CHAPTER 16

A SEX ADDICT'S DAILY BATTLES

This is the domain of addiction, where we constantly seek something outside ourselves to curb an insatiable yearning for relief or fulfillment.
— Gabor Maté, *In the Realm of Hungry Ghosts*

The warm, sparkling blue waters of Biscayne Bay, the Miami skyline in the distance. In the sunshine, the view west from Miami Beach is a magnificent picture postcard. It's a place many Canadians would love to be in January instead of shovelling snow, wearing down-filled parkas, covering their faces against flesh-freezing wind chills.

Interstate 195 is a six-lane freeway across the bay. Also known as the Julia Tuttle Causeway, it links Miami and Miami Beach. From 2006 to 2010, as many as 140 people at a time camped out under the Julia Tuttle Causeway bridge. They weren't tourists or beach bums. They lived here. They were convicted sex offenders who'd done their time in prison, got out, and had no other place to live. In Dade County the law said these sex offenders had to stay at least 2,500 feet away from where there might be children. This twenty-first-century leper colony had no toilets, no garbage cans, no fresh water source, and no electricity except from generators. It wasn't officially a prison, but it had a corrections officer who came at 7:00 every morning to do a head count and make sure nobody had escaped. In 2010, a concerned citizen noticed that an island two thousand feet away was a public park and that the Julia Tuttle colony was itself in violation of the law.

The colony doesn't exist any more, but variations on the same theme repeat themselves in communities all over North America. In just the last month, I've seen notices in the *Edmonton Journal* that contain mug shots of men I met in prison who are now out in the community. The notices tell the public to watch out for these men because they are convicted sex offenders and likely to reoffend. Notices like these remind me that we are in a very different era than when I grew up, in the 1950s, when nobody talked about sex, wife beating was not considered a crime, and drunk driving was normal. In 2013, I have conversations about sex with my six-year-old granddaughter that could never have happened in 1955. In my inner-city neighbourhood, my partner and our grandkids have no illusions that we're in a *Leave It To Beaver* world where it's safe for kids to play in a park unsupervised. Did that world ever exist except on television? We keep finding out dirty little secrets from residential school and orphanage survivors, and recent reports tell of a culture of pedophilia not only in residential schools and church rectories, but in the Boy Scouts and other places.

The problem with those notices in the newspaper is that they would have us believe that the men they talk about are devils incarnate. Yet these men have to live somewhere. They have to work and buy groceries somewhere. The success of COSA is the direct result of the community coming together to support these people instead of hiding them under a bridge and treating them like lepers.

I met quite a few sex offenders in prisons, and I've continued associations with some of them after they got out. Despite the risk of speaking out and telling his story, one of these men agreed to be part of this book. He has to live every day with the fact that if his past becomes known, he won't be able to hold down a job or find a place to live. Many ex-prisoners, and even others, would like to kill him. Yet he spends a great deal of his time and energy working with prisoners, ex-prisoners, and addicts, especially sex addicts, to show them how to live better lives in prison and in the larger community. He spoke to me in the hope that his story will help others.

\\\\\\\\\

August 26, 2011. It's 10:00 a.m., the time X and I agreed he would come to my home to talk about his life before and after the sex offence that resulted in a four-year prison sentence. I'm standing on my front porch in my central Edmonton neighbourhood. The sky is mostly clear, but the air is cool on the shady west side of the house. I glance up at the deep blue sky and the bright green canopy of hundred-year-old elm and ash trees all around. The crumbling gray pavement in front of the house sports four big black patches of fresh asphalt the city just added at our request. Our neighbourhood is on the list to repave after eighteen years of Ralph Klein-initiated austerity, but who knows when that will happen.

I look at the vacant lot south of us: a heap of concrete clumps, clay, and tree stumps left there by the builder of two-story, nearly identical, new infill houses on both sides. The rest of the houses on the block are sixty to one hundred years old. A neighbour who has lived on the corner for sixty-one years says her home was built in 1897. The street, the sidewalk, the front yards are all clean, free of litter and weeds. Every yard is different. A chain-link fence here, a low white picket fence there, an eight-foot-high hedge of lush green raspberry canes on the opposite corner.

We moved in last November. The long winter and wet, cool summer and the contractor's delays are behind us. From the porch I smell the rich, earthy heap of topsoil next to the driveway that's waiting for me to wheelbarrow it over and make a yard out of our two small patches of clay in a lot mostly covered by concrete. I look at my watch. 10:03. I wonder if X is coming or not.

Twenty-six months ago he agreed to do this interview. The first time I ask, he doesn't need persuading, but he isn't ready to set a date. The part of it we're not quite connecting on is that I'm asking him for an interview and am committed to writing it up; what he says he heard is my asking him to write up his life story. Once I figure that out, I emphasize that all I want is for him to talk to me. So he asks me for a list of questions. I haven't been that formal with anybody else I've interviewed for the book, but that sounds reasonable to me, so I agree. I decide right then to give him whatever time he needs. I know I'll see him every few months. I know I'll have plenty of other work to do on the book in the meantime. I draft a list of nine questions and email it to him on July 20, 2009.

A few months later I ask about it. He says, "Oh, I haven't had much time to write up my responses. But I'll get to it before long." I say, "X, you don't need to write anything. All I'm asking is that you talk to me. I'll do all the writing."

"I know," he says, "but I want to write up my answers first."

I raise the subject casually a few times when I see him or talk to him on the telephone. Yes, I still want to be part of the book, he says. But there's always something. He has surgery. Then he's recovering. Another time he has the flu. Then a cold. A death in the family. He's unemployed and focused on a job search. These things are all true, but in June 2011, I wonder if he's simply changed his mind. He's put the thing off so long I figure maybe he's trying to tell me no but is afraid to say it. I'm determined to put the book together by the fall, though, and I need to know if he'll be in it. His story is an important part of what I want to address in the book. I don't want to start over looking for something else, for somebody else to fill the hole there would be if he backs out. So I phone and ask him directly: Are you still interested in being in the book and, if so, when can we meet for the interview?

He agrees to meet on June 13 at 1:00 p.m. On June 10, I get an email from my daughter in Calgary. She says she and her family are coming to Edmonton for two weddings this weekend, and they'd like to visit me on Monday. So I invite them to come for lunch. Then I realize Monday is June 13! So I phone X back to reschedule. He agrees to meet on the fourteenth. Then he phones up at 10:30 the same night and asks if we can do it next week instead. Then he phones me again a couple of days later and says he's going on a camping trip, and this time he says summer isn't really a good time to do something like this; why don't we leave it till the fall? I think maybe this is never gonna happen.

Then, at 10:05 a.m. that late August morning, a twenty-year-old metallic-blue Chevy sedan pulls into the driveway. X waves to me through the windshield. I walk down the stairs, but until I shake his hand, I doubt that he's actually here, in the flesh, ready to talk to me. I invite him inside and offer him a chair at the dining-room table. He places a large, disposable McDonald's coffee cup on the table and sits down. Every other time I've seen him, he's had a Tim Hortons in hand. I know guys in prison who can drink twelve, fourteen, or more cups of coffee in a day. I often wonder how their bodies can handle that much caffeine and why they seem to need it day after day. He also lays on the table a few sheets of typescript, answers he's written to my questions.

I met X eight years ago, and he's lost maybe a hundred pounds in the meantime. He's had health problems and walks very slowly. Once I walked across a parking lot with him; I could've moved faster on my hands and knees. I notice that today he labours up the stairs onto the front porch as if he's carrying a pallet of bricks on his back. He wears a baggy cotton shirt and loose-fitting pants. His face is pale.

"How would you like to start?" I ask. "There's nothing sacred about the order of the questions I gave you. We could dive in anywhere."

"Oh, why don't we start with the first one?" he says.

X tells me about his introduction to life in prison, how he went almost immediately to the chaplain's office and found out about programs and activities he could get involved in, how the chaplain told him the key was to keep busy. He got into several programs, and I met him a few years later through one of those programs.

"I talked to him about options and how best to cope, since I'd never been to prison," X tells me. Then he jumps to question six. "One of the questions you had was, were you ever in the remand centre. I never was. I went directly. When I was charged, a detective in plain clothes came to my house on a Sunday afternoon. He invited me to come out of the house and sit in the car for a few minutes and just chit-chat. Then he told me what I was charged with."

"You were living with your family?" I ask. "What was the impact on them?"

In a breathless, nearly deadpan, voice, X says, "Horrified. Shocked. Not a clue."

His family didn't reject him out of hand, though, he says, "I guess because I just chose to be honest from the beginning about all that had been going on." He said he realized instantly that there was no way out, that he'd just be digging himself into a deeper hole if he tried to lie about what he'd done. I'd known for a few years that X had been a senior manager in a large organization. I'd also heard him talk to other prisoners in simple language, in prison lingo, since he was a prisoner himself once. As I listen to him now, I recognize how articulate and intelligent X is.

He tells me that before he was charged, he thought about suicide for some time. To cope with stress, he had bottles of vodka stashed in different places in the house, where his family wouldn't come across them. He had a high-pressure job, and the stress at work was getting harder to manage. His happy family life was a well-managed facade. He was married thirty years, a successful professional with a beautiful wife and children. But since childhood he was relentlessly attracted to adolescent males. So he drank in secret to make that go away. He couldn't talk to his wife or friends about his sexual fantasies or about the sexual relationship he'd carried on for five years with a friend of his son's, a young man of nineteen by the time it ended. He attended a church where nobody ever talked about sex except to say how wrong it was outside marriage and to condemn homosexuals to the darkest, hottest, filthiest circle of hell. He couldn't talk to anybody there either.

"I was charged in January 1997. I think it was February or March my doctor and psychiatrist arranged for me to go down to Homeward Health Centre in Guelph, Ontario, for a full assessment and treatment of sex addiction. I was down there for six weeks. Part was forensic. I wanted professional verification of addiction so I could get the help I knew I needed."

X pauses and takes a deep breath. He has his right hand on his coffee cup but doesn't raise it to his lips. "That was the wake-up call, being charged and finally being able to admit the truth to family and friends who needed to know. That was the turning point."

The truth he admits is that he's a sex addict and he's lived out deviant sexual fantasies since childhood. "Teenagers used to get together and mutually masturbate," he says, his voice cold and clinical. "That's where I learned it. So I think what was happening for me psychologically, with all the pressure of my job....I turned back to pornography. I had been involved with pornography at that time. Pornography, of course, is a trigger. Allowing yourself to fantasize is just a step away from 'acting out' and molesting someone."

"So that was the offending behaviour. I can look at it now and call it what it is and was. But at the time..." His voice fades away to a whimper. Tears form in his eyes and his chest shudders as he suppresses a sob. "It's the type of behaviour you're so fearful of letting out, of telling anybody about it..."

I give him a moment to pull himself together. The silence lingers. I start to feel more and more uneasy about pushing him to expose himself to me like this. I ask, "Has it been helpful to you to stir up all these things? I hope I didn't open any old wounds."

"It was good," he says, still fighting back the tears. He takes another deep breath. "I don't think there's anything more healing than truth. It made me think about it, of course, but it also gave me a way to express how I look at it now as opposed to then. I can look at it now in the cold light of day as it were and recognize that's where I was. I know I'm not there now. That's the thankful part. It was breaking the cycle that enabled me, I think...Yeah."

His voice breaks. More tears form in his eyes. He still has his hand on his coffee cup, but he hasn't taken one sip since he got here. I take a deep breath and decide I won't intervene, that I'll give him all the space and time he needs. "It was the change. Because when you have to look up at the cold, hard ceiling of that prison cell and know that you put yourself there...Well, I didn't see any alternatives but to look seriously at how to change. That's why the programs, the psychological programs, the sex offender program they put you through there and so on..."

"It was very scary at the time because you don't know the other ten guys in the room who are with you. You know they're all sex offenders in the program... It's the fact that you have to sit in the room, listen to other people's stories, and have some empathy for them. You have a lot of fear in you when it comes to your turn, you know? Do I really want to tell people what I've done and where I've been? And no, we don't. But then somehow you find... The program people have a way of helping people through things like that with probing questions. So when it came to my turn, I was able to tell people my story. The part I never wrote about—I talked a bit about it in general terms, but what do you do about this nowadays? Now I'm out. I'm free. I recognize I have the ability to offend again or not. So how do I manage that? It's an addiction," he says. "It's always there before me."

"So how *do* you manage it?" I ask.

He tells me he has a pastor friend who was the first one to visit him when he went into prison. Before COSA even got started, he and this pastor developed a relationship as if they were a circle of two. The pastor is somebody he can be open with about his shame, his fears, his temptations, his depression, his ongoing battle with sex addiction.

As far as involvement in his church, X says, "I've signed a letter of understanding with my pastor as to what my limitations are, what I participate in and don't participate in. I don't participate in any youth projects or get involved with the Sunday school or that sort of thing."

So I ask, "But you're not legally restricted?"

"No, I'm not. But I know my offending behaviour from the past, and unless I want to go back to jail, I have to take avoidance measures."

"Like an alcoholic who's been dry for a while and wants to stay that way," I say. "He's not gonna hang out in a bar."

"Yeah. So there's places I don't go," he says. "I don't go to swimming pools. I don't go to early shows where kids would be involved. I always go with somebody else, another adult. The other person doesn't necessarily have to know of my offending behaviour, but I make sure I'm with somebody."

I remember that X lives very close to his daughter, her husband, and their children. I remember seeing the glow in his eyes and the smile on his face whenever he talked about his grandchildren. He tells me, "In respect to my grandkids, I don't volunteer to babysit, nor do I allow myself to be alone with them." He recognizes that his own grandchildren are potentially a sexual temptation for him.

I have one grandson who just turned one. My partner, Sara, has two grandchildren, now five and seven, and she and I are raising them. I raised three of my own children, too, from birth to adulthood. I've always loved being around kids, playing with them, letting my own inner child out to play, toying with words as if they were Silly Putty, tossing smaller kids up in the air and catching them, twirling them around as if I were a whirligig. I've always enjoyed acting like a whirligig. How could I do any of that if kids were a sexual temptation for me?

Nonetheless, last fall I had to wait three months for a police check so I could officially be with my partner's two grandchildren after Social Services had placed them in her care. The police check used to take only a week or so, but in the summer of 2010 the federal government added a step. This was because of Graham James, the junior hockey coach who gained notoriety and a prison sentence for sexually molesting NHL player Sheldon Kennedy in the 1980s. James received a pardon, after serving time in prison and being offence-free for five years. Then former NHL star Theo Fleury revealed he was a James victim too, and pedophilia was in the news again.

Getting a police check now requires every person to submit fingerprints if his or her gender and birthdate matches that of anyone on the national sex offender registry. When I talked to the clerk at Edmonton Police Headquarters about this, she confirmed what I suspected: there are now so many on the registry that virtually every male applicant for a police check has to be fingerprinted. The long delay has had an impact on clearances for volunteers, for first-aid teachers, for a wide variety of people. In the fall of 2011, while I was working on this part of the book, the *Edmonton Sun*'s front-page headline and full-page photo was about a Canadian Forces veteran of over twenty years who, because of the James scandal, had to wait four months to start work as a security guard, all because of this clearance procedure.[25]

X continues to speak in a forced monotone. I've spoken that way myself when I feel an aching sadness or fear in my gut and wrestle to keep it from breaking my sentences into sobs and moans. "I've talked to my family about my offending behaviour," he says, "so they know not to expect me to be a babysitter. This was a teenager I was involved with. It wasn't a baby, but still, the same principles have to apply. I have to maintain a healthy distance." He says he's "somewhat reconciled" with his daughter and her family and with both of his sons, but he's not welcome at the home of one son because his son's wife won't have him.

He was dismissed from a workplace where for eight years he held down a low-level job related to his field of expertise. X had to settle for a job driving a delivery van after somebody outed him. A person found out about his record, informed the supervisor, and X was out of a job. No recourse. No appeal. No chance to work anything out. It didn't matter how long he'd gone without reoffending or how long ago his prison sentence ended or the fact that he'd been pardoned.

After the delivery job ended, X spent many months struggling with depression and working to get job interviews. Nothing came up. With the economy stagnant and jobs hard to find for everyone,

---

25 The police check process was streamlined after the experience of that first year under the new policy.

what are the chances a pardoned sex offender over sixty would be able to find work that would pay enough to keep him going? X didn't tell me how long he could survive without work, but he did say that after his divorce and being unemployed and under-employed for years, he will probably have to work until the day he dies. Retirement is something he can only dream about. I wonder how many years living with his sex addiction and its consequences will have taken off his life when his time comes.

X tells me they didn't do criminal record checks on job appli-cants when he got that first job after prison, but now they do. He says they have two types of checks: the first for people who have no direct contact with clients; the second for anyone who would be working with vulnerable children directly. He says he only applies for jobs that require the lower level criminal record check, which he can pass because he's been pardoned.

I ask X what goes through his mind when high-profile pedo-philes like Graham James hit the news.

"I cringe," he says. "I really feel sorry for the victims. I also feel sorry for people like James, because I can imagine what kind of life he's gone through, where he's gotten to the point of offending against young people. I know there's more to a person than just the offence. There's the background of what got them into offend-ing to begin with. And there's always a root cause. Usually it's being abused yourself."

So I ask him, "Were you abused?"

"No, I can't say I was outright abused," he says. "I did have an uncle who made sexual innuendo on a fairly regular basis." The uncle would repeat a jingle that contained a thinly veiled sexual come-on. He'd sing "Nellie, put your belly close to mine" in a sug-gestive way. "He supposedly said it in jest, but then as a teenager, going through hormone changes and all of that, I always thought, 'Is he meaning something or what?' He'd say it in front of my mom and dad. He'd say it in front of his wife."

He says nobody actually molested him, but "what I do know from the psychology of what went on in my early life is that my father was not there for me. He spent most of his time being sick. For eighteen years that I knew him, he was sick. He had a benign brain tumour. He spent a lot of time in hospital. My mom's attention was not on my brother and me but on Dad, caring for Dad, back and forth to the city on the train, every day. So when I was a kid, both my parents were not there for me. I guess I felt lost and lonely."

He pauses, reaches for his cup of cold McDonald's coffee, and then withdraws his hand again. "Of course, my masturbation and sexual activity with my friends had negative feedback for me, too....I guess it's that old story of lookin' for love in all the wrong places, right?"

"It's an odd conception of love, too," I say.

"Yeah," he shakes his head and clenches his teeth. "It's sick. It really is. So you know, I guess in my later teenage years...I thought I could just cut it cold and quit. I really was in love with my wife. So I thought, well, 'I can change night from day.' For a long, long, long time that worked." He shrugs. "I don't know what triggered it. I think it was seeing porn on some channels...when I was travelling and on my own. Then I got busy doing other things and had kids. It seemed as long as I was busy it wasn't so much of a problem."

"I don't know what triggered it that time. I think one day I was in a store, and there was porn. It opened the door again. I thought, 'Well, I can keep this under control.' No, you can't. When I came out of prison and got a computer, I went back to porn for a while. I thought, 'Well, this isn't helpful.' And I finally broke the cycle again. Talking with my pastor friend, having to admit that helped break the cycle. So it's a struggle to keep on with keeping on."

X shares with me the letter he wrote to his ex-wife a number of years ago. In it he says, "What I did to you was very wrong. None of this has been about you; it has been about me focusing only on myself, meeting my 'needs' in inappropriate, wrong, and hurtful ways." He says his actions are "inexcusable," that he's deeply sorry for all the pain he's caused her. He says, "The terrible fact is, I know there is nothing I can do or say to change the past, even though I would in a moment if I could." He tells her she was the "woman of [his] dreams" for over thirty years and wishes her well in her new life. Most of the letter, though, is his frank disclosure to her of what he learned in prison about himself and the reasons he behaved as he did. He says "living with lies, secrets and in silence keeps us sick," and "for healing to occur, I need to be open and honest."

The letter continues, "The part you did not see was that on the inside I was always in turmoil. From my teen years onward, I have had very real problems coping with my secret sexual side. Yes, I had strict moral guidelines from my parents, but early in my teen years, homosexual experiences somehow provided relief from the chaos and pain of my own childhood. My sexual experience both with myself and with my friends (boys) always brought plea-sure and seemed harmless enough, because no physical violence was ever involved. At the time I had no clue of the psychological damage caused. Pornography fed my fantasizing.... My sexual behaviour made me more and more dependent on the excitement and euphoria. I did not realize it at the time, but I came to crave the sexual excitement as a way of relieving stress and tension and coping with the chaos in my life."

As I listen to him talk about his sex addiction, I realize I'm about the same age he is. I flash back to the living room in my home in suburban Kansas City in the mid-fifties. I'm nine years old. I'm sit-ting on the rug, looking at the books on the shelf above the *World Book Encyclopedia* I often pulled out, mostly to look at the pictures. I find a thick, heavy book with a burgundy cover. I don't remember seeing it there before. I lay it on the floor and start flipping through it. It's a health reference book. The black-and-white pictures show bandaged knees, splints on arms and legs, blisters on lips, rashes on backs, hair falling out. The whole range of common injuries and illnesses. Then there's a series of pictures of a baby's head. The head is between two legs and the sequence shows it first as a patch of hair, then like a big, hairy egg, and then it has a face, a neck, and even arms, a chest, legs, and feet. And it looks like it's coming out somebody's rear end. What the hell?

My heart starts racing. I suddenly realize this is a big secret, forbidden knowledge, something evil. I shut the book and slip it back in its place on the shelf. If Mom catches me looking at this, she'll tell Dad, and I'll get a whipping. He'll take out his belt and bend me over a chair and whack my butt until it's red and hurts too much for me to sit down. Worse yet, God is looking over my shoulder. He's ashamed of me. But despite the guilt and shame and fear, I can't help but wonder how babies get started and what the difference is between men and women.

Another time, I'm with a group of little boys my age, maybe seven or eight, and somebody suggests we look inside each other's pants, just for fun. We're in a neighbour's backyard. We huddle together in a corner between the house and a hedge. The shadows are dark, and we can't see any windows where anybody can look out and see us. It's just a game, but we all know we'd better not get caught. I pull the elastic waistband on my shorts out for the others to take a look, and the others all take turns pulling or unzipping and looking. I know I'm committing another mortal sin, another reason for God to send me to hell for eternity if I don't grovel to a priest about it before I get run over by a truck.

Afterwards, I withdraw into my room in a cold sweat, ashamed of my body, too sad to cry because I made Jesus get nailed to the cross and have the skin whipped off his back. I just made Satan happy that he's got me to live with him in the centre of the biggest, hottest bonfire there ever was, to live forever with my skin burning off, my lungs on fire, and no way out, ever. I'm only seven years old. Waiting five minutes for a bus is a long time. How long is forever? My imagination hits a black, blank wall. All I can think is, "I am a bad boy. I've got to beg Jesus to help me again." But the shame of telling a priest what I did makes it hard to go to confession too. When I finally do confess, I can breathe again. Even now, fifty-eight years later, the memory of that fear and shame is as real to me as my own skin.

Unlike X, as an adolescent I never saw any pornography. But I was still curious about sex. I noticed that my sisters' breasts grew year by year. When I was fourteen, I snuck out with my twenty-year-old brother to see Sean Connery and Pussy Galore in *Goldfinger*; we told our mom we were going to play in a park. I went to an all-boys' high school, and on the hour-long bus ride every morning, my penis got stimulated by the up and down motion as the bus and its worn-out shock absorbers heaved over bumps and dips. I knew those erections were sinful, but they kept happening every day, despite my best intentions.

My dad had a subscription to *Time* magazine. When *Time* ran a cover story on pornography, I got a lecture from my dad forbidding me to read it, but I did anyway, when he was at work. I knew *Playboy* was evil, and I never bought one. I wanted to know what women looked like under their clothes, but I knew that kind of curiosity was wrong. I saw one pornographic movie in my life, when I was sixteen. I drove from my suburban home to the Strand Theatre in a Kansas City, Missouri, slum with my best friend, Bryce Jones. We wanted to see for ourselves what all the fuss was about. What is this sex thing anyway, and why are all the adults so crazy about it? My parents never talked about sex except to say *"No!"* At sixteen, I was more naive about sex than the average eight-year-old is today. I was shocked at how the movie linked sex and violence. The movie was *The Master Beater*, a cheaply made black-and-white flick about a pimp who used and discarded women like toilet paper. I left the theatre dazed and disgusted. Girls don't have penises after all! How weird is that? On the way home, Bryce and I joked about the men in the theatre who watched the whole thing with newspapers on their laps to cover up their erections.[26]

---

26 Looking back, I am shocked that neither one of us was outraged at the movie's premise that hitting and threatening violence against women were good things. But this was the sixties, when wives were still considered the husbands' property and jokes about wife beating were common. I never saw my dad hit my mom, but I also never saw her stand up to him on anything. His voice was the one that dominated evening conversations; she mostly kept her mouth shut when he was around.

Girls don't have penises, but nobody, not even my friends, told me what my own penis had to do with making babies. I had to figure that out from books. Nobody told me that penises did anything other than get hard and cause embarrassing bulges in pants. I was almost out of high school before I realized that babies didn't come out a woman's rectum! Of course, I also was raised to believe girls were like the Blessed Virgin Mary and that they never did anything as earthy and animalistic as take a crap.

Like X's dad, mine was gone most of the time. He worked long hours, and when he was home in the evenings, he was too tired to pay attention to me. There were four of us kids, and so the attention I got from Mom and Dad was always divided by four. What was the difference between me and X? If I had associated with friends who masturbated together, would I have become a sex addict too? Did he simply have a stronger sex drive than I did? Why was he sexually attracted to boys and I wasn't? Was his sexual development somehow stunted, flash-frozen at fifteen for the rest of his life? Why wasn't mine?

As I look at X sitting across from me, his eyes mostly downcast, his voice breaking at almost every sentence, I wonder. He had to be over forty years old when he carried on that sexual relationship with his teenage victim. That boy was a friend of his son's. What happened to that boy when he grew up? When I ask X about the victim, he cries. He struggles to get a word out. He says his oldest son and the victim are still buddies, that his son actually set up a meeting between the two of them. He tells me the law didn't allow any contact with the victim until after X was pardoned. The meeting took place in a Boston Pizza when the victim was twenty-six years old. X says the meeting was positive and healing for both of them, but he doesn't say any more; the pain is obviously still too great. He does say they talked for three hours, that X asked for forgiveness and his victim forgave him. X came away from the meeting more determined than ever that there would be no more victims, that he would do whatever he could to reach out to sex offenders like himself to convince them that life is still worth living.

X tells me he met with a distant relative who was convicted of possessing child pornography. The man was happy to realize he wasn't alone, but then he tells X, "So what have I got to live for? Everybody's turned against me." X tells him, "First, you need to accept that you brought it on yourself. Next, realize there's only one way out of it, and that's straight ahead. It means you're gonna have to follow a process for recovery. It's not that you have any choice." X tells me, "I heard his story from him.... It's not that he was abused either, but sex filled an unmet need."

Then X laments that there's so much shame attached to what he's done that there's no way he can help anybody publicly. So many teens are struggling with sexual behaviour, but he can't go into high schools and tell them about his experiences. Those students, and their teachers, would no more ask him into their classrooms than they'd invite the bubonic plague. Instead, X quietly gets involved in a variety of community programs to help other adults struggle with their own demons. He keeps his addiction and his past a secret, though, or he wouldn't be able to accomplish anything. In fact, his own life could be in danger.

"Your victim forgave you," I remind him, "but have you forgiven yourself?"

X grits his teeth. "Every day." He says, "The issue is affirmation. You have to change the tape in your head, if you will, the tape that says you're a terrible person. I have affirmations that I carry, that I still have at my bedside." These are pieces of paper he picks up to tell himself, "I am a loved person," and "I treat people with dignity and respect." X pulls a brass coin out of his pocket and hands it to me. It's half again as big as a loonie. This is cool, he says. "I carry it with me all the time." Across the top it says, "If you can dream it you can do it," and it has three quotations from St. Paul's Epistle to the Philippians on it. He says he often pulls it out to look at; sometimes just holding it is enough. And he has some favourite songs, like "I am forgiven," that he hums to himself or plays on a CD player.

I ask him what he does when temptation comes. "I don't know if I should tell you this or not, but I'm going to anyway," he says with

newfound resolve. "It's something I learned as a biblical principle....
God can hear the thoughts that go through your mind [but] Satan can't
hear you unless you speak out loud to him. If you speak out loud, you
speak against the evil thoughts he's putting in your mind. You speak
in the name of Jesus..." X's voice breaks. Tears well up in his eyes
again. "It is amazing how, when you do that, when you say the words
out loud: 'I command you to leave me, Satan, leave my body, soul,
mind, spirit; leave my house...'" He pauses and wipes away more
tears, takes a deep breath, and tries to go on. He pauses again and
again to weep. "I post angels," [pause] "at the four corners to keep
you and your evil" [pause] "demons away. And I command that in
the name of Jesus. In the scripture it says, if you speak it in heaven, it
is so on earth. And if you use the name of Jesus to rebuke sin and sinful thoughts, it's amazing how there's a presence and a peacefulness
that comes." [pause] "It sounds maybe a little off. I don't know. I do
know it works. I do know that when I have said those things out loud,
I feel instantly at peace and sinful thoughts subside."

We both take a deep breath. Then he says, "Once you've had a
chance to go through this in more detail and think about it, maybe
there'll be more questions or a need for a further get together." He
laughs, "I won't procrastinate."

When he gets up from the table, I take the half-full coffee cup
from him, dump it down the sink, and throw the cup away. I walk
him out the front door to his car and wave to him as he drives off.
I notice that on our new driveway—concrete poured just three
months ago—there are five drops of oil that weren't there before.
Real life is always messy, isn't it?

Later that night when my partner and I are in bed talking about
our day, I tell her about X's visit. She shudders. She tells me that
having a sex offender in our house gives her the creeps, even
though neither she nor our grandkids were anywhere near at the
time. She says to me, "Didn't you just want to run right into the
bathroom and take a shower after he left?"

"No, I didn't," I tell her. "But it sure was a difficult interview."
After I turn out the light beside our bed, I wonder if X is going

to be able to sleep tonight after telling me so many secrets. The interview was difficult for me, but X risked his life to tell me these things. He trusted me with his life, hoping his story would help others caught in sexual bondage find a reason to keep on living and make a positive contribution to society. I am deeply honoured to have X so explicitly entrust his life to me. I am blessed to have such a friend.

I know he has to keep his identity secret. I know, too, that unless people like my partner can hear his story, can see X as a human being and a brother, we'll keep living in gated communities and behind fortified mental barriers to protect us from those parts of ourselves we hide away, like a mad uterus in *Jane Eyre*'s attic or an aroused penis in a cell.

WHAT DOES "HUMAN" *REALLY* MEAN?

*What a piece of work is a man! How noble in reason! how
infinite in faculty!...in action how like an angel! in apprehen-
sion how like a god! the beauty of the world!*
—William Shakespeare, *Hamlet*

I t's minus thirty degrees Celsius in Edmonton, minus forty-two
with the wind chill. Men in buttoned-up wool overcoats grit their
teeth against the north wind that howls down 107th Street. They
bow their tuque-covered heads and jog the fifty metres from the
Government Centre bus terminal to the Legislature pedway door.
Women clutch their purses to their chests with one hand and cinch
their fur-lined parka hoods around their heads with the other.
Their watering, burning eyes guide each sleek, calf-length leather
boot up and over an ice-crusted, two-foot-high snowdrift at the
100th Avenue curb.

The January sun is a dim orange ball, barely above the south-
eastern horizon, the south rim of the frozen North Saskatchewan
River's valley. Steam billows from all three Rossdale Power Plant
smokestacks. A long procession of cars, trucks, and buses on 97th
Avenue inches along the glistening ice ruts that stretch east to the
James MacDonald Bridge and up the hill to the 84th Street traffic
circle. A black, overstuffed scarecrow pedals a bicycle across the

High Level Bridge, puffs of water vapour chugging from its neoprene face.

But that cyclist isn't me. Too cold. Too slippery. Today I bus to the Legislature where I work. To keep in shape and force my reluctant heart to exercise, during my lunch hour I pedal the indoor bike in the small exercise area under the front steps of the building. One room has barely enough room for two treadmills; another room has two stationary bikes and a set of barbells.

As I approach the outer door, I hear one of the treadmills rumbling. There's an intermittent groan too, a person struggling to breathe. I glance over to see if the person is clutching his heart. I see a face I've often seen on television and around the building: Premier Ralph Klein. He doesn't look up. He's sweating and evidently not having much fun, but I gather I don't need to phone for an ambulance.

In the tiny change room, while I put on my shorts, T-shirt, and runners, he comes in, strips naked, slings a white towel over the side of the shower stall, turns on the water, and fills the place with steam. Everybody in Alberta knows the premier likes beer, and his distended gut is one of the side effects. Everybody in the country knows he doesn't like morning meetings. Only a few people know he exercises to keep his body as fit as it is. He's the man who, several years after this, on the night of December 12, 2001, had too many drinks, visited a shelter for homeless men in Edmonton, threw some coins on the floor in front of some men there, and told them to go out and get jobs. His problems with alcohol were front-page news for a few months and then faded away again.

Five or six years after I see the premier naked, I'm in a small log building inside the fence at the Edmonton Max. I'm carrying a white towel and wearing gym shorts, nothing else. The room is filling with steam that hisses and billows off the red-hot rocks in the centre. I look around. An Aboriginal Elder. An Elder's helper. Fourteen D-unit prisoners. A few are tall and thin like me. A couple are short and round like Premier Klein. Some are murderers, some are sex offenders, most have mental health issues, many have drug and alcohol addictions, yet when we all take our clothes off and let our guard down, it's hard to tell the difference.

Some differences are evident when we talk. My language is more polished, my vocabulary bigger, my sentences longer, and I don't use the F- and D-words like they do. We talk about M2W2, of course, and I find a few more prisoners who want to get into the program. We talk about the weather, the Oilers' playoff chances, the prisoners laid up with the flu back in their cells who wanted to come but couldn't. Then the Elder reminds us we are all in the presence of the Creator, the one who made all of us, in the presence of our ancestors in the spirit world, who are here with us and care about us. For a while, we're all one, a small community of men who could be anywhere on earth. When it's over, I put my street clothes on and exit through the main gate; they go back to their eight-by-twelve concrete bunkers.

The next time I go into the visiting room with a group of volunteers, the difference between insiders and outsiders is obvious. We come through the outside door in street clothes; the prisoners come through the inside door in T-shirts, jeans, and runners. In the winter they wear identical green canvas jackets with their names printed on the front.

The last few years I ran M2W2 at the Max, I started every visit with a round of introductions. I asked them to say their names, and each month I'd ask them to say a different thing about themselves: what their favourite dessert is, why they like or hate winter, what song means something to them, what's a happy memory from childhood. It was always hard to keep people on track, especially the prisoners. Some would only say their names. Some would ramble on. Often, other prisoners would ignore the person talking and have their own conversations. One time one of the volunteers gave his name, then looked around the room, and said he came to the Max to visit because he could easily have been one of them. "The only difference between you and me is that you got caught," he said.

I didn't ask him whether he'd murdered or raped anybody, as some of the prisoners had. More likely he was talking about cheating on income tax, breaking the speed limit, running a stop sign, or using his special farmer's gasoline discount to fuel his car instead of his tractor. Or maybe he was referring to something like what the Catholic Church calls social sin. That's the idea that when we support and participate in the evils of an economy, a political-social structure that is racist, sexist, elitist, or in any other way unjust, we are committing a sin. We do this when we use a cellphone, computer, or video game system made with coltan, the mining of which has poisoned central African rivers, reduced the population of eastern mountain gorillas, and caused a deadly military conflict. We do this when we buy clothing made in Burma, where the military dictatorship exploits clothing workers and uses the profits to prevent peaceful assembly and to support violent repression of the Burmese people. We do this when we support an economic system that robs from the poor to give to the rich, that pays financial speculators upwards of a billion dollars a year, and that does not provide work for ordinary people even as it forecloses on their home mortgages. We do this when we buy from corporations who keep their prices low by buying from sweatshops, by denying their workers the right to organize for better pay and benefits, or by having low environmental standards. We do this whenever we accept without question the reports we read in the newspapers or the self-serving announcements of political leaders.

When I was a catechist in the Rite of Christian Initiation of Adults (RCIA) program at St. Theresa's Church in Mill Woods, I often volunteered to lead discussions of social justice. A few times I started off asking: "Has any of you here killed anybody today?" I was always met with blank stares. Then I would talk about an issue of the day. Sometimes it was people in Africa dying of malnutrition, dysentery, and AIDS because they have to pay western banks exorbitant interest on loans their dictators took out, even though the money went to private accounts in Switzerland. Or it might be Aboriginal people in Canada struggling with addictions and poverty because our governments and churches abused them in residential schools. Or young women starving themselves to death to conform to the perverse advertising and television imagery of somebody's ideal female body. Or George W. Bush lying about weapons of mass destruction in Iraq to justify a war. The correct answer to my question was yes; each one of us has played a part in killing someone, and we keep doing it every day.

When I started writing this book, I had a naive notion that there were simple reasons to explain why and how someone ends up in prison. Many of the people I talked to who work in restorative justice, including some prison staff, said prisoners are victims of dysfunctional families and social injustice. Most prisoners I talked to said they had miserable childhoods. One learned from his father how to mainline heroin when he was six years old. Many grew up thinking it was normal for everybody in the home to be drunk, to throw beer bottles at each other, to toss furniture and spouses through the living room window. Some were sexually abused or raped by fathers, uncles, or family friends. Many were poor. One told me that while his classmates were learning elementary and junior high physical education, he was getting his exercise crawling through the basement windows of houses and carting out valuables he could sell to support himself and his father's drug habit. Of course, some prisoners had childhoods not much different from mine.

Many prison staff I ran into clearly believed that even the guys with radically dysfunctional childhoods still made free choices, that they behaved like predatory animals when they were free and deserved to be locked up in cages and treated like animals. Corrections Canada's mission statement talks about working to return prisoners to the community, but with prison unions pushing for more security and the Harper government building more prisons—and shutting down all prison farms—instead of funding more programs, that statement looks like public relations doubletalk.

Nonetheless, prison staff and the Conservatives have a valid point: our communities need protection from violent criminals. Even the prisoners themselves agree that if they're serious about leading better lives, they can't blame society for what they did, even if they were handicapped by poverty and horrible child-hoods. After all, people with the same handicaps have made other, healthier choices. To complicate the matter further, several of the prisoners I talked to, including two who tell their stories in this book, were not socially disadvantaged in a significant way; their families provided them with relatively normal starts in life.

In *A Short History of Progress*, Ronald Wright looks at anthro-pologists' discoveries about the evolution of the human race and concludes that every one of us in our privileged Western world owes our present lifestyle to millennia of wars, brutality, and even genocide by our forebears. He says, "prehistory, like history, tells us that nice folks didn't win, that we are at best the heirs of many ruthless victories and at worst the heirs of genocide. We may well be descended from humans who exterminated rival humans — cul-minating in the suspicious death of our Neanderthal cousins some 30,000 years ago." War, violence, mass murder, and racism, he implies, are as human as a Mozart piano concerto, the Eiffel Tower, and the Red Cross.

At a meeting of M2W2 volunteers in 2002, we had a discussion of the war in Afghanistan and the American invasion of Iraq, which led us to talk about peace. Some of us referenced the Gospels and noted that as Jesus was a man of peace, we should be too, and that going into prisons to visit was one way of helping make peace in the world. One of the more conservative volunteers agreed that Jesus was fundamentally a man of peace, but he added that Jesus could do what he did because he was way better than we are; we have to muddle through violence and war because that's the way the world is for ordinary mortals. Likewise, prisoners have told me over and over that I can't expect them to be non-violent, since they live in a violent place. They have to be violent in self-defence. I have told them it's not a black-and-white thing. Alternative to Violence workshops aim to reduce violence one small step at a time, not to leap suddenly from one extreme to the other.

Besides that, the world outside the prison walls is a violent place too. It's a place where armies clash, where civilians fund wars by their labour, where other civilians pay by loss of life, loss of children, loss of limbs, loss of housing, loss of virtually everything they had, even to stay alive. It's a place where Henry Kissinger wins the Nobel Peace Prize for negotiating the end of a war in southeast Asia that he helped prosecute, killing over three million people in the process. It's a place where it's honourable and glorious — some would say even Christ-like — to kill for one's country, a place where draft dodgers like me are shamed and disowned by their families and communities for refusing to kill people who are less a threat to me than my own government is.

I strongly believe reducing violence is not only possible but necessary in prison and outside it. We can't do it by building more prisons, imposing longer sentences, and having larger coils of razor wire separating prisoners from the larger community. We can only do it if we look into another's eyes, touch another's hand — shaking hands is the one normal physical contact allowed when volunteers and prisoners meet — hear another's story, and realize the other person is a lot like us.

BIBLIOGRAPHY

Alighieri, Dante. *The Divine Comedy*. Translated by Henry Wadsworth Longfellow. New York: Collier, 1962.

Bergner, Daniel. *God of the Rodeo: The Quest for Redemption in Louisiana's Angola Prison*. New York: Random House, 1999.

Botting, Gary. *Wrongful Conviction in Canadian Law*. Toronto: LexisNexis, 2010.

Campbell, Kim. *Time and Chance: The Memoirs of Canada's First Woman Prime Minister*. Toronto: Doubleday, 1996.

Caron, Roger. *Bingo: Four Days in Hell*. Agincourt, ON: Methuen, 1986.

_____. *Go-boy! The True Story of a Life behind Bars*. Don Mills, ON: McGraw-Hill Ryerson, 1978.

Cleaver, Eldridge. *Soul on Ice*. New York: Dell, 1968.

Culhane, Claire. *No Longer Barred from Prison: Social Injustice in Canada*. Quebec City: Black Rose Books, 1991.

Dellinger, David. *From Yale to Jail: The Life Story of a Moral Dissenter*. New York: Pantheon, 1993.

Derksen, Wilma L. *Have You Seen Candace?* 2nd ed., rev. Winnipeg, MN: Amity Publishers, 2002.

Dostoyevsky, Fyodor. *Crime and Punishment*. Translated by Constance Garnett. New York: Dell, 1959.

Dumas, Alexandre. *The Count of Monte Cristo*. Translated by Robin Buss. London: Penguin, 2003.

Frankl, Viktor. *Man's Search for Meaning*. Translated by Ilse Lasch. Boston: Beacon Press, 2006.

Gonnerman, Jennifer, James Sterngold, Sasha Abramsky, Stephanie
    Mencimer, David Goodman, and Justine Sharrock. "Slammed." *Mother
    Jones*, July/August 2008. 44–63. [A series of articles about prisons in the
    United States.]

Gordimer, Nadine. "Once Upon a Time." *Jump and Other Stories*. London:
    Bloomsbury Publishing, 2003 [1991]. 23–30.

Griffiths, Jay. *A Sideways Look at Time*. New York: Penguin Putnam, 1999.

Henton, Darcy. "Behind Bars: Maximum Security + The Remand Centre."
    Alberta Views, April 2006. 27–35.

Hugo, Victor. *Les Miserables*. Translated by Norman Denny. London:
    Penguin, 1976.

King, Stephen. *Rita Hayworth and Shawshank Redemption*, in *Different
    Seasons*. New York: Signet, 1982.

Lezin, Katya. *Finding Life on Death Row: Profiles of Six Inmates*. Boston:
    Northeastern University Press, 1999.

Lozoff, Bo. *We're All Doing Time: A Guide for Getting Free*. Durham, N.C.: The
    Human Kindness Foundation, 1985.

Mandela, Nelson. *Long Walk to Freedom*. London: Abacus, 1994.

Maté, Gabor. *In the Realm of Hungry Ghosts: Close Encounters with Addiction*.
    Toronto: Knopf Canada, 2008.

Milgaard, Joyce, with Peter Edwards. *A Mother's Story: The Fight to Free My
    Son, David*. Toronto: Doubleday Canada, 1999.

Miseck, Lorie. *A Promise of Salt*. Regina, SK: Coteau Books, 2002.

Morris, Ruth. *Stories of Transformative Justice*. Toronto: Canadian Scholars
    Press, 2000.

Prejean, Helen. *Dead Man Walking: An Eyewitness Account of the Death
    Penalty in the United States*. New York: Random House Inc., 1993.

*Report of the Commission of Inquiry into the Wrongful Conviction of David
    Milgaard*. http://www.justice.gov.sk.ca/milgaard/.

Sabo, Donald F., Terry Allen Kupers, and Willie James London. *Prison
    Masculinities*. Temple University Press, 2001.

Solzhenitsyn, Aleksandr. *The Gulag Archipelago, 1918-1956: An Experiment in
    Literary Investigation*. New York: Harper & Row, 1974.

Stoesz, Donald. *Glimpses of Grace: Reflections of a Prison Chaplain*. Victoria,
    BC: Friesen Press, 2010.

Toews, Barb. *Restorative Justice for People in Prison*. Intercourse, PA: Good
    Books, 2006.

Tolle, Eckhart. *The Power of Now: A Guide to Spiritual Enlightenment*.
    London: Hodder and Stoughton, 1999.

Wright, Ronald. *A Short History of Progress*. Toronto: House of Anansi, 2004.

Zehr, Howard. *The Little Book of Restorative Justice*. Intercourse, PA: Good Books, 2002.